**W9-DDO-548**

# Lao Tzu's *Tao Te Ching*

# Lao Tzu's *Tao Te Ching*

*A Translation of the Startling New Documents Found at Guodian*

ROBERT G. HENRICKS

Columbia University Press
New York

Columbia University Press
*Publishers Since 1893*
*New York    Chichester, West Sussex*
Copyright © 2000 Columbia University Press
All rights reserved

Library of Congress Cataloging-in-Publication Data

Lao-tzu
    [Tao te ching.  English]
    Lao Tzu's Tao Te Ching : a translation of the startling new
documents found at Guodian  /  Robert G. Henricks.
        p.   cm  —  (Translations from the Asian Classics)
    Includes bibliographical references and index.
    ISBN 0–231–11816–3
    I. Henricks, Robert G., 1943–  .  II. Title.  III. Series
BL1900.L26E5  2000                              99–37496
299'.51482—dc21                                CIP

Casebound editions of Columbia University Press books are printed
on permanent and durable acid-free paper.

Printed in the United States of America

c 10 9 8 7 6 5 4 3 2 1

*For the two women I love, who, for reasons
I do not understand, also seem to love me—*

*Pat and Anna*

# Preface

Before proceeding to the introduction, the reader should be aware of two things. First, photographs and transcriptions of the bamboo slip manuscripts found at Guodian in 1993 were made public in May 1998. That means that scholarly work on these slips has just begun, and many articles are in the process of being published. Thus some of my colleagues will surely argue that this book is premature and that translation of the "Bamboo Slip *Laozi*" should await the publication of the scholarship now under way.

This is a fair criticism. Many of the opinions expressed and conclusions reached in this book must be regarded as preliminary and tentative. A few years from now, I am bound to consider changing some words and lines in the translation and my understanding of what these slips are and how they are related to the complete text of *Laozi* is bound to evolve. Nonetheless, I believe that the significance of this new find warrants bringing it to the attention of general readers and Sinologists who do not focus on early China as soon as possible. Changes to this translation, where they are needed, can be published in a second edition if there is sufficient interest.

Second, in May 1998, I co-hosted, with Sarah Allan, an International Conference on the Guodian *Laozi* at Dartmouth College. This was scheduled to coincide with official release of the book *Guodian Chumu zhujian* (郭店楚墓竹簡, Bamboo Slips from the Chu Tomb at Guodian) (Beijing: Wenwu Press, 1998). At this conference, Professor Allan and I were joined by thirty-one scholars from all over the world—specialists on the *Laozi*, early Daoism, and early Chinese history, language, literature, and philosophy—for the world's first academic discussion of this latest find. The stimulating exchange of ideas at the conference helped me in writing this book to an immeasurable extent. This discussion makes liberal use of the papers presented at that conference and the handouts provided by some participants. When I have used someone else's ideas, I have tried to give credit where it is due.

Of the people attending the conference I must single out at least five to whom I am deeply indebted: (1) Peng Hao (彭浩), curator of the Jingzhou Museum in Hubei province, who kindly gave me a copy of his initial transcription of the Guodian *Laozi* materials, including the piece called "Taiyi shengshui" (太一 生水, The Great One Gave Birth to Water). He also reviewed changes that I made to the transcription and provided useful advice. He is sharp, unassuming, and clever—a delightful person with whom I hope to work for many years. (2) Tomohisa Ikeda (池田知久), professor of Chinese philosophy at Tokyo University, who is a prolific scholar, probably known best in the West for his work on the "Wuxing" (五行, The Five Ways of Conduct) manuscript from Mawangdui. Professor Ikeda produced a detailed, line-by-line study of the "Guodian *Laozi*," along with his own transcription, which he freely distributed to everyone attending the conference. It is with his permission that I cite from these "notes" (*biji*, 筆記), although he considers this work preliminary and has no plans to publish his work in this form. (3) Xing Wen (邢文), lecturer in archaeology at Beijing University, who is a young, exceptionally talented scholar whom I met several years ago when he was doing research at Harvard. We have kept in touch via e-mail ever since. As I worked on my translation, we had many fruitful exchanges, especially in regard to the structure and meaning of "Taiyi shengshui." (4) William Boltz, professor of Asian languages at the University of Washington, to whom I am indebted for help with phonological issues both during and after the conference and for referring me to the valuable work on archaic pronunciations by Dong Tonghe (董同龢). (5) Finally, I am grateful to Sarah Allan, the Burlington Northern Professor of Chinese Studies at Dartmouth College, who initially proposed that we host this conference and who knew all the right people in China to make it happen.

*Robert G. Henricks*
*Hanover, NH*
*January 1999*

# A Note on the Romanization

In this book I follow the trend in the field, using the pinyin system of romanization instead of the more familiar but dated Wade-Giles system. This may initially confuse some readers, who will find "Laozi" where they expect to see "Lao Tzu" and *Dao de jing* where they expect to see *Tao te ching*. But readers will find that the initial consonants in the pinyin system, in most cases, more accurately reflect the Mandarin pronunciation. Thus *Tao te ching*, correctly pronounced, has always been "dow" (as in "Dow Jones Industrials"), "duh" (as in the word "dummy"), "jing" (as in "Jingle Bells"). The problematic initial consonants when reading words in pinyin are "z" (which reads like "dz"), "zh" (which is close to "j"), "c" (which in the Wade-Giles system would be "ts' "), "x" (which sounds like an initial "sh"), and "q" (which sounds like an initial "ch").

Using the pinyin system, the title of this book becomes *Laozi's* Dao de jing: *A Translation of the Startling New Documents Found at Guodian.*

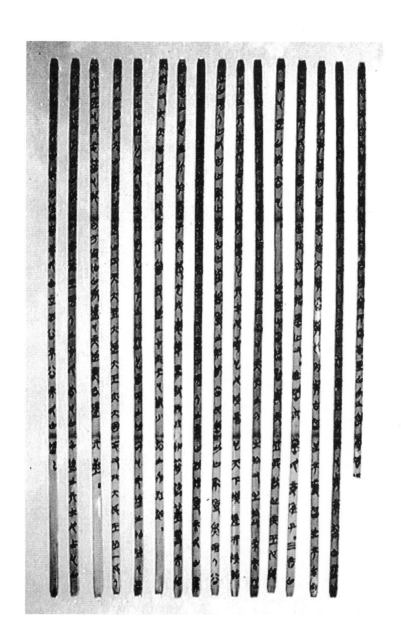

*Bamboo slips from "Laozi A".*
*From a color slide, courtesy of Peng Hao, Associate Director of the Jingzhou Museum.*

# Introduction

Few controversies in modern Chinese history have lasted longer and involved more scholars than that concerning Lao Tzu, the man, and Lao Tzu, the book. It has lasted for forty years, engaged dozens of debaters, and produced half a million words. And the battle is still continuing, both in China and in the West.

—Wing-tsit Chan, *The Way of Lao Tzu*, 1963

Archaeologists made a major find in 1973 with the discovery of two copies of the *Laozi* (老子) among a library of texts in a tomb at Mawangdui (馬王堆), South-Central China. Since this tomb had been sealed in 168 B.C., these were by far the earliest copies of this important text scholars had ever examined.[1] In content, these copies of *Laozi* generally correspond to later editions we have of the text. Although these copies lack the chapter divisions found in current editions,[2] they contain all eighty-one chapters; in fact the chapter sequence, with three exceptions, is exactly what we expect it to be.[3] However, for reasons still in contention, Parts I and II of the book—sometimes called the "Dao" part of the book (chapters 1–37) and the "De" part of the book (chapters 38–81), respectively—are reversed in the Mawangdui copies. This edition of the *Laozi*, in a sense, is a *De dao jing* instead of a *Dao de jing*. But in 1993 an earlier version of *Laozi* was found in a tomb at Guodian (郭店), Hubei province, and this new form of the text promises to be even more important than the Mawangdui copies for all readers interested in the history of how this text was composed. Study of the *Zhujian Laozi* (竹簡老子, Bamboo Slip *Laozi*), as this is called by the Chinese,[4] is bound to bring back into focus an issue that has been hotly debated during the twentieth century: Exactly when—and by what means—did the book we know as the *Laozi* come into being?

The traditional Chinese position on this—which remains a popular view in the West—is that the entire book was written by a single person called the "old Master" (Laozi), who lived at the time of Confucius, that is, around 500 B.C.[5] This position is based largely on the official "Biography of Laozi," written by Sima Qian (司馬遷), the Grand Historian of China, included in his *Shiji* (史記, Records of the Grand Historian), a work completed around 100 B.C.[6]

This position was vigorously challenged by a distinguished group of young scholars writing in China in the 1920s and 1930s.[7] The majority view of those scholars was that the book was clearly produced during the "Warring States" period (403–222 B.C.); it could not have been written by someone who lived at the time of Confucius, that is, in the "Spring and Autumn" period (722–481 B.C.).[8] Many regarded it as a book that had been written in the first half of the fourth century.[9]

But the most serious challenge to the traditional view came in 1963 with publication of D. C. Lau's translation: *Lao Tzu: Tao Te Ching*.[10] In Appendix 2 of this book ("The Nature of the Work"), Lau persuasively argued that the *Laozi*, in reality, "is an anthology, compiled by more than one hand," in which "pre-existing passages" from various sources, passages that might make quite different points but share a word or a phrase in common, have been combined by editors over the years to form what we now see as eighty-one "chapters."[11] He uses as an example the first two sections of chapter 5 in the text, arguing that "There is no connexion between the two passages other than the fact that they are both about 'heaven and earth.'"[12] Citing his translation, the sections in question read: (1) "Heaven and earth are ruthless, and treat the myriad creatures as straw dogs; the sage is ruthless, and treats the people as straw dogs." (2) "Is not the space between heaven and earth like a bellows? It is empty without being exhausted; The more it works the more comes out."

On the date of the text, Lau felt that "some form of the *Lao tzu* existed by the beginning of the third century B.C. at the latest."[13] But Lau's contemporary and longtime colleague at the University of London, Angus Graham, in a book published toward the end of his career, argued that the *Laozi* appeared anonymously in China around 250 B.C.[14]

While the views of Lau and Graham remain influential here in the West, in China, within the past decade, there has been a remarkable reversion in scholarly writings to the traditional view. In his translation and study of the *Huangdi sijing* (黃帝四經, Four Classics of the Yellow Emperor), Chen Guying (陳鼓應), for example, flatly declared that, in his opinion, "*Laozi* is the work of one

person and one time."[15] Li Xueqin (李學勤) concurred, arguing in part that the
Mawangdui "Huang-Lao" (黃老) materials rely on the *Laozi*. But Li also re-
cycled evidence first used in the 1920s and 1930s to show that Confucius knew
Laozi and in fact criticized some of the things he said in his book.[16]

Why is the "Bamboo Slip *Laozi*" important to the discussion of this particular
issue? First, the tomb in which these materials were found dates to around 300
B.C. (for more detail on this, see below); thus these materials are even older than
the Mawangdui copies. But what has been found at Guodian is not a complete
copy of the text, raising the possibility that the "complete text" as we know it
today did not yet exist at that time. Also, only sixteen of the thirty-one chapters
found on these slips are "complete"; as for the rest, in some cases a few lines are
missing (when we compare these versions with later editions), and in others all
that we find is the beginning or middle part of a chapter, to which, it would
appear, other sayings were added at some later date. What is now chapter 64 in
the text is here seen clearly as two, distinct "chapters," the first twelve lines constituting one "chapter," the second nine to ten lines constituting another.

Perhaps most important of all, the seventy-one slips on which we find sayings
of *Laozi* originally constituted three different "bundles" (*zu*, 組), distinguished
by the size and style of the slips. These three groups have been labeled "*Laozi*
A," "B," and "C" (*jia*, 甲 ; *yi*, 乙 ; *bing*, 丙, respectively). But none of these has
a title. And the fact that these sayings were grouped into three different bundles
might suggest that, in the minds of those making the copies, they were actually
three different "books." We have no way of knowing if any one of these bundles,
or all three bundles taken together, were understood by the tomb occupant and
his contemporaries, as a book that they knew as the *Laozi*. Finally, in bundle
"C," in addition to the slips containing sayings from the *Laozi*, there are fourteen slips constituting a cosmological essay, called—based on the opening lines
of the piece—"Taiyi shengshui" (The Great One Gave Birth to Water).

In short, the basic questions to be answered about these bundles found at Guodian are (1) What are they? (2) Exactly how are they related to the text that we
now know as the *Laozi*? and (3) Where do they fit in terms of the overall history
of the development of this text?

We will return to these questions. But first we must say more about the tomb
and the site of the tomb in which these new slips were found. Second, we must
carefully review the contents of each of these "bundles" and discuss the punctuation marks on the slips and the question of "chapter divisions."

The "Bamboo Slip *Laozi*" was found in "Chu tomb no. 1" (楚墓一號) at Guodian. Guodian village is presently part of Jingmen city (荊門市) in Hubei province, but during the Warring States period it was the locus of a cemetery on Mount Ji (紀山, Jishan), a cemetery that served the inhabitants of the city of Ying (郢). Ying was the capital of the ancient state of Chu, and it was located about 9 kilometers directly south of Jishan. According to Liu Zuxin (劉祖信), director of the Jingmen City Museum, one of the archaeologists who excavated the tomb, there are twenty some "groups" of tombs that remain on Jishan, amounting to more than 300 grave mounds: all of these await excavation.[17] The exploration of tomb No. 1 in October 1993 was not part of a long-range plan; the decision to carry this out was made because the tomb had been robbed, more than once in recent years, and water was getting into the tomb through a passage cut by one of the thieves.[18]

The date of the tomb is discussed in detail in the site report published in the journal *Wenwu*.[19] The conclusion reached there is that the tomb dates to the middle or late middle part of the Warring States period—that is to say, the late fourth or early third century B.C. Since the tomb is clearly a "Chu" tomb in orientation, style, and design, burial must have occurred before 278 B.C., the year in which Chu was defeated by Qin (秦), and the city of Ying was destroyed. But the types of objects put into the tomb and the artistic motifs that adorn the grave goods suggest a late fourth-century date. Strong parallels are noted with bronzes and pottery items found at "Baoshan tomb no. 2" (包山二號) in Jingmen, which dates to 316 B.C., and "Wangshan tomb no. 1" (望山一號) in Jiangling (江陵), for which the date is 332 B.C.[20]

The identity of the tomb occupant is unknown. However, since there was a mound over the grave, he was clearly a member of the aristocracy, not a commoner. But since there were not multiple layers of coffins—simply one inner coffin (*guan*, 棺) and one outer coffin (*guo*, 槨)—early ritual texts would place the occupant among the *shi* (士) class, the lowest rank of the aristocracy.

But there is an additional clue to this person's identity. One of the items found in the grave is an "eared cup" (*erbei*, 耳杯), which is inscribed with the words "Teacher of the Eastern Palace" (*donggong zhi shi*, 東宮之師). As Li Xueqin has pointed out, since the "Eastern Palace" was the residence of the "heir apparent" (*taizi*, 太子), there is a good reason to believe that the person buried herein was his tutor.[21] If our dating of the tomb is correct, the deceased was the tutor of either Xiong Wan (熊完), who assumed control as King Kaolie (考烈王) in 262 B.C., or Xiong Heng (熊横), who became King Qingxiang (頃襄) of Chu in 298 B.C.

## The Texts Found in the Tomb

This would be consistent with the types of texts put into the tomb. Instead of the "almanacs" (*rishu*, 日書), records of divination, and "inventories" of items sent along with the dead (*qiance*, 遣策) that we find in other Chu tombs,[22] the bamboo slips put into this tomb constitute a philosophical library, the type that might well have belonged to a teacher. Of the more than 800 slips found in the tomb, 730 slips have writing on them, and the documents "*Laozi*, A, B, and C," account for only 71 of those slips. When the rest were sorted by specialists, fifteen other texts were distinguished in the collection and named as follows:[23] (1) "Taiyi shengshui" (The Great One Gave Birth to Water),[24] (2) "Ziyi" (緇衣, Black Robes), (3) "Lu Mugong wen Zi Si" (魯穆公問子思, Duke Mu of Lu Asked Zi Si), (4) "Qiongda yishi" (窮達以時, Success [in Developing Virtue] Depends on Living at the Right Time), (5) "Wuxing" (五行, The Five Ways of Conduct), (6) "Tang Yu zhi dao" (唐虞之道, The Ways of Yao and Shun),[25] (7) "Zhongxin zhi dao" (忠信之道, The Way of Loyalty and Sincerity), (8) "Cheng Zhi wenzhi" (成之聞之, Cheng Zhi Once Heard It Said), (9) "Zun deyi" (尊德義, Venerate Virtue and Righteousness), (10) "Xing zi ming chu" (性自命出, Human Nature Emerges from Fate), (11) "Liu de" (六德, The Six Virtues), and (12–15) "Yucong" (語叢, 1, 2, 3, and 4, Collected Sayings, I, II, III, and IV).

With the exception of "Taiyi shengshui"—like the *Laozi* a Daoist text—these materials are largely Confucian. Even more striking, it is possible that as many as eight of these texts belonged to the now-lost *Zi Si zi* (Master Zi Si), the collected writings of Zi Si (492–431 B.C.)—Confucius's grandson—and his disciples, which in Han times consisted of twenty-three *pian* (篇, sections or chapters).[26] "Ziyi," which is now *pian* (chapter) 33 in the *Liji* (禮記, Record of Rites), has long been regarded as the work of Zi Si, and Li Xueqin has suggested that the main text (*jing*) of "Wuxing" might be his writing as well, with the commentary (*zhuan*) the work of his disciples.[27] The fact that "Ziyi" and "Wuxing" were apparently bundled together in the present collection seems to support this thesis.[28] Also bundled together were "Lu Mugong" and "Qiongda yishi." Zi Si was the teacher of Duke Mu of Lu who died in 377 B.C.[29] Finally, bundled together, on slips of the same length and style as those used for "Ziyi" and "Wuxing,"[30] were the selections "Cheng Zhi wenzhi," "Zun deyi," "Xing zi ming chu," and "Liu de."

Thus the Guodian texts are a gold mine of information not only for scholars working on the *Laozi*; from them we can learn a great deal about the thought of Zi Si and the development of Confucian thought in the period between Confucius and Mencius, that is, from the fifth to the early fourth century B.C.[31] It is important to have translations and studies of these new texts as soon as possible.

### *Laozi* A, B, and C

#### *Laozi* A

The document labeled "*Laozi* A" is the largest of the three groups, consisting of thirty-nine slips. The slips are 32.3 cm long, "cornered" at the top, and the distance between the two cords that had kept the slips tied together is 13 cm. The original sequence of the slips cannot be determined since they are not numbered, and there is no indication of which slip was first and which was last. Because the content of the *Laozi* passages is familiar to us, wherever a passage or chapter continues from the bottom of one slip to the top of the next, we know that the latter followed the former. But when a chapter ends at the bottom of a slip, we do not know which of a number of possible slips came next.

*Laozi* A includes five slips where a chapter begins at the top of a slip. Thus, these thirty-nine slips can be grouped into five different "units," a unit of slips being a group of slips that we know were in sequence. Using the chapter numbers from our current editions of the *Laozi* (no chapter numbers are used on the slips themselves), the "chapter" sequence in these five units is as follows:

*Unit 1 (slips 1–20)* begins with what to us is chapter 19 in the *Laozi*, which is followed by materials from chapters 66, 46, 30, 64 (part 2), 37, 63, 2, and 32.

*Unit 2 (slips 21–23)* begins with what we recognize as chapter 25 and is followed by the middle lines of chapter 5.

*Unit 3 (slip 24)* consists of a single slip on which we find the first six lines of what is now chapter 16.

*Unit 4 (slips 25–32)* begins with the first half of what is now chapter 64 and is followed by chapters 56 and 57.[32]

*Unit 5 (slips 33–39)* consists of four chapters, now numbered as chapters 55, 44, 40, and 9.

This sequence of the five units is the one used in *Guodian Chumu zhujian*. This is not necessarily the *original* sequence of these units. We do not yet know—and this is true of the "units" in all three of our bundles—which unit came first, which unit came last, and the original order of the units in between. In other words, it is not necessarily true that "chapter 19" was the first chapter in *Laozi* A and that chapter 9 was the last: *Laozi* A might have begun with chapter 55, or chapter 16, and so on.[33] (However, as shown below, there is reason to believe that the final unit in *Laozi* A was either 4 or 5, and that unit 4 was directly preceded by unit 1.)

Noting the sequence of chapters—or parts of chapters—within each of these units, it is clear that this arrangement of the chapters in *Laozi* is unlike anything we have ever encountered before.[34] Were the chapters that form each of these units simply chosen at random? Is this simply a collection of someone's favorite sayings that were copied down with no thought given to the sequence of the material?

That might be one's initial impression. But as Wang Bo (王博) has pointed out, in reality, the chapters in each of these units seem to be grouped together by theme.[35] The chapters in units 1 and 4 are all concerned in one way or another with "ruling the state" (*zhiguo*, 治國); in units 2 and 3, we find "cosmological" observations—descriptions of the Dao (道, the Way) and its relation to the ten thousand things. In unit 5, the main theme is "self-cultivation" (*xiushen*, 修身), with advice on how to live a long, healthy life.

Wang also suggested that all the chapters in *Laozi* B are concerned with "self-cultivation," while those in *Laozi* C—not counting the "Taiyi shengshui" selection—return to the matter of "ruling the state." This is a thesis readers should keep in mind when reading the translations.[36] In addition, reflection needs to be given to the sequence of chapters and parts of chapters in each of the units—is there significance to this particular order? This is something that has not as yet been addressed.

## *Laozi* B

*Laozi* B consists of eighteen slips. The slips are 30.6 cm long, level on top, and the distance between the cord marks is 13 cm. Here too, we can distinguish some units in the collection, although we do not know how these units were arranged when the slips were still tied together.

*Unit 1 (slips 1–8)* begins with what is now chapter 59 in the text, followed by portions of chapters 48 and 20. The unit ends with the full text of chapter 13.

*Unit 2 (slips 9–12)* consists of a single selection—chapter 41.

*Unit 3 (slips 13–18)* begins with what are now the middle six lines of chapter 52, followed by chapters 45 and 54 in their entirety.[37]

## Laozi C

*Laozi* C consists of twenty-eight slips. Chapters from the *Laozi* account for fourteen of the slips, with "Taiyi shengshui" constituting the rest. These slips are 26.5 cm long, level on top, and the distance between the cord marks is 10.8 cm. As noted above, "Taiyi shengshui" is treated as a separate text in *Guodian Chumu zhujian*, though the editors note the possibility that these slips were originally part of *Laozi* C.[38] There seems no reason to doubt that this was true, since the "Taiyi" slips are the same length and style as the slips in *Laozi* C, and the calligraphy is the same.

*Unit 1 (slips 1–3)* consists of chapters 17 and 18 in the *Laozi*.

*Unit 2 (slips 4–5)* is now chapter 35 in the *Laozi*.

*Unit 3 (slips 6–10)* is an abbreviated version of what is now chapter 31.

*Unit 4 (slips 11–14)* consists of the second half of what is now chapter 64 in the text, but this is a different version of the same set of lines found in unit 1 in *Laozi* A.

*Unit 5 (slips 1–8, on p. 13)* is "Taiyi shengshui," part 1.

*Unit 6 (slip 9, on p. 13)* is "Taiyi shengshui," part 2.

*Unit 7 (slips 10–14, on pp. 13–14)* is "Taiyi shengshui," part 3.[39]

As mentioned above, these "units" were not necessarily in this order in the original bundle of slips, and one of the things we need to ponder—both as scholars and as readers—is other ways in which these units could be arranged. In that way we might well discover a sequence that makes better sense in terms of the overall presentation of ideas in each of these documents.[40]

## Punctuation and the Issue of Chapter Divisions

The division of the *Laozi* into its current eighty-one chapters was apparently done by Liu Xiang (劉向, c. 79–c. 6 B.C.). Liu Xin (劉歆), his son, quotes his father as saying:

> When we collated the text of the *Laozi*, the imperial copy had two sections [*pian*], the Grand Historian's copy had only one section, while my own copy also had two sections. Taken together, internal and external copies

provided a total of five sections; 143 chapters. We removed duplications, which amounted to three *pian*—62 chapters—establishing a text in two parts with 81 chapters. The 'upper book' was put first, with 37 chapters, while the 'lower book' came second, with 44 chapters.[41]

The evidence seems to suggest that this division of the text into eighty-one chapters had nothing to do with determining where the text *should* be divided based on ideas and rimes. Rather, it was apparently based on "Yin and Yang" considerations: "81" is the perfect "Yang" number, the product of nine times nine. Throughout Chinese history, other ways were proposed for dividing the text. Yan Zun (嚴遵 [or Zhuang Zun, 莊遵]), for example, divided the text into seventy-two chapters, while Wu Cheng (吳澄, 1249–1331) in the Yuan dynasty argued that the correct number of chapters should be sixty-eight.[42] Nonetheless, eighty-one remained the most popular number of chapter divisions, and it is the number of chapters we find in most editions of the *Laozi* today.

Looking back on what we know of the text before Liu Xiang made his divisions—there is no punctuation in copy B of the Mawangdui manuscripts that would indicate chapter divisions. But in part II of copy A, there are black dots (·) in the text that seem to indicate where new chapters begin. There are eighteen of these dots; in most cases these confirm current chapter divisions. But there are exceptions: (1) the first two lines of chapter 46—"When the world has the Way, ambling horses are retired to fertilize fields. When the world lacks the Way, war horses are reared in the suburbs"—are set off from the rest of the chapter as a separate saying. (2) Chapter 51 is regarded as two distinct sayings (lines 1–5 and 6–10); they appear to have been put together because both sayings begin with the words "The Way gives birth to them" (*dao sheng zhi*, 道生之). (3) The opening lines of chapter 52—"The world had a beginning which can be considered the mother of the world"—are distinguished from the middle part of the chapter, that is, the lines that begin "Block up the holes, Close the doors." (4) The first line of chapter 72—"When the people don't respect those in power, then what they greatly fear is about to arrive"—is treated as a separate saying from the rest of the chapter. (5) Chapter 75 is here presented as two separate sayings (lines 1–6, and 7–11); again, these are sayings that begin in similar ways ("The reason why people starve," and "The reason why people take death lightly"). It is also possible that chapter 64 was regarded as two distinct sayings in copy A as it is in the Guodian slips. But the silk is rotted away at the start of line 10, where punctuation might have occurred.[43]

The Guodian slips are peppered with punctuation. We can distinguish four different marks or signs: (1) a sign consisting of two short strokes or lines (=); any character followed by these lines should be repeated. If a phrase or line is to be repeated, this sign is normally placed after each character in that phrase or line. (2) A short, thin line—like a hyphen or dash (__). These lines are normally used internally in chapters to distinguish different parts of the chapter in much the same way—and in many of the same places—as a mark that resembles a backward comma—printed as (∠)—was used in copy A of the Mawangdui manuscripts. (3) The sign that normally marks the end of a chapter is a small, black square (■) placed on the right side of the slip following the final character in the final line of the chapter. (4) There is a sign found only in *Laozi* A—Ƨ— where it occurs at the end of chapters 9 and 57; this may indicate the end of a *pian* in the document as a whole.[44] Wang Bo has proposed—and I agree—that units 1 and 4 (which ends with chapter 57) formed one of these *pian*, with units 2, 3, and 5 (which ends with chapter 9) constituting the other.[45]

Although punctuation normally helps clarify chapter divisions, the punctuation marks noted above unfortunately are *not* used consistently throughout our sources; in some cases—in chapters 46 and 30, for example—the thin line normally used internally in chapters at the end of sentences or sections seems to indicate the *end* of the chapter. In addition, marks are sometimes used where they do not belong, being inserted one line or one character too soon (see notes to chapters 15 and 30). Consequently, there will probably be disagreements on what constitute chapter boundaries in these new sources.

That said, if one uses this punctuation cautiously, while paying attention to other indicators as well,[46] how does the material on the Guodian slips seem to be divided in terms of chapters? Conclusions here are tentative in many cases, but my results can be summarized as follows (for a more detailed, chapter-by-chapter discussion of this problem, see appendix III):

1. *Chapters that are already complete.* The following chapters in later editions are *already* understood to be "chapters" in the Guodian slips, and, generally speaking, the Guodian versions vary little in content and length from what we find in later editions. In most cases the wording is almost exactly the same. The chapters in question are 2, 9, 13, 19,[47] 25, 35, 37, 40, 41, 44, 54, 55, 56, 57, 59, and 66. Keeping in mind that material from only thirty-one chapters of the *Laozi* is represented in the Guodian slips, the number of chapters that are "complete"— sixteen—is not insignificant. Also, since all but four of these chapters—9, 37, 44, and 59—were understood by D. C. Lau to be the products of editorial work,

if Lau was correct, then the editing of these particular chapters must have been done before 300 B.C., in fact, probably *well* before 300 B.C.[48]

2. *Chapters that are slightly longer in later editions.* Here I would include chapters 15, 30, 31, 45, 46, and 48.[49] In each of these cases we find a few additional lines at the beginning or end of the chapter in later editions. In chapters 15 and 45, those lines are already "in place," so to speak, in the Guodian slips, but they are distinguished from the main body of the chapter by punctuation.

3. *Passages to which a good deal has been added to form the chapter as we find it in later editions.* What later become chapters 5, 16, 20, 52, and 63 are partial and incomplete in the Guodian slips. From chapter 5 we have only the middle lines of the chapter, which begin "The space between heaven and earth—is it not like a bellows?"[50] In later editions, this section is preceded by four lines and followed by two. Similarly, the middle lines of chapter 52 ("Close the gates, block the holes") form a chapter in *Laozi* B, but in later editions, parallel sayings of four lines each precede and follow these lines.[51] From what would turn into chapters 16 and 20—both quite long—we have only the six or seven lines with which later forms of these chapters begin. Finally, in the Guodian slips the initial and final three lines of chapter 63 are smoothly seamed together to form a "chapter"; in later editions nine lines have been inserted between these six.

4. *Two chapters, which in later editions are one.* What is now chapter 64 is clearly two chapters in the Guodian slips. As noted, two rather different versions of the second half of chapter 64 are found in *Laozi* A and *Laozi* C. Chapter 32, in later editions, might also belong in this group, since punctuation indicates that the first four lines are distinct from lines 5–12. But connections between these two sections are such that the punctuation mark may be an error (see the translation below).

5. *One chapter, which in later editions is two.* Chapters 17 and 18 are clearly a single chapter in the Guodian slips; they are in sequence, with the first line of "chapter 18" beginning with the word *gu* (故, therefore). This is clearly the case in the Mawangdui copies of *Laozi* as well.

## Interesting Cases: Chapters 19, 30, and 63

There are quite a few chapters in the Guodian corpus that are either word-for-word identical to later editions, or contain the occasional variant, but variants that do not greatly change our understanding of that chapter's message. Naturally, there are exceptions, which are sure to be the focus of a good deal of research and writing. The following comments briefly on three of those chapters.

1. *Chapter 19*: The Guodian form of this chapter is potentially very significant; there has already been a good deal of discussion about it. This chapter normally reads:

1   Eliminate sageliness, get rid of knowledge,
2   And the people will benefit a hundredfold.
3   Eliminate humanity, get rid of righteousness,
4   And the people will return to filial piety and compassion.
5   Eliminate craftiness, get rid of profit,
6   And there will be no robbers and thieves.

7   These three sayings, regarded as a text [*wen*, 文] are not yet complete.
8   Thus we must add to them the following things:

9   Manifest simplicity and embrace the genuine.
10  Lessen self-interest and make few your desires.

Many scholars over the years, the present author included, have argued that the first line of chapter 20—"Eliminate learning and you will have no distress" (*juexue wuyou*, 絕學無憂)—should be the last line of chapter 19. Like lines 9 and 10, this is a four-character line, set out in the same grammatical pattern—verb-object verb-object.[12] If there are "three sayings" that are not complete, surely three lines are needed at the end of the chapter. But in the Guodian slips, there is a full stop (■) at the end of line 10, which is followed by the beginning of chapter 66. Moreover, the line in question—"Eliminate learning and you will have no distress"—occurs in *Laozi* B (B:3), where it is the first line in the the the initial section of what is now chapter 20.

But that is not the crucial thing in this new version of chapter 19. What is important in this form of the chapter is that there are significant variants in lines 1, 3, and 7. In place of "sageliness" (*sheng*, 聖) in the Guodian slips we find the character 攴; in place of *ren* (仁) and *yi* (義, humanity and righteousness), we find the characters 慮 and 慮; and in place of the word *wen* (文, text) in line 7, we find the character 貞. In the Wenwu transcription, 攴 is read as a phonetic loan (*jiajiezi*, 假借字) for the word *bian* (辯, argumentation); the character 慮 is understood as a variant writing of 偽 (*wei*, hypocrisy), and the character 慮, there written 慮, is understood to mean 詐 (*zha*, deceit), since the phonetic element in the character 慮 appears to be 且 (*qie*), which in archaic times was pronounced the same way as 詐. Finally, the character 貞 in line 7 is understood to mean 辨 (*bian*, distinctions).[13] So, our translation of the Guodian form of the chapter—in which lines 5 and 6 occur before lines 3 and 4—would be something like this:

1 Eliminate knowledge, get rid of argumentation,
2 And the people will benefit one hundredfold.
3 Eliminate craftiness, get rid of profit,
4 And there will be no robbers and thieves.
5 Eliminate hypocrisy, get rid of deceit,
6 And the people will return to filial piety and compassion.

7 But these three sayings, regarded as a distinction, are not complete.
8 And perhaps we should add to them the following things.

9 Manifest simplicity, embrace the genuine,
10 Lessen self-interest, and make few your desires.

"Sageliness" and "humanity and righteousness" are valued by the Confucians: For Confucius himself, "humanity" (*ren*, often translated as "benevolence") was the queen of the virtues. Thus, the Guodian form of this chapter—in which these words do not occur—at first sight appears to be much less "anti-Confucian" than the chapter 19 in all later editions of *Laozi*.

What does this mean? What are we to make of these changes? Put it this way: Is the Guodian chapter the *original* form of the chapter, which was changed at some point to make the chapter more pointedly anti-Confucian? Or, is the wording in later editions the original wording, meaning that the Guodian chapter was altered by someone who wished to downplay the anti-Confucian tone of the book? Recall that the other texts found in this tomb were predominantly Confucian.[14]

This revelation will generate a lot of discussion, as well it should. One question raised is whether these two questions sum up all our options. It is conceivable, after all, that there never was an "original" version of the *Laozi*. That is, given the work of Michael LaFargue and others who point to signs of "orality" in so many parts of this book (three- to four-line series that are metric, parallel, and rimed), it is possible that slightly different versions of some of these chapters, or portions of chapters, circulated in China before any form of the text was written down.[15] Moreover, different versions of parts of the text could have been written down, *for the first time*, at different times in different parts of the country. The two versions of part 2 of chapter 64 included in the Guodian slips could be one indication that this was so.

If it is the case, nonetheless, that one of these versions of the opening lines of chapter 19 *was* changed, I am inclined to think that the Guodian wording is the original wording and that the words "sageliness" and "humanity and righteousness" were later inserted as substitutions, possibly as a way of making the chapter a statement against the philosophy of Mencius (fl. 350 B.C.). As we know, Mencius was fond of talking about "*ren* and *yi*," and, unlike his master Confucius, he believed that everyone had the potential to become a "Sage."[56]

Before leaving this chapter, let me note that I do not agree with the Wenwu transcription of the odd characters in lines 1, 3, and 7. My choices are explained below in the notes to my translation, but, for the moment at least, I would read 支 as 辨 (*bian*, distinctions),[57] 惥 as 化 (*hua*, transformation) as it is read elsewhere in the text, and 慮 as a variant writing of 慮 (*lu*, deliberation, forethought, or planning).[58] Finally, I am inclined to understand 貞 in line 7 as a variant writing of 使 (*shi*, duty, mission, or agenda), which is the way it is read in chapter 55 (*Laozi* A, A:17).[59] Thus, my translation reads:

1    Eliminate knowledge, get rid of distinctions,
2    And the people will benefit one hundredfold.
3    Eliminate artistry, get rid of profit,
4    And there will be no robbers and thieves.
5    Eliminate transformation, get rid of deliberation,
6    And the people will return to filial piety and compassion.

7    But these three sayings regarded as your mission are not complete.
8    And perhaps we should add to them the following things:

9    Manifest simplicity, embrace the genuine,
10   Lessen self-interest, and make few your desires.

I understand this as advice for someone who is planning to rule. And the advice—as is commonly true in the *Laozi*—is the opposite of what a ruler might think he *should* do. Should he not be a promoter of "knowledge," who encourages artistic endeavors and actively "transforms" the people through education, making them morally good? Should he not be someone who "deliberates" and "carefully thinks over" the daily affairs (*shi*, 事) of running the state?[60] In the political thought of the *Laozi* the answer to these questions is "No." As we find

out in chapters 37 and 57, the Daoist ruler "does nothing, and the people transform on their own" (*wuwei er min zihua,* 無爲而民自化).[61] If this reading is
right, chapter 19 is still very "anti-Confucian," but it is not yet "anti-Mencian."[62]

2. *Chapter 30:* Punctuation separates the last line of chapter 46 (A:3) from the
first line of chapter 30 (A:4), but the mark used is the thin line normally found
inside a chapter at the end of a sentence or section. In this case, since chapters 46
and 30 are clearly distinct in terms of ideas and message, this mark must indicate
the end of a chapter.

The Guodian version of chapter 30 consists of nine lines, but in later editions
this is a much larger chapter. What is striking about this version of chapter 30 is
that it really seems to be a "bare bones" form of the chapter, containing the lines
needed to make the point and no more. Perhaps the best way to show this is to
highlight the lines added in later editions by italicizing them in the translation.[63]

1   One who uses the Way to assist the ruler of men,
2   Does not desire to use weapons to force his way through the land.
    *Such deeds easily rebound.*
    *In places where armies are stationed, thorns and brambles will grow.*
    *Great wars are always followed by famines.*[64]
3   One who is good at such things achieves his result and that's all.
4   He does not use the occasion to make himself stronger still.

5   He achieves his result but does not brag about it;
6   He achieves his result but is not arrogant about it;
7   He achieves his result but is not conceited about it.
    *He achieves his result, yet he abides with the result because he has no choice.*

8   This is called "achieving your result but not being vicious."
9   Such deeds are good and endure.

    *When things reach their prime, they get old;*
    *We call this "not the Way."*
    *What is not the Way will come to an early end.*

Line 9 in the Guodian form of the chapter ends the chapter with a fitting
comment; the three lines tacked on to this in later editions seem only tangentially
related to the main point of the chapter.[65]

The other change made in later editions is that the final line in the Guodian version—"Such deeds are good and endure" (*qi shi hao chang*, 其事好長)—was changed to "Such deeds easily rebound" (*qi shi hao huan*, 其事好還) and was transposed to become line 3 in the chapter.[66]

3. *Chapter 63:* This version of what we know as chapter 63 of the text includes the first three lines of the chapter and the last two lines of the chapter, conflates lines 4 and 13, and omits the rest (a total of nine lines, i.e., the bulk of the chapter). Line 4 normally reads "Regard the small as large and the few as many" (*daxiao duoshao*, 大小多少), with line 13 reading "Those who regard many things as easy will necessarily end up with many difficulties" (*duoyi bi duonan*, 多易必多難). The combination here reads "In affairs large or small, the more things you take to be easy, the more difficulties there are bound to be" (*daxiao zhi duoyi bi duonan*, 大小之多易必多難). So the translation of the chapter becomes:

1  Act without acting;
2  Serve without concern for affairs;
3  Find flavor in what has no flavor.

4  In affairs large or small, the more things you take to be easy
   the more difficulties there are bound to be.
5  Therefore even the Sage regards things as difficult,
6  And as a result in the end he has no difficulties.

Now the apparent "gap" in this chapter—in which the entire middle part of the chapter is missing (about fifty characters)—could be explained by sloppy copying. That is, as the copyist was writing this down, he skipped over the one or two slips on which the middle part of the chapter was written.[67] The first two words in line 4— 大小 (*daxiao*)—were at the bottom of one slip, while line 13—多易必多難 (*duo yi bi duo nan*)—was at the top of another slip, but a slip that was two more slips to the left. The problem with that solution is that line 4 in the Guodian slips is *fully integrated* by the possessive particle 之 (*zhi*), making it likely that the nine additional lines in later additions were inserted into what was originally this short, unified statement.

It is also important to note that one of the lines omitted in this form of the chapter—"Repay resentment with kindness" (*bao yuan yi de*, 報怨以德), normally line 5 in the chapter—is often brought forth as evidence that the *Laozi* was in existence at the time of Confucius, the argument being that when Confucius is asked to comment on this saying in *Analects* 14:34, the source of the saying must be chapter 63 in the *Laozi*.[68] Clearly this argument is not supported by what must be recognized as the earliest, known form of the chapter.

## The Philosophy of the "Bamboo Slip *Laozi*"

Since the Guodian slips contain material from only thirty-one of the present eighty-one chapters in the *Laozi*, in attempting to understand what these three bundles are, we must pay attention to what is and is not included in these bundles in terms of the "philosophy" of the text. In other words, given the range of ideas, concepts, terms, and phrases that are familiar to us from current editions of the *Laozi*, are those ideas, terms, phrases, and so on, all present in this selection of sayings, or are some things left out? Do the passages cited mention the Dao, the "Way"? Is the Way fully described as the source of heaven and earth and the ten thousand things? Is it referred to as the "mother" of the ten thousand things, who nourishes and develops each of those things, bringing it to maturity? Is the Way described as something that cannot be heard or seen, as something that seems to "do nothing" (*wuwei*, 無爲), while at the same time there is nothing that is left undone? Are people urged to "lessen" or "make few" their desires, and to "desire not to desire," trying instead to "know when they have enough" (*zhi zu*, 知足)? And what of the "Sage," or the Sage ruler (*shengren*, 聖人)? Is he said to be someone who is thoroughly selfless, someone who "completes his affairs" yet wants no credit for all that he does? Is he someone who "serves with no concern for affairs" (*shi wushi*, 事無事)? Do our chapters include those chapters that celebrate the power of "water," seeing it as a model of how the weak wins out over the rigid and strong? Is the "female" mentioned as being important with attention paid to the feminine, passive mode of action? Do we find the distinction made between "Being" (*you*, 有) and "Non-being" (*wu*, 無) that we find in the complete form of the text? And so on.

Actually, this is a surprisingly well-rounded treatment of Daoist thought as we know it from the *Laozi* given the fact that we are dealing with only two-fifths of the text. Six of the ten chapters in the *Laozi* in which *wuwei* (nonaction, to do nothing) is mentioned are included in the Guodian slips; both chapters that mention *wushi* ("serve without concern for affairs") are here.[69] All the chapters, save one, in which the word 樸 (*pu*, genuine, natural, uncarved wood) occurs are included in the Guodian corpus (15, 19, 32, 37, 57, but not 28), and two of the three chapters in which 知足 (*zhizu*) is mentioned in the *Laozi* are found in this collection (44 and 46, but not 33). Both chapters urging readers to 知止 (*zhizhi*, to know when it is time to stop), 32 and 44, are also here.

Still some terms are conspicuous by their absence, and some ideas are not developed or do not receive very full treatment. Whether these "omissions" are significant is one of the things that needs to be studied. In the meantime, following are some of the omissions that I have noted.

1. Of the chapters in the *Laozi* that go into detail in discussing the Dao—chapters 1, 4, 6, 14, 25, 34, 51, and 52 (opening lines)—only one is present in the Guodian slips, chapter 25.

2. In the *Laozi*, the Dao is sometimes referred to as the "One"; the key chapters on this are 10, 14, 22, 39, and 42. *None* of these is included in these sources.

3. Of the chapters that mention the "Way of heaven" (*tiandao*, 天道, or *tian zhi dao*, 天之道), only one is represented—chapter 9. The other chapters in which this phrase occurs in the *Laozi* are 47, 73, 77, 78, and 79. (Note that the Guodian bundles contain nothing from the *Laozi* beyond chapter 66. Could chapters 67–81 in the *Laozi* represent writings from some other source?)[70] In this regard, we might also mention that the "antiaristocracy" chapters, which accuse the rich of living it up at the expense of the poor, are also in this later section—chapters 72, 75, 79, 80, and 81—which do not show up on the Guodian slips.

4. Very little is made of the effectiveness of the feminine mode of behavior or of the passive and weak overcoming the active and strong. The key chapters on this are 28, 36, 43, 61, 76, and 78. Related to this in a way, the chapters in which water is used as a prominent symbol—chapters 8, 34, 43, and 78—are also missing from the Guodian slips. (But water *does* play a significant cosmological role in "Taiyi shengshui" in *Laozi* C.)

5. Only two of the five chapters in which the Dao is referred to as "mother" are found in our slips—chapters 25 and 59. The other references to the "mother" are in chapters 16, 20, and 52, but in the parts of those chapters that are not found in the Guodian slips. In addition, as Xing Wen has already noted, the "mother/infant" metaphor—as a way of describing the relationship of the Way and the ten thousand things—does not appear in these slips.[71] The key chapters are 20, 34, and 52; again, we have *some* lines from 20 and 52, but not *these* lines. Related to this, readers are urged several times in the *Laozi* to "be like an infant" (*ying'er*, 嬰兒 or *chizi*, 赤子); the "*ying'er*" lines—in chapters 10, 20, and 28—are not included in this selection.[72]

6. Finally, one of the common phrases in the *Laozi* is "Therefore the Sage." Often at the end of chapters, following maxims that tell us how things should or should not be done, we find the words "Therefore the Sage (does so-and-so)" or "Therefore the Sage (says so-and-so)." In all cases, these lines are regarded by D. C. Lau as editorial comments.[73] Of the twenty chapters in the *Laozi* in which this phrase occurs—chapters 2, 3, 7, 12, 22, 26, 27, 29, 47, 57, 58, 63, 64, 66, 70, 72, 73, 77, 78, and 79—only five are present in the Guodian slips (2, 57, 63, 64, and 66), and it is omitted in this version of chapter 66.[74]

## Conclusion—What *Is* the "Bamboo Slip *Laozi*"?

The main question for us to answer is: What is this collection of slips called the "Bamboo Slip *Laozi*," or the "Guodian *Laozi*"? In the mind of the tomb occupant and his contemporaries, what was in these three bundles of slips? Did any one of them, or any combination of them, constitute a "text" in their minds? If so, would they have said the name of that text was the *Laozi*? Regardless of how that question is answered, since this is not a complete version of *Laozi*, and many "chapters" in these bundles are not complete, *and* the chapter sequence, where it can be known, is unrelated to what we find in our modern editions, where do we locate these materials in the overall history of the text?

Before I take a stand on these issues or present my current thoughts on them, let me begin by presenting some of the proposals already made by others, in the order in which they were published.

1. In one of the earliest articles published on the Guodian find, Cui Renyi (催 仁義) took the position that these bundles are actually three different books or collections of sayings and that taken together they constituted one of the sources used by someone to produce the book that we now know as the *Laozi*.[75] (This is a daring proposal for a scholar in China to make, and I salute him for having the courage to do so.) In addition, he argued that a *De dao jing*, of the sort found at Mawangdui, was nonetheless in existence shortly after this time since Han Feizi (c. 280?–233 B.C.) cites from a *Laozi* in which the De and Dao sections were in that order.[76]

2. Li Xueqin argued in 1998 in a newspaper article that the "Guodian *Laozi*" was one of many editions of the *Laozi* circulating in early China.[77] He connected this particular version with the "Guan-Lao" (關老) branch or school of Daoism, in which the concept "Taiyi" (the Great One) played a significant role. (So for Li, the "Taiyi shengshui" in *Laozi* C is clearly meant to be part of the "text.")

The basis for assuming that there was such a "school" with this particular emphasis is found in chapter 33 of the *Zhuangzi* (莊子) in which we find the words:

> Deeming the root to be quintessential—in contrast with the crudity of the things which grow from it—deeming it inadequate to be guided by accumulation of precedents—serenely swelling alone with the daemonic-and-illumined [*shenming*, 神明]—some of the ancient tradition of the Way is to be found in these, and Guan Yin and Old Dan [Lao Dan = Laozi] got wind of them and delighted in them. They founded them in that which forever is nowhere anything, and recognized as the sovereign of them the Supreme One [*zhu zhi yi taiyi*, 主之以太一], they deemed gentleness and weakness, modesty and inferiority to be their manifestations, and emptiness, tenuity, not damaging the myriad things, to be their substance.[78]

What Li's thesis does not explain is why, if this is an "edition" of the *Laozi*, it is not complete: Why are so many chapters omitted? The other stumbling block for many of us in the West is the assumption that Guan Yin (關尹) was a historical person (assuming that "Guan Yin" is one and the same as Yin Xi [尹喜, the "Keeper of the Pass"— *guanling*, 關令], the person who, Sima Qian tells us, asked Laozi to write this book in the first place.)[79]

3. A fascinating thesis has been developed by the scholar Guo Yi (郭沂).[80] Guo believes that the chapter sequence in the Guodian bundles is superior to the chapter sequence in current editions of the *Laozi*, since in many cases, as noted, sequential chapters are here connected by theme. In addition, as he correctly points out, the initial lines of chapter 48 combined with the initial lines of chapter 20, which directly follow, make very good sense as a single, unified chapter. He also sees a connection with the *Zhuangzi* in terms of construction. This *Laozi*, like the *Zhuangzi*, is divided into three *pian*, which might be called—as they are in the *Zhuangzi*— "Nei pian" (內篇, Inner Section)—*Laozi* A, "Wai pian" (外篇, Outer Section)—*Laozi* B, and "Za pian" (雜篇, Miscellaneous Section)—*Laozi* C.[81] (Actually, *Laozi* C *is* rather "miscellaneous" in character, the chapters seem less focused in terms of theme, and one thing included is a second version of the same lines from 64 that are already found in *Laozi* A.)

But Guo's most creative thesis is that there were actually two different *Laozi*s in ancient China. The first was written, as Sima Qian tells us, by Li Er (李耳), or Li Dan (李聃), around the time of Confucius, and Guo's conviction is that it is precisely that text—the "Three-Section *Laozi*"—that has been found at Guodian. The second, the forerunner of all modern editions, was written by the second Dan Sima Qian mentions, Dan (儋) the Grand Historian of Zhou, who met with Duke Xian of Qin in 374 B.C.[82] The first *Laozi* was taken over in full by this second Dan, but to this he added materials of his own. All the chapters in our complete editions of the *Laozi* that deal with the "arts of ruling" (*wang shu*, 王術), and all the chapters with a "Legalist" feel to them were contributed by this second author, according to Guo.[83]

4. Xing Wen (邢文), like his mentor Li Xueqin, argues that the "Guodian *Laozi*" was a different version of the *Laozi* from the one that served as the ancestor of our current editions (*jinben Laozi*, 今本老子).[84] It belonged to a different lineage, a different line of textual transmission. Like Li, Xing believes "Taiyi shengshui" is an important part of this form of the text and belongs in *Laozi* C. In fact, in Xing's opinion, the "Great One," assumes the cosmological role played by the "One" in our current editions of the *Laozi*.[85] Another distinction between the two forms of the text is that the Way as "mother" is, as noted, hardly mentioned in the Guodian chapters; missing too is the "mother/child" metaphor developed in current editions (in the second half of chapter 20, in chapter 34, and in the initial lines of chapter 52).

What is the author's position? What would he call this newly discovered material were he "forced to give it a name"? Let us begin with the question—did these three bundles taken together constitute a book, a book called the *Laozi*? Would the tomb occupant and his contemporaries have called it that? It is possible. But since none of the manuscripts has a title, there is no way to confirm or deny it. Nor am I convinced that the three taken together were understood as a "text," since I can think of no reason why a unified text would include two different versions of the same exact chapter (i.e., the second part of chapter 64).[86] But was there a version of the *Laozi* in existence at this period of time, from which the materials we find on these slips were selected? The deliberate grouping of chapters into units according to theme, as noted in *Laozi* A and *Laozi* B, makes this a plausible option. However, if that is true, I would argue that any *Laozi* that served as the source for these slips was not yet "complete." It contained some chapters to which other lines would later be added (e.g., chapter 30) and passages that would later be sizable "chapters," through the addition of what appear to be unrelated sayings (e.g., chapters 5, 16, 52). But, given the differences in the length and style of the slips in each of these bundles, it seems likely that these slips were copied from at least three different sources and possibly more. It is even possible that individual chapters—or units of chapters—in each of the bundles were copied from different original sources. How else can we explain the fact that, in unit 1 of *Laozi* A, *dao* (the "Way") is written 行 until we reach chapter 32 in the unit (the final chapter), when it suddenly changes to 道?[87]

Does that mean, then, that the book of *Laozi*, the complete text,[88] did not yet exist in 300 B.C.? Not at all. In fact it is likely that at least one version of the *Laozi*, the complete text, and possibly more than one version, was in existence by 300 B.C., if not earlier. But this conclusion has nothing to do with the Guodian slips. It is based on two things. The first is that the similarities and differences of the Mawangdui copies, which were made around 200 B.C.,[89] are such that they appear to represent two lines of transmission from a common ancestor. Since it takes time for two lines to diverge to the extent exhibited in the Mawangdui copies, I have no trouble believing their common ancestor was in circulation between 300 and 250 B.C., and possibly earlier. The second thing that supports this conclusion is that the *Han Feizi* chapters "Jie Lao" (解老) and "Yu Lao" (喻老) appear to mean "Explaining the *Laozi*" and "Illustrating the *Laozi*," respectively, and, although we do not know for sure when these were written, given Han Feizi's dates—?280–233 B.C.—we cannot be too far off course if we put that at c. 250 B.C. Of course, we cannot be sure that the *Laozi* Han Feizi knew and cited was the complete text as we know it today, since he only comments on lines from a total of 23 chapters. (Curiously, only five of these chapters are found in the Guodian slips: chapters 41, 46, 54, 59, and 64.)

On the Guodian slips—all that we know for certain is that they were buried around 300 B.C.; we do not know, for example, when they were "copied," when they were made. They might have been made shortly before the funeral to accompany the deceased. But if these slips constituted the library of the deceased, they were probably made much earlier, perhaps as early as 350 B.C.[90] However, that does not help us date the sayings on the slips, since the Guodian slips appear to be "copies" of "copies." That is, they do not represent "original writing," or someone's ideas or words written down for the first time. Moreover, they are not the products of oral dictation. The scribes who made these slips were "looking at" their sources—presumably other slips—as they were writing.[91] So, the slips that served as the source or sources for the Guodian slips—when were *they* made? We have no way of knowing. Beyond this—if we agree that at least some of this material circulated orally before it was written down—lies the even more difficult question of when that material was first "composed."[92]

# Translation of the "Bamboo Slip *Laozi*"

# Translator's Notes

1. The transcription on which this translation is based was done by Peng Hao (彭浩), who kindly sent me a copy of his original work. This is the same transcription that served as the basis for the transcription published in Jingmenshi bowuguan, *Guodian Chumu zhujian* (郭店楚墓竹簡). Where I have altered Peng Hao's original, I have done so on the basis of: (1) Qiu Xigui's (裘錫圭) notes to *Guodian Chumu zhujian;* (2) Tomohisa Ikeda's (池田知久) transcription in "Jingmenshi bowuguan *Guodian Chumu zhujian* biji" (荊門市博物館《郭店楚墓竹簡》筆記), which was distributed to participants at the international conference on the "Guodian *Laozi*"; and (3) my own reading of the original characters based on the photographs of the slips. Some of my renderings may seem overly "literal," but I believe that initial transcriptions should be as faithful to the original as possible, agreeing with Boltz that the "transcription should reflect exactly what is written and nothing more."[1] The "Modern Equivalents" are the "characters" currently used for the "words" that, in my judgment, the author(s) or editor(s) intended. In most but not all cases, my renderings agree with the indentifications proposed by the editors of *Guodian Chumu zhujian*.

2. The original punctuation marks are indicated in the transcription, with the exception of the sign that indicates repetition (=). The "small lines" that normally indicate a pause or break within a chapter are indicated by the sign __; for the "black squares" that normally mark the end of a chapter, I use ▬.

3. Italicized words and lines in the translation indicate gaps in the text where slips are broken. I have indicated what I think the missing characters probably were by putting those characters in [brackets] under the heading "Modern Equivalents."

4. For "archaic pronunciations," I have mainly relied on Tōdō Akiyasu's (藤堂明保) reconstructions, for which see his *Kanwa daijiten* (漢和大字典).

However, wherever archaic rime categories had to be checked, my authority was Dong Tonghe (董同龢), *Shanggu yinyun biaogao* (上古音韻表稿).

5. Dotted lines in the translation (....) indicate places where lines have been added in later editions (for which see the comparative text in appendix II). Solid lines in the translation (___) mean that, based on the punctuation marks used in the Guodian slips, this "chapter" was probably understood at the time these copies were made as two, distinct passages (used in chapters 15, 32, and 45).

6. Where mention is made in the notes of the "Xiang'er lineage" or the "Heshanggong lineage" and so on, what is intended is a group of editions from various time periods, which originated in the Xiang'er (想爾) recension of the *Laozi* or the Heshanggong (河上公) recension of the *Laozi*. Shima Kunio (島邦男), in his seminal study *Rōshi kōsei* (老子校正) distinguished a total of six such recensions and lineages, and it is to his work that I refer in those notes. For the distinctions between "text" and "recension" and "lineage" and "edition," see Harold D. Roth, "Text and Edition in Early Chinese Philosophical Literature."

7. Finally, in appendix II, the Wang Bi (王弼) edition consulted was the edition in popular use. However, it is clear from the combined efforts of Shima Kunio, Rudolf Wagner, and William Boltz that this is not the form of the text used by Wang Bi himself.[2]

*Laozi* A

1    Eliminate knowledge, get rid of distinctions,

2    And the people will benefit one hundredfold.

3    Eliminate artistry, get rid of profit,

4    And there will be no robbers and thieves.

5    Eliminate transformation, get rid of deliberation,

6    And the people will return to filial piety and compassion.


7    But these three sayings, regarded as your mission, are not complete.

8    And perhaps we should add to them the following things:²


9    Manifest simplicity, embrace the genuine,

10   Lessen self-interest, and make few your desires.


## Comments and Notes

LINES 1–6:

In all other editions of the *Laozi*, the line sequence is 1–2, 5–6, 3–4. Moreover, and of greater importance, in other editions line 1 normally reads "Eliminate sageliness, get rid of knowledge" (絕聖棄知), while line 5 (or line 3) reads "Eliminate humanity, get rid of righteousness" (絕仁棄義). While it might seem, therefore, that the Guodian lines in this chapter are less blatantly "anti-Confucian"—since "sageliness" "humanity," and "righteousness" are the highest of Confucian values—I do not think that is true, as I have argued in the introduction. "Morally transforming the people through education" (*jiaohua*, 教化) and "carefully deliberating daily affairs" (*lushi*, 慮事) are both things we would expect of a good ruler. Qiu Xigui would have us read line 5: "Eliminate hypocrisy (悥 = *wei*, 僞), get rid of deception (慮 = *zha*, 詐)."³ But in my opinion this misses the point; the author is urging rulers to "eliminate" things that would normally be thought of as good. In line with this, I here translate *qiao* (巧, 攷) not as "craftiness," as is commonly done but, rather, as "artistry." The reference is to the kind of "artistic skill" that results in "goods that are hard to obtain" (*nan de zhi huo*, 難得之貨). The opposite of *qiao* (巧), as we see in chapter 45 (B:7), is *zhuo* (拙, clumsy or unskilled).


LINE 7:

In later editions, in place of the character 叓 , we find 文 (*wen*, text or passage). The editors of the Wenwu transcription, following Li Jiahao (李家浩), understand this character as *bian* (弁), which they regard as a phonetic loan for *bian* (辨, distinction). But this same character occurs in chapter 55 below (A:17), where it is read as *shi* (使, to cause or control).[4] Reading *shi* here as a noun, we would translate it as "order," or "mission," or "charge," which works well if we understand the chapter as advice to a would-be ruler.[5]

LINES 9–10:

It has long been thought that the first line of chapter 20 should really be read as the last line of chapter 19: thus line 11 would be "Eliminate learning and have no undue concern" (絕學無憂). Like lines 9 and 10, this is a four-character phrase; moreover, lines 9, 10, and 11 look like they might be rimed (*pu,* 樸; *yu,* 欲; and *you,* 憂). In addition, this would provide "three" sayings to be added to the "three" sayings in the opening part of the passage (lines 1–6). But the opening lines of chapter 20—beginning with "Eliminate learning and have no undue concern"—form a distinct unit (B:3) in the Guodian materials.

|   | *Transcription* | *Modern Equivalents* |
|---|---|---|
| 1 | 𢫦智弃支 | 絕知棄辨 |
| 2 | 民利百伓■ | 民利百倍 |
| 3 | 𢫦攷弃利 | 絕巧棄利 |
| 4 | 朓恖亡又■ | 盜賊無有 |
| 5 | 𢫦愳弃慮 | 絕化棄慮 |
| 6 | 民复季子■ | 絕復孝慈 |
| 7 | 三言以爲貞不足 | 三言以爲使不足 |
| 8 | 或命之或虖豆■ | 或令之有所屬 |
| 9 | 見索保譻 | 視素抱樸 |
| 10 | 少厶須欲■ | 少私寡欲 |

## A:2 (Chapter 66)⁶

1     That which allows the rivers and seas to serve as kings of the small valley streams,

2     Is their ability to be below the small valley streams.

3     Therefore, they can serve as the kings of the small valley streams.

4     The Sage's presence at the front of his people, results from putting himself behind them.

5     The reason he is above them is that in his words he is below them.

6     But although he is on top of his people, they do not regard him as heavy;

7     And although he is in front of his people, they do not regard him as posing a threat.

8     All under heaven delight in advancing him while never tiring of him.

9     Because he does not compete,

10    No one in the world can compete with him.

### Comments and Notes

LINES 1–2:

In virtually every edition of the *Laozi*, the word "can" or "to be able" (*neng*, 能) occurs in line 1 but not in line 2. Line 1, then, normally reads: "The reason rivers and seas *can* serve as the kings of the small valley streams." The Guodian form of line 2 is unique; in other editions this is simply "Is that they are good at being below them" (以其善下之).

LINES 4–7:

In later editions, lines 4 and 6 begin with "Therefore." Also, in most later editions, lines 4 and 5 are reversed. Of greater importance, the addition of the word "desire" (*yu*, 欲) to lines 4 and 5 in later editions turns these lines into hypothetical or conditional statements, implying what a ruler *should* do *if* he wants to be in front of and on top of his people: "Therefore in the Sage's desire to be over the people, He must in his words be below them. And in his desire to be out in front of the people, he must in his self be behind them."⁷ In the Guodian form of the text, these are statements of fact.

LINE 8:

Like the Mawangdui copies, the Guodian slips omit the word "therefore" from the start of this line where it is commonly found in other editions.

LINE 9:

In the Mawangdui copies, this line is in the form of a question: "Is it not because he is not contentious?" But this is a declarative statement in almost all later editions, as it is here in the Guodian slips.

## A:2 (Chapteг 66)

| | Transcription | Modern Equivalents |
|---|---|---|
| 1 | 江海所以爲百浴王 | 江海所以爲百谷王 |
| 2 | 以亓能爲百浴下 | 以其能爲百谷下 |
| 3 | 是以能爲百浴王 | 是以能爲百谷王 |
| 4 | 聖人之才民前也以身後之 | 聖人之在民前也以身後之 |
| 5 | 亓才民上也以言下之 | 其在民上也以言下之 |
| 6 | 亓才民上也民弗厚也 | 其在民上也民弗後也 |
| 7 | 亓才民前也民弗害也 | 其在民前也民弗害也 |
| 8 | 天下樂進而弗詀 | 天下樂進而弗厭 |
| 9 | 以丌不靜也 | 以其不爭也 |
| 10 | 古天下莫能叒之靜 | 故天下莫能與之爭 |

1    Of vices—none is more onerous than wanting too much.

2    Of defects—none brings more sorrow than the desire to gain.

3    Of disasters[9]—none is greater than not knowing when one has enough.

4    The contentment one has when he knows that he has enough—

5    This is abiding contentment indeed.

*Comments and Notes*

In later editions this chapter begins with the lines: "When the world has the Way, ambling horses are used to fertilize fields. When the world lacks the Way, war horses are reared in the suburbs." In the Mawangdui copies, these lines have already made their way into the text in front of "Of vices . . ." But they are distinguished as a separate saying by punctuation in Mawangdui copy A.[10]

LINE 1:

Line 1 is omitted in some forms of the text. Also, in most cases, "none is more onerous [*hou*, 厚] than" is simply "none is greater [*da*, 大] than." Finally, for "wanting too much" (*shenyu*, 甚欲), other editions have "having things that can be desired" (*keyu*, 可欲).

LINE 2:

The phrase "none brings more sorrow [*can*, 憯] than" is normally "none is greater [*da*, 大] than" in later editions, but the Mawangdui copies have *can* as well.

LINES 2 AND 3:

These are reversed in later editions. But note that the Guodian sequence seems best, since line 3 leads naturally into line 4.

## A:3 (Chapter 46, lines 3–7)

| *Transcription* | | *Modern Equivalents* | |
|---|---|---|---|
| 1 | 辠莫厚虎　甚欲 | 罪莫厚乎　甚欲 |
| 2 | 咎莫僉虎　谷尋 | 咎莫憯乎　欲得 |
| 3 | 化莫大虎不智足 | 過莫大乎不知足 |
| | | | |
| 4 | 智足之爲足 | 知足之爲足 |
| 5 | 此互足矣— | 此恆足矣 |

1    One who uses the Way to assist the ruler of men
2    Does not desire to use weapons to force his way through the land.

...................................
...................................
...................................

3    One who is good at such things achieves his result and that's all.
4    He does not use the occasion to make himself stronger still.

5    He achieves his result but does not brag about it;
6    He achieves his result but is not arrogant about it;
7    He achieves his result but is not conceited about it.

...................................

8    This is called "achieving your result but not being vicious."
9    Such deeds are good and endure.[12]

...................................
...................................
...................................

*Comments and Notes*

LINE 2:

The Guodian form of the line is unique in adding the word "desire"; other editions simply say "Does not use weapons . . . "

LINES 2 AND 3:

In most later editions, three lines have been inserted between lines 2 and 3: (1) "Such actions quickly lead to revenge"; (2) "In places where armies are camped, thorns and brambles will grow"; and (3) "After great battles, there are always years of misfortune." The last of these lines is also omitted from the Mawangdui copies, while the first of the lines—"Such actions quickly lead to revenge" (其事好還)— is the final line of the chapter in the Guodian slips (but the wording is not exactly the same).

LINE 4:

The Mawangdui copies use the imperative negative *wu* (毋) here, phrasing this in terms of an order: "Do not use this occasion . . . "

LINES 5 –7:

In the Mawangdui copies, and in the Xiang'er lineage, the line sequence is 6, 5, 7; in most other editions, the line sequence is 6, 7, 5. Of greater importance, the imperative negatives *wu* (毋) and *wu* (勿) are used in these lines in later editions, again turning the lines into "orders," that is, "do it this way." In the Guodian slips we find the negative *fu* (弗), which simply negates the verb and implies an object that follows the verb. However, in passage C:3 (now chapter 31), *fu* is used in a line which clearly must be read as a directive—"Never regard them (weapons) as beautiful things" (*fu mei ye,* 弗美也). So we cannot be sure that *fu* was not intended as an imperative negative in these lines as well.[13]

LINES 7 AND 8:

Between lines 7 and 8, later editions add a line that normally reads "He achieves his result but only because he has no choice."

LINE 9:

That this is the final line of this "chapter" in the Guodian slips is indicated by punctuation. (For the placement of this punctuation mark see the introduction.) Later forms of the chapter, including the Mawangdui copies, have three additional lines: "When things reach their prime they get old. We call this 'not the Way.' What is not the Way will come to an early end." These lines are not entirely inappropriate here since the theme of the chapter is "stopping in time," reaching your goal but not forcefully going beyond it.

|  | *Transcription* | *Modern Equivalents* |
|---|---|---|
| 1 | 以衍䘹人宔者 | 以道佐人主者 |
| 2 | 不谷以兵強於天下 | 不欲以兵強於天下 |
| 3 | 善者果而已 | 善者果而已 |
| 4 | 不以取強▬ | 不以取強 |
| 5 | 果而弗戔 | 果而弗伐 |
| 6 | 果而弗喬 | 果而弗驕 |
| 7 | 果而弗猻▬ | 果而弗矜 |
| 8 | 是胃果而不強 | 是謂果而不強 |
| 9 | 丌事好▬長 | 其事好長 |

## A:5 (Chapter 15)[14]

1  Those who were good at being noble in antiquity[15]
2  Were without doubt subtle and profound, mysterious and penetratingly wise.[16]
3  So deep that they cannot be known.[17]

.......................................

4  For this reason we praise them in the following way:

5  Hesitant were they![18] Like someone crossing a river in winter.
6  Cautious were they! Like someone wary of his four neighbors.[19]
7  Deferential were they! Like guests.
8  Accommodating were they! Like melting ice.
9  Natural and genuine were they! Like wood that hasn't been carved.
10  Undifferentiated were they! Like muddy water.

.......................................

---

11/1  Who can be muddy, yet through tranquility gradually clear?[20]
12/2  Who can be still, yet through motion gradually stir?
13/3  The one who embraces this Way does not desire to be overly full.

.......................................

.......................................

*(lines 11–13 seem to be regarded as a separate passage)*

## Comments and Notes

LINE 1:

In place of "good at being noble" (*shan wei shizhe,* 善爲士者), many editions of the *Laozi*, including the Mawangdui copies, have "good at following (or practicing) the Way" (*shan wei daozhe,* 善爲道者). The only lineage that consistently uses the Guodian form of this line is that based on the Xiang'er recension.[21]

LINE 2:

In no other edition does this line begin with *bi* (必, were without doubt, were necessarily).

LINES 3 AND 4:

All other known editions we have of the text insert the line "It is only because they cannot be known" between these two lines.

LINE 4:

In all later editions, the word *song* (頌, to sing out their praises) is replaced by *rong* (容, to describe).²² Moreover, line 4 normally includes the word *qiang* (強), yielding the translation "Therefore, were I *forced* to describe them . . . "

LINE 10:

Later editions add a line to this sequence of lines, either before or after line 10: "Broad, all-embracing were they! Like a valley." Since the word "muddy" connects lines 10 and 11, this line should be before line 10 if it is used.

LINES 11 AND 12:

The words "who can" (*shu neng*, 孰能) are omitted from these lines in the Mawang-dui copies; this is also often the case in samples from the Xiang'er lineage. Thus both lines become statements: "Muddy water, through tranquility, gradually clears." The punctuation mark at the end of this line, as noted above, is clearly in error; it should have been put at the end of line 10. Lines 11–13 are rimed.

LINE 13:

The word "overly" (*shang*, 尚) is not attested in other editions. Of more importance, most later editions add two lines to the end of this chapter. These are normally phrased: 夫唯不盈, 故能蔽不新成. Translations of these lines vary greatly. One way to read the lines would be: "It is precisely because he is not full that he therefore can wear out without being renewed."²³

## A:5 (Chapter 15)

| | Transcription | Modern Equivalents |
|---|---|---|
| 1 | 古之善爲士者 | 古之善爲士者 |
| 2 | 必非溺玄造 | 必微妙玄造 |
| 3 | 深不可志＿ | 深不可識 |
| 4 | 是以爲之頌 | 是以爲之頌 |
| | | |
| 5 | 夜虖　奴㝎涉川＿ | 豫乎　如冬涉川 |
| 6 | 猷虖丌奴愄四哭＿ | 猶乎其如畏四鄰 |
| 7 | 敢虖丌奴客＿ | 嚴乎其如客 |
| 8 | 鬳虖丌奴瀪＿ | 渙乎其如釋 |
| 9 | 屯虖丌奴樸＿ | 屯乎其如樸 |
| 10 | 坉虖亓奴濁 | 坉乎其如濁 |
| | | |
| 11 | 竺能濁以束者牞舍清█ | 孰能濁以靜者將徐清 |
| 12 | 竺能庀以迬者牞舍生 | 孰能安以動者將徐生 |
| 13 | 保此衍者不谷尙呈 | 保此道者不欲尙盈 |

1    Those who act on it ruin it,
2    Those who hold on to it lose it.²⁵
3    Therefore the Sage does nothing, and as a result he has no disasters;
4    He holds on to nothing, and as a result he loses nothing.

5    The rule to follow in approaching all matters, is—
6    If you're as careful at the end as you were at the beginning
7    You will have no disasters.

8    The Sage desires not to desire and places no value on goods that are hard to obtain.
9    He teaches without teaching, and backs away from matters in which the masses go to excess.

10   As a result, the Sage is able to help the ten thousand things to be what they are in themselves, and yet he cannot do it.

*Comments and Notes*

LINES 1 AND 2:
In most editions of the *Laozi*, the first "it" (*zhi*, 之) in both of these lines is implied but omitted. Here the character is included as it should be.

LINE 5:
This line could also be read "When you get close to completing affairs." Read either way it differs considerably from what is normally said in this place: "In people's performing their duties, they always ruin things when they are right at the point of completion."

LINE 6:
This line begins with "Therefore" or "Therefore we say" in the Mawangdui copies.

LINE 8:
In most editions, this line begins with a "Therefore."

LINE 9:

In all other editions—and in passage C:4 below—"He teaches without teaching" or "He teaches not to teach" (*jiao bujiao,* 教不教) is instead "He learns to unlearn" (*xue buxue,* 學不學).

LINE 10:

The opening words—"As a result the Sage"—are omitted in later editions, and the point made at the end in all other editions is that the Sage "dare not do it" (*fu gan wei,* 弗敢爲), even though he "is able" (能) to do it.

|    | *Transcription* | *Modern Equivalents* |
|----|-----------------|----------------------|
| 1  | 爲之者敗之 | 爲之者敗之 |
| 2  | 埶之者遠之 | 執之者失之 |
| 3  | 是以聖人亡爲古亡敗 | 是以聖人無爲故無敗 |
| 4  | 　　　亡埶古亡遊 | 　　　無執故無失 |
| 5  | 臨事之紀 | 臨事之紀 |
| 6  | 誓㒺女门 | 愼終如始 |
| 7  | 此亡敗事矣 | 則無敗事矣 |
| 8  | 聖人谷不谷不貴難㝵之貨 | 聖人欲不欲不貴難得之貨 |
| 9  | 　　學不學㥛衆之所所㳂━ | 　　教不教復衆之所過 |
| 10 | 是古聖人能專萬物之自㲋而弗能爲 | 是故聖人能輔萬物之自然而弗能爲 |

## A:7 (Chapter 37)²⁶

1   The Way constantly takes no action.

..............................

2   Marquises and kings can maintain it,
3   And the ten thousand things transform on their own.²⁷

4   Once they have transformed, should desires arise,
5   You must quell them using the nameless natural state [*pu*].
6   You must also know when you have enough.
7   Knowing [when you have enough], you will be tranquil,²⁸
8   And the ten thousand things will be stable all on their own.

*Comments and Notes*

LINE 1:

In the Mawangdui copies—and they are the exception—this line is "The Way is constantly nameless." But "takes no action" (*wuwei*, 亡 爲) must be the original reading since the *wei* (*ɦɪuar) at the end of the line is meant to rime with "transform" (*hua*, 化, *huăr) at the end of line 3. Lines 5 and 6 also rime ("original state" [*pu*, *pʻŭk] and "enough" [*ʐu*, *tsiuk]), as do lines 7 and 8 ("tranquil" [*jing*, *dzieŋ] and "stable" [*ding*, *deŋ]).

LINES 1 AND 2:

Later editions tend to insert the following line between lines 1 and 2: "And yet there is nothing left undone." This line is also omitted in the Mawangdui copies.

LINES 2 AND 3:

This is normally posed as a conditional statement: "*Were* marquises and kings able to maintain it, the ten thousand things would transform on their own." But the conditional "if" or "were" (*ruo*, 若) is omitted here in line 2, while line 3 begins with the conjunction "and" (而). Note, however, that in passage A:10 below (chapter 32), in very similar lines (lines 3 and 4), the statement assumes its normal conditional form. The omission of *ruo* in line 2 might be a copy mistake.

LINE 5:

This is the only known form of the text in which this line does not begin with "I would . . . " (*wu jiang*, 吾將 . . . ).

LINE 6:

The phrase "the nameless natural state" is normally repeated at the start of this line. In addition, in place of the words "You must also know when you have enough," the Mawangdui copies have "I will then not be disgraced"; all other editions have "I will then have no desires."

LINE 7:

Keeping with the wording used in line 6, the Mawangdui copies here have "Not being disgraced, I will be tranquil" while other editions have "Not desiring, I will be tranquil."

LINE 8:

As the last word in the line, most later editions—including that represented by the Mawangdui copies—have "upright" or "correct" (*zheng*, 正) instead of "stable" (*ding*, 定).

## A:7 (Chapter 37)

| | *Transcription* | *Modern Equivalents* |
|---|---|---|
| 1 | 衍互亡爲也 | 道恆無爲也 |
| 2 | 侯王能守之 | 侯王能守之 |
| 3 | 而萬勿牀自愿 | 而萬物將自化 |
| 4 | 愿而雄复 | 化而欲作 |
| 5 | 牀貞之以亡名之斀 | 將鎮之以無名之樸 |
| 6 | 夫亦牀智足 | 夫亦將知足 |
| 7 | 智以束 | 知[足]以靜 |
| 8 | 萬勿牀自定■ | 萬物將自定 |

1    Act without acting;
2    Serve without concern for affairs;
3    Find flavor in what has no flavor.

4    In affairs large or small, the more things you take to be easy,
     the more difficulties there are bound to be.
5    Therefore even the Sage regards things as difficult,
6    And as a result in the end he has no difficulties.

*Comments and Notes*

LINE 4:

In later editions, line 4 is divided to form two separate lines. The second half of the line—"The more things . . . "—is line 13 (in a chapter of fifteen lines). To the first part of the line—"In affairs large or small" (*daxiao*, 大小)—are added the characters 多少 (*duoshao*), the whole then being read "Regard the small as large and the few as many."

My translation of lines 4–15 as they are found in copy A of the Mawangdui manuscripts reads as follows (I have italicized the words that are omitted in the Guodian form of the chapter):³⁰

4    Regard the small as large *and the few as many.*
5    And repay resentment with kindness.³¹
6    Plan for the difficult while it is easy;
7    Act on the large while it is minute.
8    The most difficult things in the world begin as things that are easy;
9    The largest things in the world arise from the minute.
10   Therefore the Sage, to the end does not strive to do the great,
11   And as a result, he is able to accomplish the great.
12   Those who too lightly agree will necessarily be trusted by few;
13   *And* those who regard many things as easy will necessarily end up with
     many difficulties.
14   Therefore, even the Sage regards things as difficult,
15   And as a result, in the end he has no difficulty.

## A:8 (Chapter 63, lines 1–4, 13–15)

| *Transcription* | *Modern Equivalent* |
|---|---|
| 1  爲亡爲 | 爲無爲 |
| 2  事亡事 | 事無事 |
| 3  未亡未 | 味無味 |
| 4  大少之多惥必多雞 | 大小之多易必多難 |
| 5  是以聖人猷雞之 | 是以聖人猶難之 |
| 6  古冬亡雞 ■ | 故終無難 |

1    When everyone in the world knows the beautiful as beautiful, ugliness comes into being.

2    When everyone knows the good, then the not-good comes into being.

3    [In this way we must understand] the mutual production of being and non-being,

4    The mutual completion of difficult and easy,

5    The mutual formation of long and short,

6    The mutual filling of high and low,

7    The mutual harmony of tone and sound,[33]

8    And the mutual following of front and behind.

..........................................

9    Therefore the Sage abides in affairs that entail no action,

10   And spreads the wordless teaching.

11   The ten thousand things arise, but he does not begin them.[34]

..........................................

12   He does things for them, but he does not make them dependent.

13   He brings things to completion, but he does not dwell on his achievements.

14   But it is precisely because he does not dwell on them

15   That they therefore do not leave him.

*Comments and Notes*

LINES 3–8:
In the Mawangdui copies, this series of nominative phrases is completed with the stative verb—"These are all constants" (*heng ye*, 恒也). Since that line is omitted in this form of the text, we can only make sense of this series if something like "In this way we must understand" is implied at the start of the series. In most other editions, lines 3–8 stand on their own as statements (e.g., "Being and non-being produce each other.").

LINES 11–12:

Like the Mawangdui copies, the Guodian slips omit the line commonly added between these two lines: "He gives birth to them, but he does not own them."

| *Transcription* | *Modern Equivalents* |
|---|---|
| 1  天下皆智斂之爲斂也亞已 | 天下皆知美之爲美也惡已 |
| 2      皆智善    此亓不善已 | 皆知善    則不善已 |
| | |
| 3  又亡之相生也 | 有無之相生也 |
| 4  戁悬之相成也 | 難易之相成也 |
| 5  長耑之相型也 | 長短之相形也 |
| 6  高下之相浧也 | 高下之相盈也 |
| 7  音聖之相和也 | 音聲之相和也 |
| 8  先逡之相墮也 | 先後之相隨也 |
| | |
| 9  是以聖人居亡爲之事 | 是以聖人居無爲之事 |
| 10      行不言之孝 | 行不言之教 |
| | |
| 11 萬勿复而弗忹也 | 萬物作而弗始也 |
| 12     爲而弗志也 | 爲而弗恃也 |
| 13     成而弗居 | 成而弗居 |
| | |
| 14 天唯弗居也 | 夫唯弗居也 |
| 15 是以弗去也 ■ | 是以弗去也 |

## A:10 (Chapter 32)[35]

1    The Way is constantly nameless.

2    Though in its natural state it appears to be unimportant,[36]
     No one in heaven or earth dares to make it his subject.[37]

3    Were marquises and kings able to maintain it,

4    The ten thousand things would submit to them on their own.

---

5/1   Heaven and earth come together and send forth sweet dew.

6/2   No one causes this to be so; of itself it falls equally on them.

7/3   When we start to "regulate" or "put into order" there will be names.[38]

8/4   But when names have indeed come into being,

9/5   We must also know that it is time to stop.

10/6  Knowing [when] to stop is the way to avoid harm.

11/7  The Way's presence in the world,

12/8  Is like the relationship of small valley streams to rivers and seas.

(lines 5–12 seem to be regarded as a separate passage)

### Comments and Notes

LINE 4:

Punctuation at the end of line 4 would seem to indicate that lines 1–4 and lines 5–12 should be regarded as two distinct passages or "chapters," and the connection between the first four lines and the rest of the chapter is far from apparent.[39] Nonetheless, in later editions these two "chapters" are regarded as one; note that lines 11 and 12 might say metaphorically what is said more directly in lines 1–4. In addition, I suspect that the condition in which we "have names" (*you ming*), introduced in line 7, is meant to contrast with the "namelessness" (*wu ming*) of the Way as set out in line 1. Thus it is possible that the punctuation at the end of line 4 is an error.

| *Transcription* | *Modern Equivalents* |
|---|---|
| 1 | 道互亡名 | 道恆無名 |
| 2 | 僅唯妻天陛弗敢臣 | 樸雖細天地弗敢臣 |
| 3 | 侯王女能獸之 | 侯王如能守之 |
| 4 | 萬勿牆自賓■ | 萬物將自賓 |
| 5 | 天陛相會也以逾甘露 | 天地相會也以逾甘露 |
| 6 | 民莫之命而自均安 | 民莫之命而自均安 |
| 7 | 訂折又名 | 始制有名 |
| 8 | 名亦旣又 | 名亦旣有 |
| 9 | 夫亦牆智走 | 夫亦將知 |
| 10 | 智走所以不訂 | 知止所以不殆 |
| 11 | 卑道之才天下也 | 譬道之在天下也 |
| 12 | 猷少浴之彔江海■ | 猶小谷之與江海 |

## A:11 (Chapter 25)[40]

1 There is a form that developed from primordial chaos
2 That was born before heaven and earth.
3 Silent and still,[41] it stands on its own and does not change.

.......................................

4 It can be regarded as the mother of all under heaven.
5 Not yet knowing its name,
6 We refer to it as the Dao.[42]
7 Were I forced to give it a name, I'd call it the Great.

8 The "Great" means "overflowing";
9 "Overflowing" means "going far";
10 "Going far" means "to return."

11 Heaven is great; the earth is great; the Way is great; and the king too is great.
12 In this realm[43] there are four greats, and the king counts as one of them.

13 Humanity takes as its model the earth;
14 The earth takes as its model heaven;
15 Heaven takes as its model the Way;
16 And the Way takes as its model that which is so on its own.

*Comments and Notes*

LINE 1:

In all other editions we have of the text, this line begins: "There was something [*wu*, 物] that developed from primordial chaos." The character here is ⿰爿首, which Qiu Xigui suggests might be read as *dao* (道), that is, "the Way."[44] But in his notes to "Wuxing," he proposes a reading of *zhuang* (壯) for this character.[45] Thus it might be a phonetic loan for the *zhuang* (狀) that means "shape" or "form." In modern editions of *Laozi*, the Way is called "the formless form" (無狀之狀) in chapter 14.[46]

The translation is tentative since the final character in the line—瀩—remains unidentified. Later editions have the word *shi* (逝, to depart) in this location. However, Peng Hao has drawn my attention to the fact that the same character, without the "water" radical, occurs in part IV of the "Collected Sayings," where it is transcribed as *kui* (憒, chaos or chaotic).[47] In his note on that character, Qiu Xigui argues that the phonetic element must be either *dui* (𣫭) or *xian* (臽).[48] *Kui* (瀩) might be a good reading if the phonetic is *dui*; *han* (涵, all-embracing) might work well if the phonetic is *xian*. But there is another possibility. In *Chuxi jianbo wenzibian* [楚系簡帛文字編], Teng Rensheng (滕壬生) lists several samples of this character, which he transcribes as 瀩 (p. 813). Transcribed in this way, the phonetic element then might be *qian* (臤), in which case our mystery character would have belonged to the *yuan* (元) category in terms of rime. This would be significant because the words "going far" (*yuan*, 遠, \*ɦɪuǎn) and "return" (*fan*, 反, \*pɪuǎn) in the following lines were also *yuan*-rime words and because in other places where we find this same pattern in the *Laozi*—"a *yue* b, b *yue* c, c *yue* d"—in chapters 16 and 55, character "b" establishes the rime category for the whole set of lines. Our problem then would become: is there a "water" radical word in the *yuan* rime group that would be fitting here? One possibility would be *yuan* (源, \*ŋɪuǎn, the source): "By 'Great' we mean 'the source.'" Were this true, this might explain why Xia Song (夏竦), in his *Guwen sisheng yun* (古文四聲韻),[49] cites two *guwen* (ancient script) forms of the character 源 (*yuan*), noting the sources as "ancient editions of the *Laozi*" (*gu Laozi*, 古老子). The character 源 does not occur in any of our current editions of the *Laozi*.

# A:11 (Chapter 25)

| | *Transcription* | *Modern Equivalents* |
|---|---|---|
| 1 | 又𥡴蟲成 | 有狀混成 |
| 2 | 先天㞢生 | 先天地生 |
| 3 | 敓繆罜立不亥 | 寂繆獨立不改 |
| 4 | 可以爲天下母 | 可以爲天下母 |
| 5 | 未智亓名 | 未知其名 |
| 6 | 𡥈之曰道 | 字之曰道 |
| 7 | 虐弜爲之名曰大 | 吾強爲之名曰大 |
| | | |
| 8 | 大曰瀧 | 大曰潰 |
| 9 | 瀧曰連 | 潰曰遠 |
| 10 | 連曰反 | 遠曰反 |
| | | |
| 11 | 天大㞢大道大王亦大 | 天大地大道大王亦大 |
| 12 | 國中又四大安王尻一安 | 域中有四大安王處一安 |
| | | |
| 13 | 人灋㞢 | 人法地 |
| 14 | 㞢灋天 | 地法天 |
| 15 | 天灋道 | 天法道 |
| 16 | 道灋自肰■ | 道法自然 |

..........................................
..........................................
..........................................
..........................................

1    The space between heaven and earth—
2    Is it not like a bellows?[51]
3    Though it is empty it does not collapse;
4    When put into motion it sends forth all the more.

..........................................
..........................................

*Comments and Notes*

The four lines that precede these lines in later editions are: "Heaven and earth are not humane; they treat the ten thousand things as straw dogs. The Sage is not humane; he treats the common folk as straw dogs." The only point in common between these two sayings, as D. C. Lau has already noted, seems to be the mention of "heaven and earth."[52] This is one of the examples Lau uses in support of his argument that at least some of the chapters in the *Laozi* are made up of sayings from different sources that make different points but share a word or phrase in common. As we have noted in the introduction the Guodian evidence seems to support his point. The "straw dogs" lines are cited as a unit in the *Wenzi*, with no mention of "the space between heaven and earth."[53] The two lines that follow these lines, in the Mawangdui copies at least, are: "Much learning means frequent exhaustion. That is not so good as holding on to the mean."[54]

## A:12 (Chapter 5, lines 5–7)

|   | Transcription | Modern Equivalents |
|---|---|---|
| 1 | 天坣之勿 | 天地之間 |
| 2 | 丌猷囝箮與 | 其猶囊管與 |
| 3 | 虛而不屈 | 虛而不屈 |
| 4 | 達而愈出 ■ | 動而愈出 |

1    Take emptiness to the limit;

2    Cautiously guard the void.[56]

3    The ten thousand things, side by side they arise;

4    Sitting still we await their return.

5    Now, the forms come forth in great numbers,

6    But each returns to its root.

..................................

..................................

..................................

..................................

..................................

..................................

..................................

..................................

..................................

..................................

..................................

..................................

*Comments and Notes*

LINES I AND 2:

In line 1, where later editions have *ji* (極, extreme, limit), the character on the Guodian slips is 亙, which is transcribed as *heng* (恒, constant). But the *guwen* (ancient script) form of *heng* was virtually indistinguishable from the right side of *ji* (極),[57] and the reading of *ji* here seems preferred for continuity with later editions.[58] In line 2, where most later editions have *jing* (靜), "tranquility," the Guodian reading is *zhong* (中, center). Reading this *zhong* as *zhong* (盅) is Ikeda's suggestion,[59] but a literal reading of "Cautiously guard the center" would also be valid. In the Mawangdui and Guodian copies, these lines could be read as definitions, maybe something like "Taking emptiness to the extreme is what we mean by 'the limit,'" and "Guarding the void (or guarding the center), is what we mean by 'the deep.'" But they are never read that way by the Chinese, and it could be that the *ye*'s (也) at the end of lines 1 and 2—the feature that implies this kind of reading—were added to make these lines four-character lines to balance the rest.

LINE 4:

In later editions, this line normally reads "And by this I see their return." But the Guodian version has "sit" or "occupy/reside" (*ju*, 居) in place of "I" (*wu*, 吾) and "await" (*xu*, 須) in place of "see/observe" (*guan*, 觀).⁶⁰

LINE 5:

In later editions, this line reads "Now things come forth in great numbers" (*fu wu yunyun*, 夫物芸芸). Reading *yuanyuan* (臬臬 = 員員) as phonetic loans for 芸 芸, the Guodian version literally says "The Way of heaven [or "ways of heaven" (*tiandao*, 天道)] come[s] forth in great numbers." But this is problematic since the "each" (*ge*, 各) in line 6 should refer back to the subject of line 5; that would imply there are multiple "ways of heaven" ("*Each* returns to its root"). That seems unlikely since *tiandao*, in all other places in the *Laozi*, refers to a single "Way of heaven." It is possible to have the "each" refer back to the "ten thousand things" of line 3, but that is grammatically awkward. Nonetheless, if we assume that is the case, and read *yuanyuan* in line 5 as *yuanyuan* (圓圓, round and round), we get a valid and interesting reading: "The Way of heaven goes round and round, And each returns to its root."⁶¹ My own feeling, for the moment at least, is that the character 天 (*tian*) in line 5 should be read as 夫 (*fu*)—the two characters were virtually indistinguishable in ancient script⁶²—and that the character 道 (*dao*) is a mistake for 𢔻, the character in the opening line of A:11 (chapter 25), which seems to mean *zhuang* (狀, form).⁶³

LINE 6:

The rest of the chapter, using my translation of the Mawangdui copies, reads as follows:⁶⁴

7    This is called tranquility.
8    "Tranquility"—This means to return to your fate.
9    To return to your fate is to be constant;
10   To know the constant is to be wise.
11   Not to know the constant is to be reckless and wild;
12   If you're reckless and wild, your actions will lead to misfortune.

13   To know the constant is to be all-embracing;
14   To be all-embracing is to be impartial;
15   To be impartial is to be kingly;
16   To be kingly is to be like heaven;
17   To be like heaven is to be one with the Dao;
18   If you're one with the Dao, till the end of your days you'll suffer no harm.

|   | *Transcription* | *Modern Equivalents* |
|---|---|---|
| 1 | 至虛互也 | 至虛極也 |
| 2 | 獸中篙也 | 守盅篤也 |
|   |   |   |
| 3 | 萬勿方复 | 萬物旁作 |
| 4 | 居以須遆也 | 居以須復也 |
| 5 | 天道員員 | 夫狀云云 |
| 6 | 各遆亓董 | 各復其根 |

## A:14 (Chapter 64, part 1)[65]

1  What is at rest is easy to hold
2  What has not yet given a sign is easy to plan for.
3  What is fragile is easily broken.[66]
4  What is minute is easily scattered.

5  Act on it when it does not exist;
6  Establish order before it turns into chaos.

7  The biggest of trees
8  *grows from the tiniest* shoot;
9  A tower nine stories high
10  begins *with one pile of dirt;*[67]
11  *A height of eight hundred feet*
12  *starts from* under your foot.

*Comments and Notes*

LINE 5:
All other editions have "*before* it comes into existence" (*wei you,* 未有).

LINES 11–12:
These lines exist in two different forms, the other one being "A journey of a thousand li begins with a single step" (千里之行始於足下). Since both lines end with *zuxia* (足下, under your foot, or a single step), there is no way of knowing which line was written on the Guodian slip. But both Mawangdui copies have "A height of eight hundred feet,"[68] and Shima Kunio has shown that this was the form of the line in the Yan Zun and Xiang'er lineages, and in the original Wang Bi recension as well.[69] In any event, lines 10 and 12 rimed.[70] "A journey of a thousand li . . . " seems to have originated with the Heshanggong recension.

| *Transcription* | *Modern Equivalents* |
|---|---|
| 1 | 亓安也易柰也 | 其安易持也 |
| 2 | 亓未菲也易思也 | 其未兆也易謀也 |
| 3 | 亓纔也易畔也 | 其毳也易判也 |
| 4 | 亓幾也易後也 | 其幾也易散也 |
| 5 | 爲之於亓亡又也 | 爲之於其無有也 |
| 6 | 絧之於亓未娛 | 治之於其未亂 |
| 7 | 合□□□ | 合[抱之木 |
| 8 | □□□末 | 生於毫]末 |
| 9 | 九成之臺 | 九成之臺 |
| 10 | 甲□□□ | 起[於累土] |
| 11 | □□□□ | [百刃之高 |
| 12 | □□足下▬ | 始於]足下 |

## A:15 (Chapter 56)[11]

1   Those who understand it say nothing about it; those who talk about it do not understand it.

2   He closes the holes,
3   Blocks the gates,
4   Softens the glare,
5   Settles the dust,
6   Severs the bonds,
7   And unties the knots.

8   This is called the Mysterious Union.

9   Therefore there is no way to get intimate with him,
10   But there is also no way to shun him.
11   There is no way to benefit him,
12   But there is also no way to harm him.
13   There is no way to ennoble him,
14   But there is also no way to debase him.

15   As a result, he is the noblest thing in the world.

### Comments and Notes

LINE 1:
The references to an "it" (*zhi*, 之) in this line are omitted in later editions, resulting in translations that say something like: "One who knows does not speak, and one who speaks does not know."

LINES 2 AND 3:
The verbs are normally reversed in later editions: He "blocks" the holes and "closes" the gates.

LINE 6:
This normally reads "files down the sharp edges" (*zuo qi rui*, 挫其銳). My translation is tentative since the characters on the Guodian slips—劷 and 頯—are unknown.

Ikeda suggests reading the first as a phonetic loan for *fu* (副, \*p'ɪuək, to cut, sever), and the second as a writing of *ying* (攖, bound up, entangled).[72] Another possibility—which would not change the meaning—would be to read the second as the character 纓 (*ying*, tied up or bound) and the first as a phonetic loan for the character 刨 (*bao*, \*pok), which provides a better phonological match for the phonetic element *chu* (畜, \*t'ɪok).

LINES 4–7:

The Mawangdui copies share this sequence with the Guodian slips, but in other editions the order is normally 6–7 and 4–5. Either sequence is acceptable in terms of the rime, since the riming words are "gates" (*men*), "dust" (*chen*), and "knots" (*fen*).

## A:15 (Chapter 56)

| | *Transcription* | *Modern Equivalents* |
|---|---|---|
| 1 | 智之者弗言言之者弗智 | 知之者弗言言之者弗知 |
| 2 | 閔亓逸 | 閉其兌 |
| 3 | 賽亓門 | 塞其門 |
| 4 | 和亓光 | 和其光 |
| 5 | 迵亓訢訢 | 同其塵 |
| 6 | 銼亓䌰 | 刨其纓 |
| 7 | 解亓紛 | 解其紛 |
| 8 | 是胃玄同 | 是謂玄同 |
| 9 | 古不可尋天新 | 故不可得而親 |
| 10 | 亦不可尋而疋 | 亦不可得而疏 |
| 11 | 不可尋而利 | 不可得而利 |
| 12 | 亦不可尋而害 | 亦不可得而害 |
| 13 | 不可尋而貴 | 不可得而貴 |
| 14 | 亦可不可尋而戔 | 亦可不可得而賤 |
| 15 | 古爲天下貴■ | 故爲天下貴 |

1    Use the upright and correct to order the state;
2    Use irregular methods when using the troops;
3    But be unconcerned with affairs if you want to take over the world.

4    How do I know this is so?

.......................................

5    Well, the more taboos there are in the world, the more rebellious the people will be;
6    And the more sharp weapons the people possess, the more disordered the state will be.
7    The more people know, the more "oddities" will be produced;
8    And the more "exemplary goods" are put on display, the more robbers and thieves there will be.[74]

9    Therefore the words of the Sage put it this way:

10   I am unconcerned with affairs, and the people on their own enjoy good fortune;
11   I do nothing, and the people transform on their own;
12   I love tranquility, and the people on their own are upright and honest.
13   I desire not to desire, and the people on their own are content with the plain and unadorned.

*Comments and Notes:*

LINE 4:
Like the Mawangdui copies, the Guodian slips omit the answer to this question, which is normally found in later editions: "By this."

LINES 5–6:
The Guodian slips omit the *xia* (下, below) from *tianxia* (天下, the world) in line 5, suggesting a reading of "The more taboos *heaven* has," or "The more taboos there are about *heaven*" for the first part of the line. However, I think in this case *tian* on its own must mean "world." Alternatively, it could mean "the ruler": *Tian* could

stand for "ruler" or "father" in early texts when used in the context of social relations. At the end of this line, later editions have *pin* (貧, poor) where the Guodian slips have *pan* (畔), which we here read as *pan* (叛, to rebel). So line 5 normally reads "The more taboos there are in the world, the *poorer* the people will be." In some ways *pin* (貧, poor) seems a better choice here than *pan* (叛). For one thing, *pin* rimed better with *hun* (昏, chaotic), the final word in line 6, than did *pan*, and one expects lines 5 and 6 to rime since 7 and 8 clearly did (*qi* [起, *k'ıuəg], and *you*, [有, *ɦıuəg]).[75] In addition, the final character in line 10 (福) could be read as a variant writing of *fu* (富, wealth); in this way, lines 5 and 10 would nicely contrast. But since "taboos" are imposed to avoid "bad fortune," I think it is better to read the final word in line 10 as a variant writing of *fu* (福, good fortune); that is, the people enjoy good fortune *even though* the ruler is unconcerned with taboos and prohibitions.[76] If this choice is right, the final word in line 5 need not be *pin*, and *pan* in this case might be used in response to the "order" (*zheng*, 正) that line 1 desires, just as the mention of "sharp weapons" (*liqi*, 利器) in line 6, might refer back to line 2.[77] I continue to think that lines 1 and 2 are suggestions that "others" (Confucians and Militarists) made to rulers, while line 3 is the author's advice.[78]

LINES 5–8:

From the point of view of later editions, it would appear that a single character has been omitted from each of these lines. Instead of *tianxia* (天下, the world) in line 5, we have only *tian* (heaven); in line 6, where other editions have *bangjia* (邦家) or *guojia* (國家, the state), this version has only *bang*; in line 7, where later editions tend to have *jiqiao* (伎巧, arts and talents) or *zhiqiao* (知巧, knowledge and skill),[79] this version simply has *zhi*; and in line 8, the connective particle *er* (而) is omitted, even though the parallel structure seems to demand it. But the lines appear correct as they stand; they are all eight-character lines (omitting from consideration the introductory *fu* [夫] at the start of line 5), and the metric and symantic patterns of the set of lines as a whole are quite clever. Since the connective *er* is essentially the comma that separates the two clauses in lines 5–7, the metric pattern used in the lines is 4/3, 4/3, 3/4, 4/4. Lines 5 and 6 are grammatically strictly parallel, while line 7, in terms of meter, is the reverse of line 6. Then the first clause in line 8 (*fawu zizhang*) grammatically parallels the second clause in line 7 (*qiwu ziqi*), and, for a strong finish, the second clause in line 8 (*daozei duoyou*) uses this same grammatical pattern. Also note that symantically the subjects of the two clauses in the opening lines are reversed (i.e., "If the world is filled with . . . , the *people* are . . ; but if the *people* have . . . , the *state* then is . . . ").

LINES 10–13:

Normally, the line sequence here is 11, 12, 10, and 13.[80] But lines 10–13 might correspond line-by-line to lines 5–8, in which case the Guodian order seems the best. Following the author's advice, the people will "enjoy good fortune" (end of line 10) with no need of "taboos" (start of line 5), and they will be "upright and honest" (*zheng* [正], end of line 12) stands in contrast to their production of "oddities" (*qiwu* [奇物], end of line 7).[81]

## A:16 (Chapter 57)

|   | *Transcription* | *Modern Equivalents* |
|---|---|---|
| 1 | 以正之邦 | 以正治邦 |
| 2 | 以𢦏甬兵 | 以奇用兵 |
| 3 | 以亡事取天下 | 以無事取天下 |
| 4 | 虐可以智亓然也 | 吾何以知其然也 |
| 5 | 夫天多𪯆韋而民爾畔 | 夫天多忌諱而民彌叛 |
| 6 | 民多利器而邦慈昏 | 民多利器而邦滋昏 |
| 7 | 人多智而𢦏勿慈记 | 人多知而奇物滋起 |
| 8 | 灋勿慈章眺悤多又 | 法物滋章盜賊多有 |
| 9 | 是以聖人之言曰 | 是以聖人之言曰 |
| 10 | 我無事　而民自福 | 我無事　而民自福 |
| 11 | 我亡為　而民自蟲 | 我無爲　而民自化 |
| 12 | 我好青　而民自正 | 我好靜　而民自正 |
| 13 | 我谷不谷而民自檏乙 | 我欲不欲而民自樸 |

1    One who embraces the fullness of virtue
2    May be compared to a newborn babe.


3    Vipers and scorpions, poisonous insects and snakes will not bite him,
4    Birds of prey and fierce beasts will not strike him.
5    His bones are soft and his muscles are pliant, yet his grasp is firm.
6    He does not yet know of the mating of female and male, [yet] his penis stiffens.
7    This is because his essence is at its height.
8    He can scream all day without getting hoarse;[83]
9    This is because his inner harmony is at its height.


10    That inner harmony we call "the constant."
11    To know that harmony we call "being wise."
12    Trying to increase your life is known as "bad fortune."[84]
13    And when the mind controls the *qi*—this we call "using force."


14    When things reach their prime they get old.
15    This is called "not the Way."[85]


*Comments and Notes*

LINE 3:
This line is normally "Wasps and scorpions, vipers and snakes will not bite/sting him," but the line exists in a number of forms.[86]


LINE 4:
 This is often an eight-character line formed by two clauses, that is, something like "birds of prey do not seize him; fierce beasts do not grab him" (or, in the opposite order, "fierce beasts . . . birds of prey . . . "). But the Guodian form of the line matches that of the Mawangdui copies. It has six characters, paralleling line 3; also, characters 2 (birds, *tög), 4 (beasts, *thiog), and 6 (strike, *kʻug) probably rimed.[87]


LINE 5:
In copy B of the Mawangdui manuscripts, this line reads: "His bones and muscles

are soft and pliant." But in this sequence, characters 2 (soft, *niɔk), 4 (pliant, *niog), and 7 (firm, *kag) were phonologically similar, even though they did not fully rime.

LINE 6:

In the Wang Bi recension, the word *quan* (全, complete) is substituted for *juan* (朘, penis), which makes sense only as a phonetic loan. Where other editions have *juan*, the Guodian slips have an unknown character, 肰, which is understood to be *ran* (然). I suspect this is a variant writing of *yang* (陽), which, like *juan*, means the penis.[88]

LINE 10:

Like the Mawangdui copies, and in contrast to later editions of the *Laozi*, the Guodian slips omit the word "knowing" (*zhi*, 知) from the start of this line. Lines 10 and 11 in later editions are: "Knowing harmony is known as 'the constant.' Knowing the constant is called 'being wise.'"

LINE 15:

All other editions of the *Laozi*, including that represented by the Mawangdui copies, add a line at the end of the chapter: "What is not the Way will come to an early end." As noted above (A:4, chapter 30), lines 14 and 15 plus this additional line are also found at the end of chapter 30 in later editions.

|  | *Transcription* | *Modern Equivalents* |
|---|---|---|
| 1 | 畬悳之厚者 | 含德之厚者 |
| 2 | 比於赤子 | 比於赤子 |
| | | |
| 3 | 蟲蠆蠚它弗蓳 | 蜂蠆蟲蛇弗螫 |
| 4 | 攫鳥猷獸弗扣 | 據鳥猛獸弗扣 |
| 5 | 骨霥菫柔而捉固 | 骨弱筋柔而握固 |
| 6 | 未智牝戊之合朘悲 | 未知牝牡之合陽怒 |
| 7 | 精之至也 | 精之至也 |
| 8 | 冬日虖而不嚘 | 終日呼而不嗄 |
| 9 | 和之至也 | 和之至也 |
| | | |
| 10 | 和曰稟 | 和曰常 |
| 11 | 智和曰明 | 知和曰明 |
| 12 | 薈生曰羕 | 益生曰祥 |
| 13 | 心貞燹曰彊 | 心使氣曰強 |
| | | |
| 14 | 勿壅則老 | 物壯則老 |
| 15 | 是胃不道■ | 是謂不道 |

## A:18 (Chapter 44)[89]

1    Fame or your health—which is more dear?

2    Your health or possessions—which is worth more?

3    Gain or loss—in which is there harm?

4    When attachments are great there is bound to be waste;

5    If you store much away, you are bound to lose a great deal.

6    Therefore, if you know contentment you will not be disgraced,

7    And if you know when to stop, you will not be harmed.

8    As a result, you will live a long time.

*Comments and Notes*

Allowing for the use of synonyms, phonetic loans, and variant writings, the wording here is exactly the same as we find in other editions, with the exception of line 5, in which the words "much" (*hou,* 厚) and "great" (*duo,* 多) are reversed. Also, like the Mawangdui copies, the Guodian version omits a "Therefore" at the beginning of line 4 and puts one at the start of line 6; this in contrast to most later editions.[90] A possible point of interest is the fact that there is internal rime in lines 1–7. The riming words are: line 1, *shen* (health) and *qin* (dear); line 2, *huo* (possessions) and *duo* (more); line 3, *wang* ( loss) and *bing* (harm); line 4, *ai* (attachments) and *fei* (waste); line 5, *cang* (stored away) and *wang* (lose); line 6, *ẓu* (contentment) and *ru* (disgrace); and line 7, *ẓhi* (stop) and *dai* (harm). Also, the final word in line 8—*jiu* (long time)—rimed with the final word in line 7, *dai* (harm).[91]

|  | *Transcription* | *Modern Equivalents* |
|---|---|---|
| 1 | 名與身箸新 | 名與身孰親 |
| 2 | 身與貨箸多 | 身與貨孰多 |
| 3 | 貨與貞箸疠 | 得與亡孰病 |
| 4 | 甚炁必大賹 | 甚愛必大費 |
| 5 | 启贁必多貞 | 厚藏必多亡 |
| 6 | 古智足不辱 | 故知足不辱 |
| 7 | 智走不怠 | 知止不殆 |
| 8 | 可以長舊■ | 可以長舊 |

## A:19 (Chapter 40)⁹²

1     "Returning" is the way the Way moves;⁹³
2     "Weakness" is the way the Way works.

3     The things of the world arise from being,
4     And being comes from non-being.⁹⁴

*Comments and Notes*

LINES 3 AND 4:
A literal translation of the Guodian words would be: "The things of the world arise from being, and they arise from non-being." That is to say, the word "being" (*you*, 又/有), which is repeated in all other editions we have of the text, is not repeated on the Guodian slips. But with the Wenwu editors, I think this is a mistake; the copyist simply forgot to add the sign for "repetition" (=) after the *you* in line 3.⁹⁵ However, Chen Guying is delighted with this form of the line, since he believes that the Way *is* both "being" and "non-being"; hence it is correct to say that "the things of this world arise from being, *and* they arise from non-being." The phenomenal things of the world actually come from both.⁹⁶

|   | *Transcription* | *Modern Equivalents* |
|---|---|---|
| 1 | 返也者道　僮也 | 反也者道　動也 |
| 2 | 溺也者道之甬也 | 弱也者道之用也 |
| | | |
| 3 | 天下之勿生於又 | 天下之物生於有 |
| 4 | 　　　生於亡■ | 　　　[有]生於無 |

## A:20 (Chapter 9)[97]

1    To accumulate until you have filled it
2    Is not so good as stopping in time.
3    When swift flowing waters gather against it
4    It cannot hold out very long.

5    When gold and jade fill your chambers
6    No one can safeguard them.
7    Arrogance resulting from wealth and rank
8    On its own brings on disaster.

9    When the deed is done withdraw—
10   Such is heaven's Way.

### Comments and Notes

The theme of the chapter is consistent throughout; it is established with metaphors in the opening lines, talked of directly in lines 5–8, and repeated in the closing lines, in which we are reminded that this is, after all, the way things work in nature. When the heat of summer becomes sufficient to ripen the crops, it stops, and the weather cools down. In the Chinese, lines 4, 6, 8, and 10 rime, and the passage consists almost entirely of four-character lines.[98]

LINES 1–2:
One image that comes to mind is that of filling a cup or a vase to the brim so that it is top heavy and easily spilled. Later editions tend to say "to hold" (*chi*, 持) where we here translate "to accumulate." I am following the lead of the Wenwu editors in reading the character 朱 as *ẓhi* (植/殖), for which one definition is *ji* (積, to accumulate or build up).[99] Either word is appropriate, but "accumulate" seems to fit well with the overall theme of the chapter.

LINE 3:
This line is normally translated "To pound it out and give it a point" (in the sense of sharpening a sword or a knife), the characters being *chuai er rui ẓhi* (揣而銳之). But the characters here are *tuan er qun ẓhi* (湍而群之), where *tuan* refers to the rapid and swirling motion of water, and *qun* means "a crowd" or "to amass." While we might replace *tuan* (湍, *t'uan) with *chuai* (揣, *ts'ïuar), arguing that it is simply

a case of using a different radical, it is more difficult to see how we could get from *qun* (群, *gɪuən) to *rui* (銳, *diuad). But I suspect that the Guodian form of this line is the correct one and that the later version developed from this by mistake. What confirms this is the fact that the characters used in this line in Mawangdui copy B phonetically agree with the Guodian words, and not with the words used in later editions. The Mawangdui characters are 掜 (*tuan) 而 允 (*ğiuən) 之.[100]

But what is the point of lines 3 and 4? The answer might be provided in the following words of Li Kang (李康, c. 196–264): "When a tree stands above all the rest in the forest, the wind is sure to break it; and when a mound stands out from the shore, the fast flowing water is sure to overwhelm it [*liu bi tuan ʒhi,* 流 必 湍 之]."[101] This image certainly fits in with the point made in the rest of the chapter.

## A:20 (Chapter 9)

| | *Transcription* | *Modern Equivalents* |
|---|---|---|
| 1 | 朱而湼之 | 持而盈之 |
| 2 | 不不若已 | 不不若已 |
| 3 | 湍而羣之 | 湍而羣之 |
| 4 | 不可長保也 | 不可長保也 |
| | | |
| 5 | 金玉湼室 | 金玉盈室 |
| 6 | 莫能獸也 | 莫能守也 |
| 7 | 貴福喬 | 貴福驕 |
| 8 | 自遺智也 | 自遺咎也 |
| | | |
| 9 | 攻述身退 | 功遂身退 |
| 10 | 天之道也乙 | 天之道也 |

*Laozi* B

1    For ruling humanity and serving heaven, there is nothing so good as keeping things in reserve.

2    Only if you keep things in reserve will you early submit;[2]

3    Early submission—this means *to repeatedly build up your virtue*;

4    *If you repeatedly build up your virtue, there is nothing you* cannot overcome;[3]

5    *If there is nothing* you cannot overcome, no one knows how far you can go;[4]

6    If no one knows how far you can go, you can possess the whole world;

7    And if you possess the world's mother, you can last *and endure*.

8    *This is called* the Way *of deep roots, a firm base*, long life, and long-lasting vision.

## Comments and Notes

LINE 1:

"Keeping things in reserve" (*se*, 嗇) refers to the act of storing grain after the harvest, and, by extension, *se* also means "farmer." One school of thought reads this line: "For ruling humanity and serving heaven, there is nothing so good as being a farmer."

LINES 2 AND 3:

Where later texts advise "early submission" (*zaofu*, 早服 [or 伏 or 復]) in both lines, the Guodian slips seem to urge "preparing early" (*zaobei*, 早備). Since the focus of the chapter seems to be "nourishing life" (*yangsheng*, 養生), and long life results from conserving one's vital energies and powers (*qi*, 氣; *jing*, 精; and *shen*, 神—respectively, breath, essence/semen, and spirit), and since the earlier one starts to "prepare" the better, it is tempting to see the Guodian reading as correct.[5] However, the characters 備 (*bei*) and 服 (*fu*) were pronounced much the same in antiquity—*bɪuək and *bɪuək—so either could have served as a phonetic loan for the other. And since *bei* is consistently used as a phonetic loan for *fu* in the other Guodian texts (see "Zun deyi," "Cheng Zhi wenzhi," and part 3 of the "Collected Sayings"), I suspect it is used here in that way as well.[6]

LINE 7:

In all other editions of the *Laozi*, this line says "If you possess the mother of the state/kingdom" (有國之母), which does not make a lot of sense, since the reference must be to the Dao. The *guo* (國) in this line must be read to mean *yu* (域)—the Guodian character is 貮—and "the mother of the whole world" then corresponds to other references we find to the Dao, like "the mother of the world" (天下之母) in chapter 25, and "the mother of heaven and earth" (天地之母) in chapter 52.[7]

LINE 8:

This is normally read as two lines: 8: "This is called having deep roots and a firm base"; and 9: "It's the Way of long life and long lasting vision." That remains a valid reading. But since the word "Way" (道, *dog) at the end of the line is meant to rime with "endure" (舊, *gɪog) at the end of line 7, I think this might be better read as one line. Thus we have a single line, consisting of two-character adjective/noun phrases that appear to be phonetically balanced.[8]

*Meter and Rime:*

The attention paid to meter and rime in this passage is quite striking. The first four lines are seven-character lines, in which the phrase pattern produces a rhythm of 4/3, 3/4, 4/3, 3/4. Lines 5 to 7 are then eight-character lines with a rhythm of 3/5, 4/4, 4/4, while the final line is a thirteen-character line—twelve if we omit the final particle *ye* (也)—with a rhythm of 2/4/4/2, 1. For the rime pattern, the second and fourth words in the first line—"humanity" and "heaven"—rime (*nien and *tʻen); but the last word in the line—*se* (嗇, *sɪək)—establishes the rime that will be used in lines 2 to 6. Moreover, there is both internal and end rime in each of these lines: in line 2, "reserve" and "prepare"; line 3, "prepare" and "virtue"; line 4, "virtue" and "overcome"; line 5, "overcome" and "far"; and line 6, "far" (*gɪək) and "world" (*fɪuək). In line 7, "mother" (*muəg) still rimes with "world" at the end of the previous line, but the final word in the line, "endure"—assuming it was written as *jiu* (舊, *gɪog) and not *jiu* (久, *kuəg)— shifts the rime to one that will match with "the Way" (*dog )at the end of line 8.[9]

|   | *Transcription* | *Modern Equivalents* |
|---|---|---|
| 1 | 給人事天莫若嗇 | 治人事天莫若嗇 |
| 2 | 夫唯嗇是以暴是以 | 夫唯嗇是以早是以 |
| 3 | 暴備是胃□□□ | 早備 是謂[重積德 |
| 4 | □□□□□克■ | 重積德則 無]不克 |
| 5 | □不克則莫智丌亟 | [無]不克則莫知其極 |
| 6 | 莫智丌亟可以又阈 | 莫知其極可以有域 |
| 7 | 又阈之母可以長□ | 有域之母可以長[久 |
|   |   |   |
| 8 | □□ | 是謂 |
| 9 | □□□□長生舊見之道也■ | 深根固柢]長生舊視之道也 |

1    Those who [toil at] their studies increase day after day;
2    Those who practice the Way, decrease day after day.
3    They decrease and decrease,
4    Until they reach the point where they do nothing at all.
5    They do nothing, yet there is nothing left undone.

.....................................
.....................................
.....................................

*Comments and Notes*

LINE 1

In the Mawangdui copies, this line begins with the word *wei* (爲, to work at)—
"Those who work at their studies." But this is omitted in the Guodian slips. Paral-
lelism with the words in line 2 seems to demand it (*wei xue ʐhe* [爲學者] vs. *wei dao
ʐhe* [爲道者]), so this is probably a slip by the scribe. However, it is not grammatically necessary for the line to make sense.

LINE 4:

Punctuation at the end of this line (▬) might indicate that these four lines were
seen as a self-contained unit and that line 5 is simply a related saying or an editorial
comment. With the character *wei* added to the start of line 1, lines 1 and 2 would be
balanced, five-character lines, and lines 3 and 4 would be four-character lines (if we
omit the particle *ye* [也] from the end of line 4).

LINE 5:

This line does not occur in either of the Mawangdui copies, nor does it occur any-
where else in either of those *Laoʐi* manuscripts. This prompted the scholar Gao
Ming to argue, in several publications, that the concept of "doing nothing, and yet
there being nothing left undone" (*wuwei er wubuwei* [無爲而無不爲]), was not
in origin a Daoist notion; this is a saying that developed in Legalist texts making its
way into the *Laoʐi* at some later date.¹¹ The problem with this argument is that although this line does not *occur* in chapter 48 in the Mawangdui copies, it is not that it
was *omitted*; rather, the silk on which these words might have been written has rotted

away. But the size of the gap in both texts is large enough to accommodate the six characters in question.[12] In any event, the presence of the line here seems to resolve this issue.

The three lines added to this "chapter" in all later editions we have of the text are: "Getting control of the world, can only be done if you have no interest in matters of ruling [*wushi*, 無事]. If you are interested in matters of ruling, you'll be unworthy of getting control of the world." There is no reason why these lines should be part of this chapter, and, as noted in the introduction, the present five lines move directly into another saying on "learning," and together they might have been understood as constituting a single "chapter."

## B:2 (Chapter 48)

| | *Transcription* | *Modern Equivalents* |
|---|---|---|
| 1 | 學者日益 | 學者日益 |
| 2 | 爲道者日臭 | 爲道者日損 |
| 3 | 臭之或臭 | 損之又損 |
| 4 | 以至亡爲也＿ | 以至無爲也 |
| 5 | 亡爲而亡不爲＿ | 無爲而無不爲 |

**B:3 (Chapter 20, lines 1–7)**[13]

1   Eliminate learning and you will have no distress.

2   Pleasant agreement and angry rejection—
3   How far apart are they?
4   Beautiful and ugly—
5   What exactly is the difference between them?

6   Those who are feared by the people
7   Must also, because of this, fear others.

........................................
........................................
........................................
........................................
........................................
........................................
........................................
........................................
........................................
........................................
........................................
........................................
........................................
........................................
........................................
........................................
........................................
........................................

*Comments and Notes*

LINE 1:
For the view that this line should be the last line in chapter 19 instead of the first line of chapter 20, see the "Comments and Notes" to passage A:1 (chapter 19). But, as Xu Kangsheng has recently argued, the content of learning is really "distinctions,"

value distinctions, in many cases, which lead to disagreement and conflict, the kinds of distinctions the author here calls into question.[14]

LINE 7:

The copyist inserts punctuation (⎵) before the word "others" (*ren*, 人), which would seem to indicate that the word *ren* is the first word in the passage that follows (chapter 13), and that punctuation is followed in the Wenwu transcription.[15] In addition, in almost all later editions of the *Laoẓi*, this line simply says "Cannot not be feared" (*buke buwei*, 不可不畏). But *ren* is also found at the end of this line in Mawangdui copy B,[16] which, like the Guodian slips, also adds an *yi* (以) after the *ke* (可), the particle that brings "because of this" into the line. Thus I suspect the punctuation mark before the word *ren* was inserted one space too soon. Further support for reading the text in this way is the fact that having the character 人 be the first word in the following passage, "chapter 13," is elsewhere unattested. And, as others have already argued, concluding that the distinction between "those who fear" and "those who are feared" is not a permanent one—these "opposites" can easily turn into one another—fits very well with the chapter's overall theme.[17]

However, the evidence provided by meter and rime complicates the issue. Were we to read 畏 as the final character of the line, the chapter would balance in terms of the rhythm, having as the number of characters in each of the lines 4, 3, 4, 3, 4, 4, 6 ( = 3, 3). And the end rime, line by line, would be: (1) ·iog or iəu, (2) har, (3) fiar, (4) ·ak, (5) niak, (6) ·iuər (or iuəi), and (7) ·iuər. So if the last character in line 7 were 畏, the sound would have resonated, in a sense, with the final character in line 1. Moreover, having 人 as the first character in chapter 13 would at last provide a balanced beginning to that chapter, with five characters in lines 1 and 2. So this issue is not easily resolved. The deciding factor for me is that if 人 had been the initial character in chapter 13, there should be some sign of it in lines 3 and 7 of chapter 13, but there is not.

My translation of the additional lines in chapter 20, based on the Mawangdui copies, reads as follows:[18]

8   Wild, unrestrained! It will never come to an end!

9   The multitudes are peaceful and happy;
10  Like climbing a terrace in springtime to feast at the tailao sacrifice.
11  But I am tranquil and quiet—not yet having given a sign.
12  Like a child who has not yet smiled.
13  Tired and exhausted—as though I have no place to return.

14  The multitudes all have a surplus;

15  I alone seem to be lacking.

16  Mine is the mind of a fool—ignorant and stupid!

17  The common people see things clearly;

18  I alone am in the dark.

19  The common people discriminate and make fine distinctions;

20  I alone am muddled and confused.

21  Formless am I! Like the ocean;

22  Shapeless am I! As though I have nothing in which I can rest.

23  The masses all have their reasons [for acting];

24  I alone am stupid and obstinate like a rustic.

25  But my desires alone differ from those of others—

26  For I value drawing sustenance from the Mother.

## B:3 (Chapter 20, lines 1–7)

| | *Transcription* | *Modern Equivalents* |
|---|---|---|
| 1 | 𡖇學亡惪 | 絕學無憂 |
| 2 | 唯與可 | 唯與訶 |
| 3 | 相去幾可 | 相去幾何 |
| 4 | 㦡㦡亞 | 美與惡 |
| 5 | 相去可若 | 相去何若 |
| 6 | 人之所㬌 | 人之所畏 |
| 7 | 亦不可以不㬌＿人 | 亦不可以不畏人 |

1    "Favor" is really "disgrace"—it is like being in bondage.

2    Be wary with matters that cause great distress—treat them as if they could mean your life.

3    Why do I say "Favor is really disgrace"?

4    Receiving favor puts you in a dependent position.[20]

5    If you get it, it is like being bondage;

6    If you lose it, it is like being in bondage.

7    This is what I mean by "Favor is really disgrace—it is like being in bondage."[21]

8    *And why do I say "Be wary with matters that cause great distress—treat them as if they could mean your life"?*

9    The reason we have great distress

10    Is that we have bodies;

11    If we did not have bodies, what would we *worry about*?

12    *Therefore, with someone who values taking care of his life more than* running the world,

13    To him we can entrust the world.

14    And with someone who dotes on his life as if it *were* the whole world,

15    To him we can turn over the world.

*Comments and Notes*

LINES 1–7:

This represents a new approach to a chapter that has given commentators and translators fits for thousands of years. This interpretation might be wrong; but it at least treats line 3 as complete, and it explains why in lines 4 to 6 the author is concerned *only* with the getting or losing of "favor." Line 1 is normally translated "Regard favor and disgrace with alarm" (*chongju ruo jing,* 寵 辱 若 驚). But if *chongru* is understood as "favor *and* disgrace" when the author asks in line 3 "What do I mean by *chongju?*" we would expect him to talk about both things. He does not; he talks only about "favor." Thus I propose that we fare better by reading *chongju* as "favor *is* disgrace" or "to be favored is to be insulted/disgraced." Since that is not a claim one would normally make, he then proceeds to explain what he means.

In addition, where later editions all have "alarm" (*jing*, 驚), the Guodian slips have the character *ying* (纓/縷, to be bound up, wrapped up in cords, ensnared). Although this can be read as a phonetic loan for "alarm" (the archaic pronunciations being *kĭĕŋ, and *·ıeŋ, respectively), I see no reason to do that, since someone who has been "favored" becomes "obligated" or "tied" to his patron; in addition, his fate then becomes "wrapped up" with the fate of his patron.

But there is another possibility to consider. If the punctuation mark that follows the character *wei* (纍/畏) at the end of the previous passage was meant to indicate repetition, line 1 in this passage would then be read "*Fear* people's favor as being in bondage" (畏人寵辱若纓), or possibly "Fear favor in the same way that you fear being bound" (畏寵辱若纓).[22] With the second of these, lines 1 and 2 would then be parallel; we would have two five-character lines that both begin with a verb/object phrase and end with "若 X." Moreover, the first and last characters in each of those lines would have been phonetically close—*wei* (畏, *·ıuər) and *gui* (貴, *kıuəd); *ying* (纓, *·ıeŋ) and *shen* (身, *thien). But again, were this the case, one would expect to find the word *wei* (畏, fear) repeated in lines 3 and 7.

LINE 3:

In many later editions, including the edition represented by the Mawangdui copies, the characters 若驚 (*ruo jing*) are included at the end of this line. Understood in the usual way, this would be translated, "Why do I say 'Regard favor and disgrace with alarm'?" Although we might be tempted to think that those words were erroneously omitted, the Guodian form of the line—何謂寵辱—is actually very common, and it was continued in the Xiang'er and Heshanggong lines of the text.[23]

LINE 4:

In the Heshanggong recension, this was changed to "Disgrace is inferior" (辱為下), and on occasion a line was inserted before this: "Favor is superior" (寵為上). Clearly some readers did not understand what the author was trying to say: how could "favor" be something inferior?[24]

LINE 12:

This assumes that the Guodian form of the line matched what we find in the Mawangdui copies—故貴為身於為天下. Of the later recensions, the only one that comes close to this form of the line is the Xiang'er recension. Most later editions have "Therefore with one who values his life as much as the world" (故貴以身爲天下).[25]

LINES 12–15:
My comment on these lines in my 1989 translation bears repeating.[26]
The sentiments of chapter 13—that the person who should be entrusted with ruling the world is precisely the one who cares more for his own life than he does for the wealth, honor, and power he would have by ruling the world—show up again in the *Zhuangzi* in a section that A. C. Graham identifies as "Yangist" (representing the views of the "individualist" Yang Chu and his school). The first anecdote in chapter 28 of the *Zhuangzi* reads, "Yao resigned the empire to Hsu Yu. Hsu Yu refused it. Next he resigned it to Tzu-chou Chih-fu. 'It might not be a bad idea to make me Son of Heaven,' said Tzu-chou Chih-fu. 'However, at the moment I am worried about a serious ailment. I'm going to put it right, and haven't time just now to put the empire right.' The empire is the most important thing of all, but he would not harm his life for the sake of it, and how much less for anything else! Only the man who cares nothing for the empire deserves to be entrusted with the empire."[27]

# B:4 (Chapter 13)

| | *Transcription* | *Modern Equivalents* |
|---|---|---|
| 1 | 龍辱若纓 | 寵辱若纓 |
| 2 | 貴大患若身 | 貴大患若身 |
| | | |
| 3 | 可胃龍辱 | 何謂寵辱 |
| 4 | 龍爲下也 | 寵爲下也 |
| 5 | 尋之若纓 | 得之若纓 |
| 6 | 遊之若纓 | 失之若纓 |
| 7 | 是胃龍辱＿纓 | 是謂寵辱若纓 |
| | | |
| 8 | □□□□□若身 | [何謂貴大患]若身 |
| 9 | 虖所以又大患者 | 吾所以有大患者 |
| 10 | 爲虖又身 | 爲吾有身 |
| 11 | 返虖亡身或可□ | 及吾無身有何[患] |
| | | |
| 12 | □□□□□爲天下 | [故貴爲身於]爲天下 |
| 13 | 若可以厇天下矣＿ | 若可以託天下矣 |
| 14 | 恷以身爲天下 | 愛以身爲天下 |
| 15 | 若可以迲天下矣■ | 若可以寄天下矣 |

1    The ablest students, when they hear of the Way, with effort can get
     started on it;

2    Mediocre students, when they hear of the Way, it is as if they are lost and
     confused;

3    With the dullest of students, when they hear of the way, they laugh
     aloud at it.

4    But if they did not laugh aloud at it, it could not be considered the Way.²⁹

5    Therefore, as we find it in the fixed sayings:

6    The bright Way seems dispersed;

7    The level Way seems uneven;³⁰

8    The Way *that goes forward* seems to retreat.

9    The highest virtue seems to be [low like] a valley;

10   The greatest purity seems to be soiled;

11   Vast virtue seems insufficient.

12   Steadfast virtue seems to be *lax*;

13   *Genuine* substance seems to be flawed;

14   The greatest square has no corners.

15   The greatest vessel is slowly completed;

16   The greatest sound makes little noise;³¹

17   The greatest image is lacking in form;

18   The Way *is great yet has no name*;

19   *It is good at beginning and good at completing.*

*Comments and Notes*

LINE 1:
This is one of many lines in the *Laozi* that can be translated several different but
equally valid ways. In the "modern edition" of the *Laozi*, the second part of this
line is normally *qin er xing zhi* (勤而行之, with effort they are able to do it, or with

effort they are able to follow it). But in the Mawangdui copies this wording changes to *jin neng xing zhi* (堇能行之, are just barely able to do it). (But *jin* [堇] and *qin* [勤] are interchangeable, so this could still be "with effort they are able to do it.") In the Guodian form of the line, "it" (*zhi*) at the end of the line is replaced by *yu qi zhong* (於亓中, into it, or into its core or center).[32] Here, the second part of line 1 could be read: "are barely able to get into it," "with an effort they can get into it," or, most optimistically, "by making an effort they can travel right to its core." Unfortunately, there is no way to decide which reading is "right."

LINE 2:

Like line 1, this can be read different ways. The second half of the line, in later editions, reads *ruo cun ruo wang* (若存若亡, literally "like keep, like lose," or "some things they get, some things they don't," or "some things they remember, some they forget," and so on). But *cun* (存, *dzuən) is replaced by *hun* (昏, *muən, confused) in the Guodian slips. Since *hun* is commonly used as a phonetic loan for *wen* (聞, *mɪuən, hear) in these slips—in fact right here in these lines—we might validly translate "it is as if they hear it but then forget it." But I rather like the literal reading.[33]

LINE 5:

It is possible that "fixed sayings" (*jianyan*, 建言) was actually the name of a book, in which case we should translate: "Therefore, in the *Jianyan* we find."[34] The punctuation mark at the end of this line presumably indicates that what follows are well-known, possibly "cited," sayings. The lines that follow are metric and rimed.

LINE 6:

In almost all later editions this line says "The bright Way seems to be dark [*mei*, 昧]." But in place of *mei* (*muəd), Mawangdui copy B has *fei* (費, *p'ɪuəd), while the Guodian slips have the character 孛 (*bo*, *buət). I would suggest reading *fei* (scattered, dispersed, or diffused) as the intended word, for which *bo* was a phonetic loan.

LINES 7 AND 8:

These lines are reversed in almost all later editions.[35]

LINES 6–19:

In the Chinese, lines 6 to 8 are rimed (*buət, *lɪuəd, and *t'uəd), as are lines 9 to 14 (*kuk, *niuk, *tsiuk, *tug, *diug , and *ŋɪug), and 15 to 19 (*dhieŋ, *thieŋ, *tsieŋ, *mieŋ, and *dhieŋ).[16] Also, with two exceptions (lines 11 and 19), they are all four-character lines. In terms of symmetry, we would expect the three "Way" lines (6–8) to be followed by the three "Virtue" lines (9, 11, and 12), with all the lines that begin with "Great" (10, 14–17) grouped together. Such is not the case, but one wonders whether this represents the original sequence.

LINE 19:

We cannot be sure what the final line was in the Guodian version. But since there is space for about five characters, it must have been slightly different from what we find in later editions. Using eight characters, Mawangdui copy B, for example, says "Only the Way is good at beginning things and also good at bringing things to completion." The Chinese for my suggested translation would have been: 善始且善成.

## B:5 (Chapter 41)

| | *Transcription* | *Modern Equivalents* |
|---|---|---|
| 1 | 上士昏道董能行於丌中 | 上士聞道勤能行於其中 |
| 2 | 中士昏道若昏若亡 | 中士聞道若聞若忘 |
| 3 | 下士昏道大芺之 | 下士聞道大笑之 |
| 4 | 弗大芺不足以爲道矣 | 弗大笑不足以爲道矣 |
| 5 | 是以建言又之▄ | 是以建言有之 |
| 6 | 明道女孛 | 明道如費 |
| 7 | 遟道女纇 | 夷道如纇 |
| 8 | □道若退 | [進]道若退 |
| 9 | 上惪女浴__ | 上德如谷 |
| 10 | 大白女辱 | 大白如辱 |
| 9 | 上惪女浴__ | 上德如谷 |
| 10 | 大白女辱 | 大白如辱 |
| 11 | 生惪女不足 | 廣德如不足 |
| 12 | 建惪女□ | 建德如[偷 |
| 13 | □貞女愈 | 質]貞如渝 |
| 14 | 大方亡禺 | 大方無隅 |
| 15 | 大器曼成 | 大器慢成 |
| 16 | 大音袛聖 | 大音細聲 |
| 17 | 天象亡坓 | 大象無形 |
| 18 | 道□□□ | 道[裏無名 |
| 19 | □□□□□ | 善始且善成] |

..........................................
..........................................
..........................................
..........................................

| | |
|---|---|
| 1 | Close the gates |
| 2 | Block the holes |
| 3 | And to the end of your days you will not toil. |

| | |
|---|---|
| 4 | Open the holes |
| 5 | Excel in affairs |
| 6 | And you will never reach the end of your days. |

..........................................
..........................................
..........................................
..........................................

*Comments and Notes*

LINES 1 AND 2:
In later editions these lines are reversed.

LINE 3:
For "toil" (reading 孟 as *wu* [務]), all later editions use the synonym "labor" (*qin*, 勤).

LINE 5:
In later editions the first word in this line is *ji* (濟), which is understood to mean "meddle in" or "get involved in." But the Guodian character is 賽 (*sai*), the same *sai* that at the start of line 2 means "to block" (賽 = 塞). In their notes to the text, the Wenwu editors suggest that we read this as 寨, which means *shi* (實, to realize) or *an* (安, to rest in).[38] But there is no reason not to read this as *sai* in the sense of "to excel" or "to be successful in." The synonym *ji* might have been used to replace this to avoid confusion with the meaning of *sai* in line 2.

With 就 (*jiu*, to save) as the final character in this line in later editions, this is normally translated "And till the end of your days you will not be saved." But the final character in the Guodian slips is 逨 (= 來) (*lai*, to come), not *jiu*. Since it is likely that lines 3 and 6 are intended to rime—the meter here, line by line, is 3, 3, 4; 3, 3, 4—if we are correct in reading the last word in line 3 as *wu*, the last word in line 6 should rime with *mɪŏg. The word *lai* provides us with a close match—*mləg—but the word *qiu* (求, *gɪog, to seek, or to attain) would be better. Since the characters for *lai* and *qiu*, in antiquity as well as today, were hard to distinguish, it could be that the *lai* (逨) in the text really ought to be *qiu* (逑). But with either word the reading remains the same.

The lines that precede these in later editions are:[39]

1   The world had a beginning,
2   Which can be considered the mother of the world.
3   Having attained the mother, in order to understand her children,
4   If you return and hold on to the mother, till the end of your life you will suffer no harm.

The lines that follow in later editions are:[40]

11   To perceive the small is called "discernment."
12   To hold on to the pliant is called "strength."
13   If you use the rays to return to the source of the light,
14   You will not abandon your life to peril.
15   This is called Following the Constant.

It seems likely to me that this set of nine lines originally constituted a unified saying; note that lines 13 and 14 parallel lines 3 and 4. What connects lines 5–10 of the chapter with lines 1–4 is the common concern with "till the end of your days" or "till the end of your life" (*moshen* [没身], or *zhongshen* [終身]).[41]

| *Transcription* | *Modern Equivalents* |
|---|---|
| 1 | 閟亓門 | 閟其門 |


|  | *Transcription* | *Modern Equivalents* |
|---|---|---|
| 1 | 閟亓門 | 閟其門 |
| 2 | 賽亓㿺 | 塞其兌 |
| 3 | 冬身不丟 | 終身不務 |
| 4 | 啓亓㿺 | 啓其兌 |
| 5 | 賽亓事 | 賽其事 |
| 6 | 冬身不埭■ | 終身不來 |

## B:7 (Chapter 45)⁴²

1    What is most perfect seems somehow defective;
2    Yet you can use it, and it never wears out.
3    What is most full seems to be empty;
4    Yet you can use it, and it never runs dry.

5    Great skill seems to be clumsy;⁴³
6    Great gains seem to be losses;⁴⁴
7    Great straightness seems to be bent.

---

8/1  Activity overcomes cold;
9/2  Tranquility overcomes heat.
10/3 Pure and tranquil, you can stabilize the whole world.

(Lines 8–10 seem to be understood as a separate saying.)

*Comments and Notes*

LINES 5–7:
The line sequence here is normally 7, 5, and 6.

LINE 6:
Equally valid—"Great advances seem like retreats." In almost all later editions—where this is the last line of the series—this line is "Great eloquence seems to stammer and stutter" (*da bian ruo na,* 大辯若訥). We can trace the development of this line from the Guodian form to this later form by means of the Mawangdui copies. Mawangdui copy B, like the Guodian slips, has "loss" or "retreat" (*chu,* 絀) at the end of this line, while copy A has the unidentified character 炳. It now seems clear that this character, like the character 芮 (*rui*) in chapters 7 and 9 in copy A, was a phonetic loan for 退 (*tui,* retreat). That not being clear to a copyist, 炳 was written as 訥 (*na,* stammer), at which point the character 成 (*cheng*) (or 贏 [*ying*])⁴⁵ at the beginning of the line was changed to something that meant the opposite, "eloquence"; hence the character 辯 (*bian*).

Normally found as the final lines of chapter 45, these three lines are set off from what precedes and what follows on the Guodian slips by punctuation. And they seem to have little in common with the preceding lines in that chapter, all of which are four-character lines, and all of which begin with the word "great" (*da*, 大). Here, lines 8(1) and 9(2) are three-character lines (though they could be read as a single six-character line, just like line 10[3]). The cadence in this little passage, with each character being a syllable, is: 1, 2, 3; 1, 2, 3; 1, 2—3, 4, 5, 6. The first two words in line 10—*qing* (pure) and *jing* (tranquil)—rime with the last—*ding* (stable), and the final words in lines 8 and 9 were also close to riming with *ding*. The archaic finals were *ts'aŋ (cold), *nian (heat), and *deŋ (stable).[46]

## B:7 (Chapter 45)

| | Transcription | Modern Equivalents |
|---|---|---|
| 1 | 大成若夬 | 大成若缺 |
| 2 | 丌甬不幣＿ | 其用不弊 |
| 3 | 大浧若中 | 大盈若沖 |
| 4 | 丌甬不穿＿ | 其用不窮 |
| 5 | 大攷若仳＿ | 大巧若拙 |
| 6 | 大成若詘＿ | 大成若絀 |
| 7 | 大植若屈■ | 大直若屈 |
| 8 | 喿勅蒼＿ | 募秤飛 |
| 9 | 青勅然 | 靜勝然 |
| 10 | 清清爲天下定■ | 清靜爲天下定 |

1   What is firmly implanted cannot be pulled out;[48]
2   What is firmly embraced cannot be lost.
3   As a result, the sacrifices of your descendants will never end.[49]

4   If you cultivate it in your self, your virtue will be pure;
5   If you cultivate it in your family, your virtue will be overflowing;
6   If you cultivate it in your village, your virtue will be longlasting;
7   If you cultivate it in your state, your virtue will be rich and full;
8   If you cultivate it throughout the world, *your virtue will be widespread.*

..........................................

9    *Look at the* family *from the point of view of the family;*
10   Look at the village from the point of view of the village;
11   Look at the state from the point of view of the state;
12   Look at the world from the point of view of the world.

13   How do I know *the condition of* the whole world?
14   *By this.*

*Comments and Notes*

The message here sounds very Confucian, and the wording is reminiscent of "The Great Learning," where we find the words: "The ancients who wished to manifest their clear character [*ming de*, bright virtue] to the world would first bring order to their states. Those who wished to bring order to their states would first regulate their families. Those who wished to regulate their families would first cultivate their personal lives."[50]

LINES 4–8:
Like the Mawangdui copies, the Guodian slips omit the word "in" (*yu*, 於) in each of these lines. Thus line 4 begins, literally speaking, "Cultivate it your own person." But the preposition should be included, since the basic unit throughout the chapter is the four- or eight-character line. Without the *yu*, lines 4 to 7 are seven-character lines. In any event, there is internal rime in each of these lines, the riming words being "person" and "pure"; "family" and "overflowing"; "village" and "longlasting"; "state" and "rich and full"; and "world" and "widespread."[51]

LINES 8 AND 9:

Later editions normally have an additional line here: "Look at your self from the point of view of your self." There is a gap in the Guodian slips at this point, but it is not large enough to accommodate this additional line.

LINES 13 AND 14:

Because the bottom part of this slip is broken, we cannot be sure how this chapter ended. To a similar question in passage 16 in *Laozi* A (chapter 57), the reply of "By this" (*yi ci*, 以 此) is not given. But the present chapter could not end with an unanswered question, and the words "By this" seem appropriate if we are correct about the Confucian tone of the message: if I want to know the "condition" or "present state" of the world, I can know by knowing myself.[52]

| *Transcription* | *Modern Equivalents* |
|---|---|
| 1  善建者不朵 | 善建者不拔 |
| 2  善保者不兌 | 善抱者不脫 |
| 3  子孫以丌祭祀不毛 | 子孫以其祭祀不輟 |
| | |
| 4  攸之身丌悳乃貞 | 修之身其德乃眞 |
| 5  攸之豪丌悳又舍 | 修之家其德有餘 |
| 6  攸之旨丌悳乃長 | 修之鄉其德乃長 |
| 7  攸之邦丌悳乃奉 | 修之邦其德乃豐 |
| 8  攸之天下□□□□ | 修之天下[其德乃普 |
| | |
| 9  □□□豪 | 以家觀]家 |
| 10  以旨觀旨 | 以鄉觀鄉 |
| 11  以邦觀邦 | 以邦觀邦 |
| 12  以天下觀天下 | 以天下觀天下 |
| | |
| 13  虐可以智天□□□ | 吾何以知天[下之然 |
| 14  □□ | 以此] |

*Laozi* C

1    With regard to the very best rulers, the people below simply know they are there.

2    With regard to those one step down, they love them and praise them.

3    With regard to those another step down, they fear them.

4    And with regard to those yet another step down, they revile and insult them.²

5    When trust is insufficient, there will be no trust in return.

6    Hesitant are they! In their cautious use of words.

7    They complete their affairs and finish their tasks,

8    Yet the common folk say, "These things happened all on their own!"

9    Therefore, when the Great Way is rejected, it is then that "humanity" and "righteousness" show up on the scene;

.......................................

10   When the six relations are not in harmony, it is then that we hear of "filial piety" and "compassion";

11   And when the state is in chaos and disarray, it is then that there is praise for the "upright officials."

## Comments and Notes

LINE 7:

In the Mawangdui copies, the words "affairs" (*shi*, 事) and "tasks" (*gong*, 功) are reversed. But the Guodian order seems preferable in terms of rime. Lines 6 and 8 clearly rimed—*yan* (言, *ŋɪăn, words), with the *ran* (然) of *ȝiran* (*nian, on their own)—and "tasks" (*kuŋ) at the end of line 7 was close to riming with "trust" (*xin*, 信, *sien) at the end of line 5.³

LINE 9:

It is the "Therefore" at the head of this line that indicates this is a single passage and should not be divided into two chapters. In later editions, this "therefore" is maintained only in that represented by the Mawangdui copies.

LINES 9 AND 10:

In all later editions, a line is inserted between these lines: "When knowledge and wisdom appear, it is then that we have great hypocrisy."

LINES 9–11:

These are balanced eight-character lines, where we would expect to find internal rime with the fourth and eighth words: that is, "rejected" (*fei*, 廢) and "righteous-ness" (*yi*, 義), "harmony" (*he*, 和) and "compassion" (*ci*, 慈), and "chaos" (*luan*, 亂) and "officials" (*chen*, 臣). But that is not the case.[4]

| *Transcription* | *Modern Equivalents* |
|---|---|
| 1   大上下智又之 | 太上下知有之 |
| 2   丌即新譽之 | 其即親譽之 |
| 3   丌旣愚之 | 其即畏之 |
| 4   丌即炙之 | 其即侮之 |
| | |
| 5   信不足安又不信 | 信不足安有不信 |
| 6   猷唬丌貴言也 | 猷乎其貴言也 |
| 7   成事述社 | 成事遂功 |
| 8   而百告曰我自狀也 | 而百姓曰我自然也 |
| | |
| 9   古大道癹安又悬義 | 故大道廢安有仁義 |
| 10  六新不和安又孝孯 | 六親不和安有孝慈 |
| 11  邦豙緍燮安又正臣■ | 邦家昏亂安有正臣 |

## C:2 (Chapter 35)[5]

1    Grasp the Great Image and the whole world will come;
2    Come, and suffer no harm, for security and peace will be great.

3    Music and sweets—for these travelers stop.
4    Consequently, when the Way utters words—
5    Bland and insipid! Their lack of flavor.

6    Look at it—not enough to be seen;
7    Listen to it—not enough to be heard,
8    Yet it cannot be exhausted.

### Comments and Notes

LINES 1–3:

The first three lines are essentially balanced, six-character lines,[6] with internal rime on the third and sixth words: "image" (象,*ǵiaŋ) and "come" (往, *ɦɪuaŋ); "harm" (害, *ɦad) and "great" (大, *dad); and "sweets" (餌, *niəg) and "stop" (止, *tiəg).

LINE 4:

The "Consequently" (*gu*, 故) at the head of the line is also found in the Mawangdui copies, but it is omitted in all other later editions. In addition, the Mawangdui copies add "we say" (*yue*, 曰) after "words": "As a result, of the Way's speaking we say . . . "

LINE 8:

In later editions, the words "use it" (*yong zhi*) are added to this line so that it parallels lines 6 and 7: "Use it—it cannot be exhausted."[7] In the Guodian version, lines 6, 7, and 8 are meant to be read as a single line: "Look at it—not enough to be seen; listen to it—not enough to be heard, yet it cannot be exhausted."[8] Lines 6 and 7 remind us of the opening of chapter 14 of the *Laozi*, where we find "We look at it and yet do not see it. . . . We listen to it and yet do not hear it."

|   | *Transcription* | *Modern Equivalents* |
|---|---|---|
| 1 | 埶大象天下往 | 執大象天下往 |
| 2 | 往而不害安坪大 | 往而不害安平大 |
| 3 | 樂與餌怎客迬 | 樂與餌過客止 |
| 4 | 古道□□□ | 故道[之出言] |
| 5 | 淡可丌無味也 | 淡呵其無味也 |
| 6 | 見之不足見 | 視之不足見 |
| 7 | 聖之不足翻 | 聽之不足聞 |
| 8 | 而不可旣也 ■ | 而不可旣也 |

## C:3 (Chapter 31)⁹

...........................................
...........................................
...........................................

1    When the gentleman is at home he values the left;
2    When using weapons he values the right.
3    Therefore we say, weapons *are instruments of ill omen*;

...........................................

4    If you have no choice but to use them, it is best to be dignified and
     reverent.¹⁰

5    Never see them as things of beauty.¹¹
6    To see them as things of beauty is to delight in the taking of life.
7    And if you delight *in killing, you will not* achieve your aim in the world.¹²

8    Therefore, in auspicious affairs we honor the left;
9    While in matters of mourning we honor the right.
10   As a result, [when they go into battle] the lieutenant general stands on the left,
11   While the supreme general stands on the right.
12   This means they act as they would at a funeral rite.

13   Therefore, when *large numbers of people* are killed, stand before them in
     grief and sorrow.
14   When the battle is won, then act as you would at a funeral rite.

### Comments and Notes

LINE 3:
In later editions, chapter 31 begins with this line, normally phrased: "As for fine
weapons, they are instruments of ill omen."¹³ Then follow two lines also found at
the end of chapter 24: "But there are those who hate them. Therefore, those who
have the Way, with them do not dwell."

LINE 3:
In the Mawangdui copies, this line reads: "Therefore, weapons are not the instru-

ments of the gentleman," followed by "they are instruments of ill omen."[14] But more common in later editions is the reading: "Weapons are instruments of ill omen," followed by "They are not the instruments of the gentleman." With the critical characters missing, the Guodian line could have said either of these—that weapons are instruments of ill omen, *or* that they are not the instruments of the gentleman. I think that the former follows more logically from the preceding line.

LINE 5:
In most later editions, this line is "When victorious he (i.e., the gentleman) does not see them as things of beauty." But the Guodian form of the line is continued in the Mawangdui copies and, later, in the lineage based on the Xiang'er recension.

LINE 8:
In most later editions, there is no "Therefore" at the start of this line. But it is also present in the Mawangdui copies and the Xiang'er recension.

LINE 9:
In most later editions, the word "inauspicious" (*xiong*, 凶) is used here instead of "mourning" (*sang*, 喪). But the Mawangdui copies also have "mourning," as do many copies in the Xiang'er lineage.

LINE 13:
No other version of the *Laozi* has "Therefore" at the start of this line.

# C:3 (Chapter 31)

| | *Transcription* | *Modern Equivalents* |
|---|---|---|
| 1 | 君子居則貴左 | 君子居則貴左 |
| 2 | 甬兵則貴右 | 用兵則貴右 |
| 3 | 古曰兵者□□□□□ | 故曰兵者[不祥之器也 |
| 4 | □䢔已而甬之錟繲爲上 | 不]得已而用之恬襲爲上 |
| | | |
| 5 | 弗敚也 | 弗美也 |
| 6 | 敚之是樂殺人 | 美之是樂殺人 |
| 7 | 夫樂□□□以䢔志於天下 | 夫樂[殺不可]以得志於天下 |
| | | |
| 8 | 古吉事上左 | 故吉事上左 |
| 9 | 䘮事上右 | 喪事上右 |
| 10 | 是以支牄軍居左 | 是以偏將軍居左 |
| 11 | 上牄軍居右 | 上將軍居右 |
| 12 | 言以䘮豊居之也 | 言以喪禮居之也 |
| | | |
| 13 | 古殺□□則以忞悲位之 | 故殺[人眾]則以哀悲立之 |
| 14 | 戰勑則以䘮豊居之 ■ | 戰勝則以喪禮居之 |

1    Those who act on it ruin it,

2    Those who hold on to it lose it.

3    The Sage does nothing, and as a result he has no disasters;

4    He holds on to nothing, and as a result *he loses nothing.*

5    If you're as careful at the end as you were at the beginning, you'll have no disasters.

6    As for people's disasters—they always ruin things when they're just about to complete them.[16]

7    Therefore, the Sage desires not to desire and places no value on goods that are hard to obtain;

8    He learns how to unlearn and backs away from matters in which the masses go to excess.

9    Therefore, the Sage could help the ten thousand things to be what they are in themselves, but he dare not do it.

### Comments and Notes

LINE 3:

The word "Therefore" is normally found at the head of this line. In later editions, it is only omitted in the Heshanggong recension. (Note that it *is* present in the version of this passage preserved in *Laozi* A.)

LINES 5 AND 6:

In later editions, these lines are reversed, and the wording of line 6 is not exactly the same. For "As for people's disasters" (人之敗也) at the start of this line, we find "In people's performing their duties" (民之從事也) in later editions. (In passage A:6, lines 6 and 5 are reversed as they are in later editions, but the initial line there is "The rule to follow in approaching matters [is this]"—*lin shi zhi ji,* 臨事之紀).

LINE 8:

As in all later editions, but in contrast to the words used in passage A:6, this line begins with "He learns how to unlearn" (*xue bu xue,* 學不學). In A:6, this line

begins "He teaches without teaching" or "He teaches not to teach" (*jiao bu jiao*, 教
不教).

LINE 9:

The "Therefore" at the head of this line is omitted in later editions (but passage A:6
also includes it).[17] In common with later editions—and in contrast to what we find
in passage A:6—this line ends, however, with the words "but he dare not do it" (*er
fu gan wei* 而弗敢爲).[18]

*Rime and Meter:*

Although they belonged to different rime groups in archaic Chinese, the words "act"
(爲, *fɪuar*) and "ruin" (敗,*puăd*) in lines 1 and 3 were phonologically close; the
same is true of the words "hold on to" (執,*tiəp*) and "lose" (失, *thiet*) in lines 2
and 4. In line 5, which is essentially an eight-character line, there is internal rime
with words 4 and 8 (始, *thiəg*, begin; and 敗事, *dzïəg*, disasters). Finally, lines 7,
8, and 9 rimed (貨, *huar*, goods; 過, *kuar*, excess; and 爲, *fɪuar*, do it), and if we
remove the opening "Therefore the Sage" from line 7, and add the character 人 to
line 8 (present in all later editions), lines 7 and 8 become balanced, nine-character
lines, in three- and six- character units.

| | *Transcription* | *Modern Equivalents* |
|---|---|---|
| 1 | 爲之者敗之 | 爲之者敗之 |
| 2 | 埶之者遊之＿ | 執之者失之 |
| 3 | 聖人無爲古無敗也 | 聖人無爲故無敗也 |
| 4 | 無埶古□□□ | 無執故 [無失也] |
| 5 | 訢冬若訂則無敗事亘＿ | 慎終若始則無敗事矣 |
| 6 | 人之敗也互於丌虞成也敗之＿ | 人之敗也恆於其且成也敗之 |
| 7 | 是以□人欲不欲不貴戁尋之貨 | 是以[聖]人欲不欲不貴難得之貨 |
| 8 | 　　　學不斈遆衆之所迓＿ | 　　　學不學復衆之所過 |
| 9 | 是以能桷蓳勿之自肰而弗敢爲■ | 是以能輔萬物之自然而弗敢爲 |

## C:5 "Taiyi shengshui," Part I (slips 1–8, 10–12)[19]

**Note:** In the Wenwu transcription, the "Taiyi shengshui" selection is divided into three parts: slips 1–8 are seen as a unit, slip 9 stands alone, and slips 10–14 are treated as the third part of the text.[20] I think that slips 10–12 follow directly from the end of slip 8; I will translate and discuss slips 9, 13–14 in the next section. Here, I maintain that the "this" at the end of line 8 means both the "process" herein described and the "source of the process"—Taiyi, the "Great One." Does this mean that "Great One" is the "name" (*ming*, 名) of what we "refer to as" (*wei*, 謂) or "designate" (*zi*, 字) the "Dao"? Not necessarily. Relevant here are the lines in chapter 25 of the *Laozi*, where speaking of the source of heaven and earth, the author explains: "I do not yet know its name [*ming*, 名]; I simply 'call it' [*zi zhi*, 字之] the Dao. Were I *forced* to give it a name, I would say it's 'The Great' [*da*, 大]." Lines 10–12 make the same distinction between what something actually *is*, that is, its "name," and how we "refer to" that thing, what it is "called" (*wei*, 謂), that is, its "designation" (*zi*, 字).

*Translation*

(a) The Great One gave birth to water. Water returned and assisted Taiyi, in this way developing heaven. Heaven returned and assisted Taiyi, in this way developing the earth. Heaven and earth [repeatedly assisted each other], in this way developing the "gods above and below." The "gods above and below"[21] repeatedly assisted each other, in this way developing Yin and Yang. Yin and Yang repeatedly assisted each other, in this way developing the four seasons. The four seasons repeatedly assisted each other, in this way developing cold and hot. Cold and hot repeatedly assisted each other, in this way developing moist and dry. Moist and dry repeatedly assisted each other; they developed the year, and the process came to an end.

Therefore, the year was produced by moisture and dryness; moisture and dryness were produced by cold and hot. Cold and hot and the four seasons, were produced by Yin and Yang. Yin and Yang were produced by the "gods above and below." The "gods above and below" were produced by heaven and earth, and heaven and earth were produced by the Great One. This being so, the Great One is concealed in water and moves with the four seasons. Completing a cycle, [it starts] over again; [we regard this beginning as] the mother of the ten thousand things: first it is depleted, then it is full; we regard this beginning as the guiding principle of the ten thousand things.[22] This is something that heaven cannot destroy, the earth cannot smother, and Yin and Yang cannot produce. The gentleman knows this is referred to as ["the Way."] . . . (slips 1–8)

(b) What is below is soil; yet we refer to it [*wei zhi,* 謂 之] as the earth: what is above is air; yet we refer to it as heaven. In the same way, "the Way" is its designation [*zi,* 字]. "But, may I ask, what is its name [*ming,* 名]?" One who uses the Way to work at his tasks certainly relies on its name; for this reason his tasks are completed and he endures. When the Sage works at his tasks, he also relies on its name; as a result his deeds are achieved and he suffers no harm. With heaven and earth, "name" and "designation" both stand together. But when we move beyond these domains, we can think of nothing that would fit [as a name]. (slips 10–12)

*Comments and Notes*

Interest in the god named "Taiyi" (太 一 or 大 一, the Great One) has been considerable among scholars in China with the realization that one of the paintings found in Tomb No. 3 at Mawangdui in 1973 is a picture of Taiyi, with the deities Leigong (雷 公, Lord Thunder) and Yushi (雨 師, the Rain Master) standing to his right and his left.[23] Taiyi is portrayed as a god with a red face and red legs, antlers on top of his head, arms that appear to be wings, and a mouth that could be a bird's beak. This portrayal of god—of the "supreme" god who lives in the sky—as a fusion of bird and dragon (the antlers—dragons have horns), can be traced back to Shang dynasty times (c. 1500 B.C.).[24]

But in pre-Qin philosophical texts, "Taiyi" is simply another name for the "Dao," the Way, which is how it is used here. As Ge Zhaoguang (葛 兆 光) has recently shown, "Taiyi," "Dao," and "Taiji" (太 極, the Great Ultimate) are terms that are used interchangeably in texts of this era.[25] The term "Taiyi" itself is never used in the *Laozi.* But, as seen in the complete form of the text, the "One" seems to be used to mean the Way in several chapters (10, 22, 39, 42), and in chapter 25, as noted, the author claims that, were he forced to give it (the Way) a name, he would say it is the "Great" (*da,* 大).

Cui Renyi and Li Xueqin both believe that "Taiyi shengshui" is related to chapter 42 of the *Laozi,* which opens in the following way: "The Way gave birth to the One; the One gave birth to the Two; the Two gave birth to the Three; and the Three gave birth to the ten thousand things."[26] However, Cui thinks it is clear that chapter 42 of the *Laozi* is *based* on "Taiyi"; the former is abstract and symbolic, while the latter talks about actual things.[27] Li argues, to the contrary, that "Taiyi shengshui" must be *later* than the received edition of the *Laozi* since, although the Way is often talked about as the "One" (*yi*) in the *Laozi*, the phrase "Great One" (*taiyi*) does not yet occur.[28] Isabelle Robinet, on the other hand, has argued[29] these are two quite different cosmological views, in that, in contrast to chapter 42 of the *Laozi*—in which successive things "produce" (*sheng*, 生) one another—in "Taiyi shengshui" things are produced, but then they "return" and interact with or "assist" Taiyi, thus producing additional things.

Finally, as some scholars have already noted, cosmological schemes in which everything in the world originates from the "Great One" are found in many texts, including the "Zhongxia ji" (仲夏紀, Midsummer) chapter of the *Lushi chunqiu* (呂氏春秋, Mr. Lu's Spring and Autumn) and the "Li yun" (禮運, Changes in the Rites) chapter of the *Liji*. The relevant lines in the "Li yun" are: "For this reason, the rites must originate with the Great One [*dayi*, 大一]: It separates, forming heaven and earth; revolves, creating Yin and Yang; changes, creating the four seasons; and orders all things, creating the ghosts and the gods.[30] The *Lushi chunqiu* account begins with the words "The Great One produced the two principles [*liangyi*, 兩儀], which produced Yin and Yang. Yin and Yang changed and transformed, one ascended, the other went down."[31] Then in succession are mentioned heaven and earth, the sun and the moon, stars and constellations, the four seasons (some being hot and some cold), and finally the ten thousand things: "The ten thousand things emerged from the Great One and were transformed [*hua*, 化, given form? given life?] by Yin and Yang."[32]

*Transcription*

(a) 大一生水，水反桮大一，是以成天。天反桮大一，是以成墬。
天墬□□□也，是以成神明。神明還相桮也，是以成会易。会
易還相桮也，是以成四時。四時還桮也，是以成倉然。倉然還
相桮也，是以成浧澡。浧澡還相桮也，成哉而步。古哉者，浧
澡之所生也。浧澡者，倉然之所生也。倉然者，四時者，会易
之所生。会易者，神明之所生也。神明者，天墬之所生也。天
墬者，大一之所生也。是古大一鬻於水，行於時，迡而或□□
□□薹勿母。罷块罷淂，以忌爲薹勿經。此天之所不能殺，墬
之所不能釐，会易之所不能成。君子智此之胃□□□□□□
□。(slips 1–8)

(b) 下，土也，而胃之墬。上，燬也，而胃之天。道亦亓志也。青
昏亓名？以道從事者必厇亓名，古事城而身長；聖人之從事
也，亦厇亓名，古杠城而身不剔。天墬名志竝竝。古怂亓方不
田相□。□□□。(slips 10–12)

*Modern Equivalents*

(a) 太一生水，水反輔太一，是以成天。天反輔太一，是以成地。
天地[復相輔]也，是以成神明。神明復相輔也，是以成陰陽。陰
陽復相輔也，是以成四時。四時復輔也，是以成滄然。滄然
復相輔也，是以成滋燥。滋燥復相輔也，成歲而止。故歲者，滋
燥之所生也。滋燥者，滄然之所生也。滄然者，四時者，陰陽
之所生。陰陽者，神明之所生也。神明者，天地之所生也。天
地者，太一之所生也。是故太一藏於水，行於時，舟而又
[始，以紀爲]萬物母。一缺一盈，以紀爲萬物經。此天之所不
能殺，地之所不能埋，陰陽之所不能成。君子知此之謂[道?]。
□□□□□。

(b) 下，土也，而謂之地。上，氣也，而謂之天。道亦其字也。請
問其名？以道從事者必詫其名，故事成而身長；聖人之從事
也，亦詫其名，故功成而身不傷。天地名字並立。故過其方不
思相[當]。□□□。

## C:6 "Taiyi shengshui," Part II (slips 9, 13–14)[33]

*Translation (tentative):*

(a) The Way of Heaven values weakness. To cut away[34] at what is complete in order to add on to life is to attack using force, to punish using . . . (slip 9)

(b) [Heaven is incomplete] in the northwest. What is below it (i.e., the earth) is high and firm. The earth is incomplete in the southeast. What is above it (i.e., the sky) [is low and soft (?). When what is above is lacking,] there is a surplus below, and when what is below is lacking, there is a surplus above. (slips 13–14)

*Comments and Notes*

If we are right in connecting slips 10 to 12 of this selection with slips 1 to 8, we are left with the problem of what to do with slips 9, 13, and 14. All three slips are difficult to translate lacking a context; all three could be translated in many different ways. We must also decide whether the three are connected: Is it possible that the three formed a unit that began with slip 9? What *is* clear is that slips 13 and 14 assume the reader's familiarity with a well-known Chinese cosmological myth, a myth cited in the *Huainanẓi* as follows: [35] "In antiquity Gonggong [共工] fought with Zhuanxu [顓頊] over who would be God. [Having lost], he got angry and butted Mount Buzhou [不周之山]. Heaven's pillar then broke, and earth's cord snapped, so that heaven now dips down in the northwest. As a result, the sun and the moon, along with the stars and constellations, now move in that direction. In addition, the earth no longer fills up the space in the southeast. Thus the rivers, flood waters, and the dust and the dirt now settle in that direction."

To elaborate: Sarah Allan has persuasively argued that the ancient Chinese understood the cosmos to be in the shape of a turtle; the upper shell of the turtle was the dome of the sky, while the under shell served as the earth's surface.[36] The sky was held in place over the earth by four mountains/pillars (= the legs of the turtle), located in the northwest, northeast, southeast, and southwest. In addition, there were "cords" (*wei*, 維) connecting heaven and earth, to keep the two from separating completely should anything happen to one of the pillars (i.e., the mountains). When Gonggong broke the northwestern pillar, naturally the dome/shell then tipped in that direction, putting such stress on the "cord" in the southeast that it broke. As a result, heaven and earth are no longer level; they are closer together than they once were in the northwest, and further apart in the southeast.

While that explains what slips 13–14 might mean, what can we make of slip 9? My translation assumes that key words in the expression mean what they mean in the *Laozi*. In the *Laozi*, in the opposition of *qiang* (強, strong or force) and *ruo* (弱, weak or soft), it is the soft and the weak that overcome the strong and the firm.[37] Moreover, "to add on to life" (*yisheng*, 益生) is condemned in chapter 55 in the lines: "To add on to life is called a 'bad omen' [*xiang*, 祥]; For the mind to control the breath—that is called 'forcing things' [*qiang*, 強]."[38] Still, what is meant by "cutting away at what is complete" (*xuecheng*, 削成) is not clear without knowing more of the original passage.

Is it possible that all three of these slips are meant to be read together? It is tempting to see a connection since the word *qiang* (強) is prominent in both passages. The text for my "high and firm"—"What is below it is *high and firm*"—is *gao yi qiang* (高以強). *Qiang* translated this way is a positive thing, whereas it is condemned in slip 9. But *gao yi qiang* could be translated in different ways, since the *yi* that I translate as "and" more commonly means "by this means" or "because of." Thus *gao yi qiang* could also be read "is high as the result of violence," and the parallel line that refers to the sky might have been "is low as the result of violence." So another translation of slips 13–14 might be:

Heaven is incomplete in the northwest. What is below it (i.e., the earth) is high as the result of violence. The earth is incomplete in the southeast. What is above it (i.e., the sky) is low as the result of violence. Where what is above is lacking, there is a surplus below, and where what is below is lacking, there is a surplus above." (slips 13–14)

The "violence" would refer, of course, to the act of Gonggong. The question then would become could the words in slip 9—"To cut something off from what is complete in order to add on to life"—*also* refer to Gonggong's deed?[39] They might, especially since he broke off part of a pillar that was already "complete," and *yisheng* (to extend life) could also be translated as "to better your life." Unfortunately, the words *xuecheng*—"to cut off from what is complete"—and *yisheng*—"to better your life"—still do not *exactly* describe Gonggong's actions and his situation. As a result, I cannot yet argue with any certainty that these three slips were meant to be read together.[40]

*Transcription*

(a) 天道貴溺 ，雀成者，以益生者；伐於勈，責於 □， □□□ 。□ □□ (slip 9)

(b) 於西北，亓下高 以勈。埅不足於東南，亓上□□□。 □□□□ 者，又余於下，不足於下者，又余於上。■ (slips 13–14)

*Modern Equivalents*

(a) 天道貴弱，削成者，以益生者；伐於強，責於□， □□□ □□□

(b) 於西北，其下高 以強。地不足於東南，其上[底以強。不足於 上]者，有餘於下，不足於下者，有餘於上。■

# Appendixes

# Appendix I

*Sima Qian's "Biography of Laozi"*[1]

As for Laozi (the Old Master), he was from Quren village in Li township, in the district of Ku in the state of Chu. His surname was Li [李], his name was Er [耳], and his style was Dan [聃]. He was in charge of the royal archives in Zhou.[2]

Confucius once went to Zhou wanting to ask Laozi about the rites. Laozi replied: "As for the things you are talking about—those people along with their bones have already rotted away! All that remains is their words. Moreover, if the gentleman lives at the right time he rides in the carriage of an official; if he does not, then he moves about like a tumbleweed blown by the wind. I have heard it said that the good merchant has a well-stocked warehouse that appears to be empty; and the gentleman, though overflowing in virtue, gives the appearance of being a fool. Rid yourself of your arrogant manner, your many desires, your pretentious demeanor and unbridled ambition. None of these is good for your health. What I have to tell you is this, nothing more." Confucius left and said to his disciples, "As for birds, I understand how they can fly; with fish, I understand how they can swim; and with animals, I understand how they can run. To catch things that run, we can make nets; to catch things that swim, we can make lines; and to get things that fly, we can make arrows. But when it comes to dragons, I cannot understand how they ascend into the sky riding the wind and the clouds. Today I met Laozi, and he's just like a dragon!"

Laozi cultivated the Way and its virtue. In his studies he strove to conceal himself and be unknown. He lived in Zhou for a long time. But, seeing the decline of the Zhou, he decided to leave. When he reached the checkpoint at the pass, Yin Xi [尹喜], the official in charge of the pass, said to him, "Sir, you are about to retire. You must make an effort to write us a book." So Laozi wrote a book in two sections, explaining the ideas of the Way and its virtue in something over five thousand words, and left. No one knows how he ended.

Some people say Lao Laizi [老萊子] was also from Chu. He wrote a book with fifteen sections that explained how to apply the ideas of the Daoist school, and *he* lived at the same time as Confucius, and so on.

Laozi probably lived for more than 160 years—some say more than 200—because he cultivated the Way and nourished his life.

One hundred and twenty-nine years after the death of Confucius, as scribes have recorded, Grand Historian Dan [儋] had an audience with Duke Xian [獻] of Qin (r. 384–362 B.C.)[3] at which he said: "In the beginning, Qin and Zhou were united. But, having been united for five hundred years, we have now parted ways. Seventy years after this separation, a king who rules by right of might will emerge from this state."[4] Some say *this* "Dan" was actually Laozi; others say no. At present, nobody knows which side is right. Laozi was a gentleman who lived retired.

Laozi's son's name was Zong [宗]; Zong was a general in the state of Wei, and he was given a fief in Duan'gan.[5] Zong's son was Zhu, and Zhu's son was Gong, and Gong's great-great-grandson was Jia. Jia served during the reign of Emperor Xiaowen (r. 180–157 B.C.), and Jia's son Jie was grand tutor to Liu Ang, king of Jiaoxi. As a result, he and his family lived in Qi.

In our age, those who study the thought of Laozi belittle Confucian studies, and the Confucians belittle the ideas of Laozi. "If the ways they follow are different, there is no need to take counsel together."[6] Did he mean something like this?

Li Er said, "If you do nothing, things will transform on their own; if you are pure and tranquil, things will be correct and proper all on their own."[7]

## Comments and Notes

Note that Sima Qian offers at least two—three if we include Lao Laizi—identifications of the "Old Master": (1) Li Er, who lived at the time of Confucius, whose "posthumous name" was Dan (聃); (2) Dan (儋) the "Grand Historian" of Zhou, who met with Duke Xian of Qin, in 374 B.C. He admits that at the time of his writing (c. 100 B.C.) people disagreed which of these two was "Laozi." He does allow, however, for the possibility that these two "Dans" were actually one and the same, by saying "Laozi probably lived for more than 160 years—some say more than 200."

Some of the problems that have been noted with Sima Qian's data are as follows:[8]

1. Studies of surnames in China indicate that Li (李) was not used as a surname before the fourth century B.C.

2. In the list of Laozi's descendants, the number of generations indicated is not long enough if Laozi was someone who lived at the time of Confucius. The list might be fitting if Laozi were the second Dan mentioned, the one who lived in the early or mid-fourth century. Moreover, "Zong of Duan'gan" (段干宗), Laozi's son, is probably the Wei general Duan'gan Chong (段干崇), who is noted in the *Zhanguoce* (戰國策) as suing for peace with Qin in 273 B.C.[9]

3. It is hard to imagine that Confucius would consult with Laozi concerning the "rites," in light of Laozi's negative view of "ritual" (*li*, 禮) as expressed in chapter 38 of his book.[10] Moreover, the account we find here of what happened when Confucius met with Laozi is inconsistent with material preserved in the *Liji*, in which Confucius comments on what he had learned about funeral rites from Lao Dan ("Old Dan" being a way of referring to the "Old Master").[11]

Confucius's interview with Laozi is very important since it is one of the few pieces of evidence indicating that the *Laozi* was written by someone who lived at the time of Confucius. However, Sima Qian's account of this meeting can hardly be used as solid, historical data. This has all the markings of a story concocted by the Daoists, in which Laozi humiliates Confucius, and Confucius then acknowledges to his disciples that Laozi is his intellectual superior—he cannot understand him. As we know, there was a proliferation of stories like this, most of them ending up in the *Zhuangzi*.[12]

But what then of the *Liji* accounts in which Lao Dan does indeed seem to be a ritual specialist? D. C. Lau's conclusion here seems to be the logical one: "My conjecture is that these were later in date than the stories in the Taoist tradition, and constituted a move on the part of the Confucians to counter the successful attempts by Taoists to make Confucius a figure of ridicule."[13] But Angus Graham proposed a different way to make sense of this data.[14] Graham's thesis is that the story of a meeting between Old Dan and Confucius, in which Confucius was instructed by Old Dan in the rites, was originally transmitted by the Confucians. Whether there was an Old Dan in reality is not important; the key thing is that the story shows that Confucius was not beyond accepting instruction from others.[15] It was Zhuangzi, in Graham's opinion, who turned Old Dan into a Daoist, a Daoist who made fun of Confucius, such stories being effective, in part, because even the Confucians acknowledged that Old Dan was Confucius's teacher. When the *Laozi* made its appearance in China—around 250 B.C. in Graham's estimation—who better to identify as the "Old Master" than the person known as "Old Dan"? This, then, is the source of Li Er's "posthumous name" (Dan, 聃) and the reason the meeting of Confucius and Laozi shows up in Laozi's biography. But what is the source of the other detail that describes the life of Laozi: for example, his names, the name of his village and township and state, and the names of his descendants? Graham suggests that all this data comes from the life of the *other* Dan (儋), Dan the "Grand Historian," someone who had wisely predicted that Qin would ultimately prevail over all other states to unify China (which it did in 221 B.C.).

One final note on this matter. As I mentioned in the introduction, Guo Yi has come up with another understanding of these events. His argument is that there were really two "Old Dans" in ancient China. The first, Confucius's contemporary, wrote the "Bamboo Slip *Laozi*," which we have recently found; the second, Dan the "Grand Historian" who met with Duke Xian of Qin, is actually the person who compiled the ancestral edition of our complete, eighty-one-chapter form of the text. Guo argues that Laozi's criticisms of Confucius, as recorded in his biography, are consistent with the "Bamboo Slip *Laozi*," in which a lot is made of getting rid of desires and not being arrogant (as in chapters 19 and 30). In addition, chapter 31 (C:3 in the translation) in the "Bamboo Slip *Laozi*" demonstrates that Laozi was indeed someone who knew something about funeral rites! Finally, he suggests that the Old Dan who was in charge of the Zhou library and left Zhou when he saw the state in decline was in fact Dan the "Grand Historian." Exiting "China," he in fact went to Qin, where he met with Duke Xian.[16]

# Appendix II

*Line-by-Line Comparisons*

*Note:* Section and line numbers correspond to those used in the translation. The unnumbered lines in **Bold** print are lines that are only found in later editions. The abbreviations (MWDa, MWDb, and WB) stand for "Mawangdui copy A," "Mawangdui copy B," and the commonly used "Wang Bi" edition.

## A:1 (Chapter 19)

| 1 | 㓞智弃㚓 |
|---|---|
| MWDa | 絕聲棄知 |
| MWDb | 絕耴棄知 |
| WB | 絕聖棄智 |

| 2 | 民利百伓 ■ |
|---|---|
| MWDa | 民利百貝 |
| MWDb | 而民利百倍 |
| WB | 民利百倍 |

| 3 | 㓞攺弃利 |
|---|---|
| MWDa | 絕仁棄義 |
| MWDb | 絕仁棄義 |
| WB | 絕仁棄義 |

| 4 | 朓㤼亡又 ■ |
|---|---|
| MWDa | 民復畜茲 |
| MWDb | 而民復孝慈 |
| WB | 民復孝慈 |

| 5 | 𢝔 憑弃慮 |
|---|---|
| MWDa | 絕巧棄利 |
| MWDb | 絕巧棄利 |
| WB | 絕巧棄利 |

| 6 | 民复季子■ |
|---|---|
| MWDa | 盗賊无有 |
| MWDb | 盗賊无有 |
| WB | 盗賊無有 |

| 7 | 三言　以爲貞不足 |
|---|---|
| MWDa | 此三言也以爲文未足 |
| MWDb | 此三言也以爲文未足 |
| WB | 此三　者以爲文不足 |

| 8 | 或命之或䖷豆■ |
|---|---|
| MWDa | 故令之有所屬 |
| MWDb | 故令之有所屬 |
| WB | 故令　有所屬 |

| 9 | 見索保蕓 |
|---|---|
| MWDa | 見素抱□ |
| MWDb | 見素抱樸 |
| WB | 見素抱樸 |

| 10 | 少厶　須欲■ |
|---|---|
| MWDa | □□　□□ |
| MWDb | 少□而寡欲 |
| WB | 少私　寡欲 |

## A:2 (Chapter 66)

| 1 | 江海　所以　爲百浴王 |
|---|---|
| MWDa | □海之所以能爲百浴王者 |
| MWDb | 江海　所以能爲百浴□□ |
| WB | 江海　所以能爲百谷王者 |

| 2 | 以亓能為百浴下 |
|---|---|
| MWDa | 以亓　　善下之 |
| MWDb | 以亓　　善下之也 |
| WB | 以其　　善下之 |

| 3 | 是以能為百浴王 |
|---|---|
| MWDa | 是以能為百浴王 |
| MWDb | 是以能為百浴王 |
| WB | 故　能為百谷王 |

| 4 | 　　聖人之才民前也　以　身後之 |
|---|---|
| MWDa | 是以聖人之欲上民也必以亓言下之 |
| MWDb | 是以耴人之欲上民也必以亓言下之 |
| WB | 是以　　欲上民　必以　言下之 |

| 5 | 亓才民上也　以　言下之 |
|---|---|
| MWDa | 亓欲先□□必以亓身後之 |
| MWDb | 亓欲先民也必以亓身後之 |
| WB | 　欲先民　必以　身後之 |

| 6 | 　　亓才民上也民弗厚也 |
|---|---|
| MWDa | 故　　居　前而民弗害也 |
| MWDb | 故　　居　上而民弗重也 |
| WB | 是以聖人處　上而民不重 |

| 7 | 亓才民前也民弗害也 |
|---|---|
| MWDa | 　居　上而民弗重也 |
| MWDb | 　居　前而民弗害 |
| WB | 　處　前而民不害 |

| 8 | 　天下　樂進而弗詀 |
|---|---|
| MWDa | 　天下　樂隼而弗猒也 |
| MWDb | 　天下皆樂誰而弗猒也 |
| WB | 是以天下　樂推而不厭 |

| 9 | 以亓不靜也 |
|---|---|
| MWDa | 非以亓无諍與 |
| MWDb | 不□亓无爭與 |
| WB | 　以其不爭 |

10　古天下莫能戔之靜
MWDa　故□□□□□　靜
MWDb　故天下莫能與　爭
WB　　故天下莫能與之爭

## A:3 (Chapter 46)

MWDa　・天下有道□走馬以糞
MWDb　□□□道卻走馬□糞
WB　　天下有道卻走馬以糞

MWDa　天下无道戎馬生於郊
MWDb　天下无道戎馬生於郊
WB　　天下無道戎馬生於郊

..................................................................

1　　　皋莫厚虖甚欲
MWDa　・罪莫大於可欲
MWDb　罪莫大　可欲

2　　　咎莫憸虖　谷尋
MWDa　戱莫大於不知足
MWDb　禍□□□□□□
WB　　禍莫大於不知足

3　　　化莫大虖不智足
MWDa　咎莫憯於　欲得
MWDb　□□□□　□□
WB　　咎莫大於　欲得

4　　　　智足之爲足
MWDa　　　□□□□□
MWDb　　　□□□□□
WB　　故知足之　足

| 5 | 此互足矣__ |
|---|---|
| MWDa | 恒足矣 |
| MWDb | □足矣 |
| WB | 常足矣 |

## A:4 (Chapter 30)

| 1 | 以道䅶人宔者 |
|---|---|
| MWDa | 以道佐人主 |
| MWDb | 以道佐人主 |
| WB | 以道佐人主者 |

| 2 | 不谷以兵強於天下 |
|---|---|
| MWDa | 不　以兵強□天下 |
| MWDb | 不　以兵強於天下 |
| WB | 不　以兵強　天下 |

........................................................

| MWDa | □□□□ |
|---|---|
| MWDb | 亓□□□ |
| WB | 其事好還 |

| MWDa | □□所居楚朼生之 |
|---|---|
| MWDb | □□□□□棘生之 |
| WB | 師之所處荊棘生焉 |

| WB | 大軍之後必有凶年 |
|---|---|

........................................................

| 3 | 善者果而已 |
|---|---|
| MWDa | 善者果而已矣 |
| MWDb | 善者果而已矣 |
| WB | 善有果而已 |

| 4 | 不　以取強__ |
|---|---|
| MWDa | 毋　以取強焉 |
| MWDb | 毋　以取強焉 |
| WB | 不敢以取強 |

| | |
|---|---|
| 5 | 果而弗癹 |
| MWDa | 果而毋驕 |
| MWDb | 果而毋驕 |
| WB | 果而勿矜 |
| | |
| 6 | 果而弗喬 |
| MWDa | 果而勿矜 |
| MWDb | 果而勿矜 |
| WB | 果而勿伐 |
| | |
| 7 | 果而弗矜＿ |
| MWDa | 果而□□ |
| MWDb | 果□□伐 |
| WB | 果而勿喬 |

.......................................................

| | |
|---|---|
| **MWDa** | 果而毋得已居 |
| **MWDb** | 果而毋得已居 |
| **WB** | 果而不得已 |

.......................................................

| | |
|---|---|
| 8 | 是胃果而不強 |
| MWDa | 是胃□而不強 |
| MWDb | 是胃果而　強 |
| WB | 　　果而勿強 |
| 9 | 亓事好＿長 |

.......................................................

| | |
|---|---|
| **MWDa** | 物壯而老 |
| **MWDb** | 物壯而老 |
| **WB** | 物壯則老 |
| | |
| MWDa | 是胃之不道 |
| MWDb | 　胃之不道 |
| WB | 是謂　不道 |
| | |
| MWDa | 不道蚤已 |
| MWDb | 不道蚤已 |
| WB | 不道早已 |

## A:5 (Chapter 15)

| | |
|---|---|
| 1 | 古之善爲士者 |
| MWDa | □□□□□□ |
| MWDb | 古之仚爲道者 |
| WB | 古之善爲士者 |

| | |
|---|---|
| 2 | 必非溺玄造 |
| MWDa | □□□□ |
| MWDb | 微眇玄達 |
| WB | 微妙元通 |

| | |
|---|---|
| 3 | 深不可志__ |
| MWDa | 深不可志 |
| MWDb | 深不可志 |
| WB | 深不可識 |

| | |
|---|---|
| **MWDa** | **夫唯不可志** |
| **MWDb** | **夫唯不可志** |
| **WB** | **夫唯不可識** |

| | |
|---|---|
| 4 | 是以　爲之頌 |
| MWDa | 故　強爲之容曰 |
| MWDb | 故　強爲之容曰 |
| WB | 故　強爲之容 |

| | |
|---|---|
| 5 | 夜虖　奴含涉川__ |
| MWDa | 與呵亓若冬□□ |
| MWDb | 與呵亓若冬涉水 |
| WB | 豫焉　若冬涉川 |

| | |
|---|---|
| 6 | 猷虖丌奴愚四嬰__ |
| MWDa | □□□□畏四□ |
| MWDb | 猷呵亓若畏四嬰 |
| WB | 猶兮　若畏四鄰 |

7　　敢虖丌奴客__
MWDa　□呵亓若客
MWDb　嚴呵亓若客
WB　　儼兮其若容

8　　戁虖丌奴　　罞__
MWDa　澳呵其若凌　　澤
MWDb　澳呵其若凌　　澤
WB　　澳兮其若冰之將釋

9　　屯虖丌奴樸__
MWDa　□呵亓若榾
MWDb　沌呵亓若樸
WB　　敦兮其若樸

10　　坉虖亓奴湮
MWDa　湷□□□
MWDb　湷呵亓若濁
WB　　曠兮其若谷

...............................................................

**MWDa**　□□□若浴
**MWDb**　湉呵亓若浴
**WB**　　混兮其若濁

...............................................................

11　　竺能湮以束者牖舍清■
MWDa　　濁而情之　余清
MWDb　　濁而靜之　徐清
WB　　孰能濁以靜之　徐清

12　　竺能庀以　迬者牖舍生
MWDa　　女以　重之　余生
MWDb　　女以　重之　徐生
WB　　孰能安以久動之　徐生

13　　保此衍者不谷䇂呈
MWDa　葆此道　不欲　盈
MWDb　葆此道□□欲　盈
WB　　保此道者不欲　盈

...............................................................

| MWDa | 夫唯不欲□ |
|------|---------|
| WB | 夫唯不　盈 |

| MWDa | □以能□□□　成 |
|------|---------------|
| MWDb | 是以能斃而不　成 |
| WB | 故　能蔽　不新成 |

## A:6 (Chapter 64, part 2)

| 1 | 爲之者敗之 |
|---|----------|
| MWDa | □□□□□ |
| MWDb | 爲之者敗之 |
| WB | 爲　者敗之 |

| 2 | 埶之者遠之 |
|---|----------|
| MWDa | □　□□□ |
| MWDb | 執　者失之 |
| WB | 執　者失之 |

| 3 | 是以聖人亡爲　古亡敗 |
|---|-------------------|
| MWDa | □□□□□□也□无敗□ |
| MWDb | 是以耴人无爲□□□□□ |
| WB | 是以聖人無爲　故無敗 |

| 4 | 亡埶　古亡遊 |
|---|-----------|
| MWDa | 无執也故无失也 |
| MWDb | □□□□□□□ |
| WB | 無執　故無失 |

| 5 | 　　臨事　　之紀 |
|---|--------------|
| MWDa | 民之從事也恒於亓成事而敗之 |
| MWDb | 民之從事也恒於亓成　而敗之 |
| WB | 民之從事　常於幾成　而敗之 |

| 6 | 誓各女㕣 |
|---|--------|
| MWDa | 故　慎終若始 |
| MWDb | 故曰慎冬若始 |
| WB | 　慎終如始 |

7 此亡敗事矣
MWDa 則□□□□
MWDb 則无敗事矣
WB 則無敗事

8 　　　聖人谷不谷　不貴難㝵之貨
MWDa □□□□欲不欲而不貴難得之腸
MWDb 是以耶人欲不欲而不貴難得之貨
WB 是以聖人欲不欲　不貴難得之貨

9 孚不孚　　返衆　之所所㤅＿
MWDa 學不學而復衆人之所　過
MWDb 學不學　復衆人之所　　過
WB 學不學　復衆人之所　　過

10 是古聖人能專萬物之自炊而弗能爲
MWDa 　　能輔萬物之自□□弗敢爲
MWDb 　　能輔萬物之自然而弗敢爲
WB 　　以輔萬物之自然而不敢爲

## A:7 (Chapter 37)

1 衍互亡爲也
MWDa 道恒无名
MWDb 道恒无名
WB 道常無爲

..............................................................

WB 而無不爲

..............................................................

2 侯王　能守之
MWDa 侯王若　守之
MWDb 侯王若能守之
WB 侯王若能守之

| 3 | 而萬勿牺自愿 |
|---|---|
| MWDa | 萬物將自愿 |
| MWDb | 萬物將自化 |
| WB | 萬物將自化 |

| 4 | 愿而雒复 |
|---|---|
| MWDa | 愿而欲□ |
| MWDb | 化而欲作 |
| WB | 化而欲作 |

| 5 | 牺貞之以亡名之歔 |
|---|---|
| MWDa | □□□之以无名之楃 |
| MWDb | 吾將閴之以无名之樸 |
| WB | 吾將鎮之以無名之樸 |

| 6 | 夫亦牺智足 |
|---|---|
| MWDa | 无名之楃夫　將不辱 |
| MWDb | 无名之樸夫　將不辱 |
| WB | 無名之樸夫亦將無欲 |

| 7 | 智　以束 |
|---|---|
| MWDa | 不辱以情 |
| MWDb | 不辱以靜 |
| WB | 不欲以靜 |

| 8 | 萬勿牺自定■ |
|---|---|
| MWDa | 天地將自正 |
| MWDb | 天地將自正 |
| WB | 天下將自定 |

## A:8 (Chapter 63, lines 1–4, 13–15)

| 1 | 爲亡爲 |
|---|---|
| MWDa | ・爲无爲 |
| MWDb | 爲无爲 |
| WB | 爲無爲 |

| | |
|---|---|
| 2 | 事亡事 |
| MWDa | 事无事 |
| MWDb | □□□ |
| WB | 事無事 |

| | |
|---|---|
| 3 | 未亡未 |
| MWDa | 味无未 |
| MWDb | □□□ |
| WB | 味無味 |

| | |
|---|---|
| 4 | 大少之　　　多惖必多難 |
| MWDa | 大小多少(13)多易必多難 |
| MWDb | □□□□(13)多易必多難 |
| WB | 大小多少(13)多易必多難 |

| | |
|---|---|
| 5 | 是以聖人猷難之 |
| MWDa(14) | □□□人猷難之 |
| MWDb(14) | 是以耶人□□之 |
| WB(14) | 是以聖人猶難之 |

| | |
|---|---|
| 6 | 古冬　亡難■ |
| MWDa(15) | 故終於无難 |
| MWDb(15) | 故□□□□ |
| WB(15) | 故終　無難矣 |

**A:9 (Chapter 2)**

| | |
|---|---|
| 1 | 天下皆智𢼸之爲𢼸也亞已 |
| MWDa | 天下皆知美　爲美　亞已 |
| MWDb | 天下皆知美之爲美　亞已 |
| WB | 天下皆知美之爲美斯惡已 |

| | |
|---|---|
| 2 | 皆智善　　　此丌不善已 |
| MWDa | 皆知善　　　訾　不善矣 |
| MWDb | 皆知善　　　斯　不善矣 |
| WB | 皆知善之爲善斯　不善已 |

| | |
|---|---|
| 3 | 又亡之相生也 |
| MWDa | 有无之相生也 |
| MWDb | □□□□生也 |
| WB | 故有無相生 |

| | |
|---|---|
| 4 | 戁惖之相成也 |
| MWDa | 難易之相成也 |
| MWDb | 難易之相成也 |
| WB | 難易　相成 |

| | |
|---|---|
| 5 | 長耑之相型也 |
| MWDa | 長短之相刑也 |
| MWDb | 長短之相刑也 |
| WB | 長短　相較 |

| | |
|---|---|
| 6 | 高下之相涅也 |
| MWDa | 高下之相盈也 |
| MWDb | 高下之相盈也 |
| WB | 高下　相傾 |

| | |
|---|---|
| 7 | 音聖之相和也 |
| MWDa | 意聲之相和也 |
| MWDb | 音聲之相和也 |
| WB | 音聲　相和 |

| | |
|---|---|
| 8 | 先垕之相墮也 |
| MWDa | 先後之相隋 |
| MWDb | 先後之相隋 |
| WB | 前後　相隨 |

| | |
|---|---|
| **MWDa** | 恒也 |
| **MWDb** | 恒也 |

9    是以聖人居亡爲之事
MWDa 是以聲人居无爲之事
MWDb 是以即人居无爲之事
WB   是以聖人處無爲之事

10   行不言之孚
MWDa 行□□□□
MWDb 行不言之教
WB   行不言之教

11   萬勿逜　而弗冂也
MWDa □□□　□□□也
MWDb 萬物昔　而弗始
WB   萬物作焉而不辭

WB   生而不有

12   爲而弗志也
MWDa 爲而弗志也
MWDb 爲而弗侍也
WB   爲而不恃

13   成　而弗居
MWDa 成功而弗居也
MWDb 成功而弗居也
WB   功成而弗居

14   天唯弗居也
MWDa 夫唯　居
MWDb 夫唯弗居
WB   夫唯弗居

15   是以弗去也■
MWDa 是以弗去
MWDb 是以弗去
WB   是以不去

**A:10 (Chapter 32)**

| | |
|---|---|
| 1 | 道互亡名 |
| MWDa | 道恒无名 |
| MWDb | 道恒无名 |
| WB | 道常無名 |

| | |
|---|---|
| 2 | 僅唯妻　天陛弗敢臣 |
| MWDa | 楎唯□□□□□□□ |
| MWDb | 樸唯小而天下弗敢臣 |
| WB | 樸雖小　天下莫能臣也 |

| | |
|---|---|
| 3 | 侯王女能獸之 |
| MWDa | 侯王若能守之 |
| MWDb | 侯王若能守之 |
| WB | 侯王若能守之 |

| | |
|---|---|
| 4 | 萬勿牖自賓▬ |
| MWDa | 萬物將自賓 |
| MWDb | 萬物將自賓 |
| WB | 萬物將自賓 |

| | |
|---|---|
| 5 | 天陛相會也以逾甘霤 |
| MWDa | 天地相谷　以俞甘洛 |
| MWDb | 天地相合　以俞甘洛 |
| WB | 天地相合　以降甘露 |

| | |
|---|---|
| 6 | 民莫之命天自均安 |
| MWDa | 民莫之□□□□□ |
| MWDb | □□□令而自均焉 |
| WB | 民莫之令而自均 |

| | |
|---|---|
| 7 | 訂折又名 |
| MWDa | 始制有□ |
| MWDb | 始制有名 |
| WB | 始制有名 |

8 名亦旣又
MWDa □□□有
MWDb 名亦旣有
WB 名亦旣有

9 夫亦牕智迮
MWDa 夫□□□□
MWDb 夫亦將知止
WB 夫亦將知止

10 智迮所以不訂
MWDa □□所以不□
MWDb 知止所以不殆
WB 知止可以不殆

11 卑道之才天下也
MWDa 俾道之在天□□
MWDb 卑□□在天下也
WB 譬道之在天下

12 猷少浴之夆江海▓
MWDa □□浴之與江海也
MWDb 猷小浴之與江海也
WB 猶川谷之於江海

## A:11 (Chapter 25)

1 又楷蟲成
MWDa 有物昆成
MWDb 有物昆成
WB 有物混成

2 先天地生
MWDa 先天地生
MWDb 先天地生
WB 先天地生

| 3 | 敓 | 繆 | 蜀立 | 不亥 |
|---|---|---|---|---|
| MWDa | 繡呵 | 繆呵 | 獨立□ | □□ |
| MWDb | 蕭呵 | 漻呵 | 獨立而 | 不玹 |
| WB | 寂兮 | 寥兮 | 獨立 | 不改 |

**WB**　周行而不殆

| 4 | 可以爲天下母 |
|---|---|
| MWDa | 可以爲天地母 |
| MWDb | 可以爲天地母 |
| WB | 可以爲天下母 |

| 5 | 未智亓名 |
|---|---|
| MWDa | 吾未知其名 |
| MWDb | 吾未知亓名也 |
| WB | 吾不知其名 |

| 6 | 爭之曰道 |
|---|---|
| MWDa | 字之曰道 |
| MWDb | 字之曰道 |
| WB | 字之曰道 |

| 7 | 虐弖爲之名曰大 |
|---|---|
| MWDa | 吾強爲之名曰大 |
| MWDb | 吾強爲之名曰大 |
| WB | 強爲之名曰大 |

| 8 | 大曰瀄 |
|---|---|
| MWDa | □曰筮 |
| MWDb | 大曰筮 |
| WB | 大曰逝 |

| 9 | 瀄曰連 |
|---|---|
| MWDa | 筮曰□ |
| MWDb | 筮曰遠 |
| WB | 逝曰遠 |

| | |
|---|---|
| 10 | 逺曰反 |
| MWDa | □□□ |
| MWDb | 遠曰反 |
| WB | 遠曰反 |

| | |
|---|---|
| 11 | 天大陛大道大王亦大 |
| MWDa | □□天大地大王亦大 |
| MWDb | 道大天大地大王亦大 |
| WB | 故道大天大地大王亦大 |

| | |
|---|---|
| 12 | 國中又四大安　王尻　一安 |
| MWDa | 國中有四大　　而王居　一焉 |
| MWDb | 國中有四大　　而王居　　一焉 |
| WB | 域中有四大　　而王居其一焉 |

| | |
|---|---|
| 13 | 人灋陛 |
| MWDa | 人法地 |
| MWDb | 人法地 |
| WB | 人法地 |

| | |
|---|---|
| 14 | 陛灋天 |
| MWDa | □法□ |
| MWDb | 地法天 |
| WB | 地法天 |

| | |
|---|---|
| 15 | 天灋道 |
| MWDa | □法□ |
| MWDb | 天法道 |
| WB | 天法道 |

| | |
|---|---|
| 16 | 道灋自然 |
| MWDa | □法□□ |
| MWDb | 道法自然 |
| WB | 道法自然 |

## A:12 (Chapter 5, lines 5–7)

| | |
|---|---|
| MWDa | 天地不仁 |
| MWDb | 天地不仁 |
| WB | 天地不仁 |
| | |
| MWDa | 以萬物爲芻狗 |
| MWDb | 以萬物爲芻狗 |
| WB | 以萬物爲芻狗 |
| | |
| MWDa | 聲人不仁 |
| MWDb | 耴人不仁 |
| WB | 聖人不仁 |
| | |
| MWDa | 以百省□□狗 |
| MWDb | □百姓爲芻狗 |
| WB | 以百姓爲芻狗 |

.................................................................

| | |
|---|---|
| 1 | 天垔之勿 |
| MWDa | 天地□間 |
| MWDb | 天地之間 |
| WB | 天地之間 |
| | |
| 2 | 丌猷囡籗與 |
| MWDa | □猶囊籥輿 |
| MWDb | 亓猷囊籥輿 |
| WB | 其猶囊籥乎 |
| | |
| 3 | 虛而不屈 |
| MWDa | 虛而不涸 |
| MWDb | 虛而不涸 |
| WB | 虛而不屈 |
| | |
| 4 | 逹而愈出 ■ |
| MWDa | 蹱而俞出 |
| MWDb | 勤而俞出 |
| WB | 動而愈出 |

.................................................................

| | |
|---|---|
| MWDa | 多聞數窮 |
| MWDb | 多聞數窮 |
| WB | 多言數窮 |

| | |
|---|---|
| MWDa | 不若守於中 |
| MWDb | 不若守於中 |
| WB | 不如守　中 |

## A:13 (Chapter 16, lines 1–6)

| | |
|---|---|
| 1 | 至虛互也 |
| MWDa | 至虛極也 |
| MWDb | 至虛極也 |
| WB | 至虛極 |

| | |
|---|---|
| 2 | 獸中箐也 |
| MWDa | 守情表也 |
| MWDb | 守靜督也 |
| WB | 守靜篤 |

| | |
|---|---|
| 3 | 萬勿方复 |
| MWDa | 萬物旁作 |
| MWDb | 萬物旁作 |
| WB | 萬物並作 |

| | |
|---|---|
| 4 | 居以須　復也 |
| MWDa | 吾以觀其復也 |
| MWDb | 吾以觀亓復也 |
| WB | 吾以觀　復 |

| | |
|---|---|
| 5 | 天道昃昃 |
| MWDa | 天物雲雲 |
| MWDb | 天物秐秐 |
| WB | 夫物芸芸 |

| 6 | 各遆　　亓堇■ |
|---|---|
| MWDa | 各復歸於其□ |
| MWDb | 各復歸於亓根 |
| WB | 各復歸　其根 |

## A:14 (Chapter 64, part 2)

| 1 | 亓安也易朿也 |
|---|---|
| MWDa | ・亓安也易持也 |
| MWDb | □□□□□□ |
| WB | 其安　易持 |

| 2 | 亓未芃也易愳也 |
|---|---|
| MWDa | □□□□易謀□ |
| MWDb | □□□□□□□ |
| WB | 其未兆　易謀 |

| 3 | 亓霆也易畔也 |
|---|---|
| MWDa | □□□□□ |
| MWDb | □□□□□ |
| WB | 其脆　易泮 |

| 4 | 亓幾也易後也 |
|---|---|
| MWDa | □□□□□□ |
| MWDb | □□□□□□ |
| WB | 其微　易散 |

| 5 | 爲之於亓亡又也 |
|---|---|
| MWDa | □□□□□□□ |
| MWDb | □□□□□□□ |
| WB | 爲之於　未有 |

| 6 | 絧之於亓未燮 |
|---|---|
| MWDa | □□□□□□□ |
| MWDb | □□□□□□□ |
| WB | 治之於　未亂 |

7　　合□□□
MWDa　　□□□□
MWDb　　□□□木
WB　　合抱之木

8　　□□□末
MWDa　　□□□末
MWDb　　作於毫末
MWDc　　生於毫末

9　　九城之臺
MWDa　　九成之臺
MWDb　　九成之臺
WB　　九層之臺

10　　甲□□□
MWDa　　作於羸土
MWDb　　作於纂土
WB　　起於累土

11　　□□□□
MWDa　　百仁之高
MWDb　　百千之高
WB　　千里之行

12　　□□足下＿
MWDa　　台於足下
MWDb　　始於足下
WB　　始於足下


## A:15 (Chapter 56)

1　　智之者弗言言之者弗智
MWDa　　□　□弗言言　者弗知
MWDb　　知　者弗言言　者弗知
WB　　知　者不言言　者不知

| | |
|---|---|
| 2 | 閟亓逆 |
| MWDa | 塞亓閟 |
| MWDb | 塞亓兌 |
| WB | 塞其兌 |
| | |
| 3 | 賽亓門 |
| MWDa | 閉亓□ |
| MWDb | 閉亓門 |
| WB | 閉其門 |
| | |
| 4 | 和亓光 |
| MWDa | □其光 |
| MWDb | 和亓光 |
| WB | 挫其銳 |
| | |
| 5 | 週亓訢訢 |
| MWDa | 同亓塵 |
| MWDb | 同亓塵 |
| WB | 解其紛 |
| | |
| 6 | 劀亓纂 |
| MWDa | 坐亓閱 |
| MWDb | 銼亓兌 |
| WB | 和其光 |
| | |
| 7 | 解亓紛 |
| MWDa | 解亓紛 |
| MWDb | 而解亓紛 |
| WB | 同其塵 |
| | |
| 8 | 是胃玄同 |
| MWDa | 是胃玄同 |
| MWDb | 是胃玄同 |
| WB | 是謂元同 |
| | |
| 9 | 古不可尋天新 |
| MWDa | 故不可得而親 |
| MWDb | 故不可得而親也 |
| WB | 故不可得而親 |

| | |
|---|---|
| 10 | 亦不可尋而疋 |
| MWDa | 亦不可得而疏 |
| MWDb | 亦□□得而□ |
| WB | 亦不可得而疏 |

| | |
|---|---|
| 11 | 不可尋而利 |
| MWDa | 不可得而利 |
| MWDb | □□得而利 |
| WB | 不可得而利 |

| | |
|---|---|
| 12 | 亦不可尋而害 |
| MWDa | 亦不可得而害 |
| MWDb | □□□得而害 |
| WB | 亦不可得而害 |

| | |
|---|---|
| 13 | 不可尋而貴 |
| MWDa | 不可□而貴 |
| MWDb | 不可得而貴 |
| WB | 不可得而貴 |

| | |
|---|---|
| 14 | 亦可不可尋而戔 |
| MWDa | 亦　不可得而淺 |
| MWDb | 亦　不可得而賤 |
| WB | 亦　不可得而賤 |

| | |
|---|---|
| 15 | 古爲天下貴■ |
| MWDa | 故爲天下貴 |
| MWDb | 故爲天下貴 |
| WB | 故爲天下貴 |

## A:16 (Chapter 57)

| | |
|---|---|
| 1 | 以正之邦 |
| MWDa | ・以正之邦 |
| MWDb | 以正之國 |
| WB | 以正治國 |

| 2 | 以㦻甬兵 |
|---|---|
| MWDa | 以畸用兵 |
| MWDb | 以畸用兵 |
| WB | 以奇用兵 |

| 3 | 以亡事取天下 |
|---|---|
| MWDa | 以无事取天下 |
| MWDb | 以無事取天下 |
| WB | 以無事取天下 |

| 4 | 虗可以智亓然也 |
|---|---|
| MWDa | 吾何□□□□也㦻 |
| MWDb | 吾何以知亓然也才 |
| WB | 吾何以知其然哉 |

........................................................

| WB | 以此 |
|---|---|

........................................................

| 5 | 夫天　多卟韋而民爾畔 |
|---|---|
| MWDa | 夫天下□□諱而民彌貧 |
| MWDb | 夫天下多忌諱而民彌貧 |
| WB | 　天下多忌諱而民彌貧 |

| 6 | 民多利器而邦　慈昏 |
|---|---|
| MWDa | 民多利器而邦家茲昏 |
| MWDb | 民多利器□□□□昏 |
| WB | 民多利器　國家滋昏 |

| 7 | 人多智而㦻勿慈记 |
|---|---|
| MWDa | 人多知而何物茲□ |
| MWDb | □□□□□□□□ |
| WB | 人多伎巧奇物滋起 |

| 8 | 灋勿慈章　眺悬多又 |
|---|---|
| MWDa | □□□□□盜賊□□ |
| MWDb | □物茲章而盜賊□□ |
| WB | 法令滋彰　盜賊多有 |

| 9 | 是以聖人之言曰 |
|---|---|
| MWDa | □□□□□□□ |
| MWDb | 是以□人之言曰 |
| WB | 故　聖人　　云 |

| 10 | 我無事　而民自福 |
|---|---|
| MWDa | 我无爲也而民自化 |
| MWDb | 我无爲　而民自化 |
| WB | 我無爲　　而民自化 |

| 11 | 我亡爲而民自蠱 |
|---|---|
| MWDa | 我好靜而民自正 |
| MWDb | 我好靜而民自正 |
| WB | 我好靜而民自正 |

| 12 | 我好青而民自正 |
|---|---|
| MWDa | 我无事　民□□ |
| MWDb | 我无事而民自富 |
| WB | 我無事而民自富 |

| 13 | 我谷不谷而民自樸乙 |
|---|---|
| MWDa | □□□□□□□□ |
| MWDb | 我欲不欲而民自僕 |
| WB | 我　無欲而民自樸 |

## A:17 (Chapter 55)

| I | 畬悳之厚者 |
|---|---|
| MWDa | □□之厚□ |
| MWDb | 含德之厚者 |
| WB | 含德之厚 |

| 2 | 比於赤子 |
|---|---|
| MWDa | 比於赤子 |
| MWDb | 比於赤子 |
| WB | 比於赤子 |

| | |
|---|---|
| 3 | 蟲蠆蠆它弗蠚 |
| MWDa | 逢衛蝟地弗螫 |
| MWDb | 蠭癘虫蛇弗赫 |
| WB | 蜂蠆虺蛇不螫 |
| | |
| 4 | 攫鳥　　猷獸弗扣 |
| MWDa | 攫鳥　　猛獸弗搏 |
| MWDb | 據鳥　　猛獸弗捕 |
| WB | 猛獸不據攫鳥不搏 |
| | |
| 5 | 骨溺堇柔而捉固 |
| MWDa | 骨弱筋柔而握固 |
| MWDb | 骨筋弱柔而握固 |
| WB | 骨弱筋柔而握固 |
| | |
| 6 | 未智牝戉之合　[illegible]惹 |
| MWDa | 未知牝牡□□而朘□ |
| MWDb | 未知牝牡之會而朘怒 |
| WB | 未知牝牡之合而全作 |
| | |
| 7 | 精之至也 |
| MWDa | 精□至也 |
| MWDb | 精之至也 |
| WB | 精之至也 |
| | |
| 8 | 冬日唇而不惪 |
| MWDa | 終曰號而不发 |
| MWDb | 冬日號而不嗄 |
| WB | 終日號而不嗄 |
| | |
| 9 | 和之至也 |
| MWDa | 和之至也 |
| MWDb | 和□□□ |
| WB | 和之至也 |

| | |
|---|---|
| 10 | 和曰県 |
| MWDa | 和曰常 |
| MWDb | 和□□ |
| WB | 知和曰常 |
| | |
| 11 | 智和曰明 |
| MWDa | 知和曰明 |
| MWDb | 知常曰明 |
| WB | 知常曰明 |
| | |
| 12 | 賹生曰羕 |
| MWDa | 益生曰祥 |
| MWDb | 益生□祥 |
| WB | 益生曰祥 |
| | |
| 13 | 心叀𣪠曰弝 |
| MWDa | 心使氣曰強 |
| MWDb | 心使氣曰強 |
| WB | 心使氣曰強 |
| | |
| 14 | 勿𡒞則老 |
| MWDa | □□即老 |
| MWDb | 物□則老 |
| WB | 物壯則老 |
| | |
| 15 | 是胃不道■ |
| MWDa | 胃之不道 |
| MWDb | 胃之不道 |
| WB | 謂之不道 |

.................................................................................................

| | |
|---|---|
| **MWDa** | 不□□□ |
| **MWDb** | 不道蚤已 |
| **WB** | 不道早已 |

## A:18 (Chapter 44)

| | | |
|---|---|---|
| 1 | | 名與身筲新 |
| MWDa | | 名與身孰親 |
| MWDb | | 名與□□□ |
| WB | | 名與身孰親 |
| | | |
| 2 | | 身與貨筲多 |
| MWDa | | 身與貨孰多 |
| MWDb | | □□□□□ |
| WB | | 身與貨孰多 |
| | | |
| 3 | | 貨與貞筲疒 |
| MWDa | | 得與亡孰病 |
| MWDb | | □□□□□ |
| WB | | 得與亡孰病 |
| | | |
| 4 | | 甚忈必大贄 |
| MWDa | | 甚□□□□ |
| MWDb | | □□□□□ |
| WB | | 故甚愛必大費 |
| | | |
| 5 | | 厇蠻必多貞 |
| MWDa | | □□□□亡 |
| MWDb | | □□□□□ |
| WB | | 多藏必厚亡 |
| | | |
| 6 | | 古智足不辱 |
| MWDa | | 故知足不辱 |
| MWDb | | □□□□□ |
| WB | | 知足不辱 |
| | | |
| 7 | | 智㞢不怠 |
| MWDa | | 知止不殆 |
| MWDb | | □□□□ |
| WB | | 知止不殆 |

| 8 | 可以長舊█ |
|---|---|
| MWDa | 可以長久 |
| MWDb | □□□□ |
| WB | 可以長久 |

## A:19 (Chapter 40)

| 1 | 返也者道　僅也 |
|---|---|
| MWDa | □□□道之動也 |
| MWDb | 反也者道之動也 |
| WB | 反　者道之動 |

| 2 | 溺也者道之甬也 |
|---|---|
| MWDa | 弱也者道之用也 |
| MWDb | □□者道之用也 |
| WB | 弱　者道之用 |

| 3 | 天下之勿生於又 |
|---|---|
| MWDa | 天□□□□□□ |
| MWDb | 天下之物生於有 |
| WB | 天下萬物生於有 |

| 4 | 　生於亡█ |
|---|---|
| MWDa | □□□□ |
| MWDb | 有□於无 |
| WB | 有生於無 |

## A:20 (Chapter 9)

| 1 | 朱而涅之 |
|---|---|
| MWDa | 植而盈之 |
| MWDb | 植而盈之 |
| WB | 持而盈之 |

| 2 | 不不若　已 |
|---|---|
| MWDa | 不　□□□ |
| MWDb | 不　若亓已 |
| WB | 不　如其已 |

| | |
|---|---|
| 3 | 湍而羣之 |
| MWDa | □□□之□之 |
| MWDb | 掘而尤之 |
| WB | 揣而梲之 |

| | |
|---|---|
| 4 | 不可長保也 |
| MWDa | □可長葆也 |
| MWDb | 不可長葆也 |
| WB | 不可長保 |

| | |
|---|---|
| 5 | 金玉涅室 |
| MWDa | 金玉盈室 |
| MWDb | 金玉盈室 |
| WB | 金玉滿堂 |

| | |
|---|---|
| 6 | 莫　能獸也 |
| MWDa | 莫之　守也 |
| MWDb | 莫之能守也 |
| WB | 莫之能守 |

| | |
|---|---|
| 7 | 貴福　喬 |
| MWDa | 貴富而驕 |
| MWDb | 貴富而驕 |
| WB | 富貴而驕 |

| | |
|---|---|
| 8 | 自遺　智也 |
| MWDa | 自遺　咎也 |
| MWDb | 自遺　咎也 |
| WB | 自遺其咎 |

| | |
|---|---|
| 9 | 攻述身退 |
| MWDa | 功述身芮 |
| MWDb | 功遂身退 |
| WB | 功遂身退 |

| | |
|---|---|
| 10 | 天之道也乙 |
| MWDa | 天□□□ |
| MWDb | 天之道也 |
| WB | 天之道 |

| | |
|---|---|
| 1 | 給人事天莫若嗇 |
| MWDa | □□⌐□□□□ |
| MWDb | 治人事天莫若嗇 |
| WB | 治人事天莫若嗇 |

| | |
|---|---|
| 2 | 夫唯嗇是以景是以 |
| MWDa | □□□□□□□ |
| MWDb | 夫唯嗇是以蚤服 |
| WB | 夫唯嗇是謂早服 |

| | |
|---|---|
| 3 | 景備是胃　□□□ |
| MWDa | □□□□□□□ |
| MWDb | 蚤服是胃　重積□ |
| WB | 早服　謂之重積德 |

| | |
|---|---|
| 4 | □□□□□不克■ |
| MWDa | □□□□□□□ |
| MWDb | □□□□□□□ |
| WB | 重積德則無不克 |

| | |
|---|---|
| 5 | □不克則莫智丌互 |
| MWDa | □□□□□□□ |
| MWDb | □□□□□□□ |
| WB | 無不克則莫知其極 |

| | |
|---|---|
| 6 | 莫智丌互可以又陝 |
| MWDa | □□□□□可以有國 |
| MWDb | 莫知亓□□□有國 |
| WB | 莫知其極可以有國 |

| | |
|---|---|
| 7 | 又陝之母可以長□ |
| MWDa | 有國之母可以長久 |
| MWDb | 有國之母可□□久 |
| WB | 有國之母可以長久 |

| 8 | □□ |
|---|---|
| MWDa | 是胃 |
| MWDb | 是胃 |
| WB | 是謂 |

| 9 | □□□□長生舊見之道也■ |
|---|---|
| MWDa | 深槿固氏長□□□□道也 |
| MWDb | □根固氏長生久視之道也 |
| WB | 深根固柢長生久視之道 |

## B:2 (Chapter 48)

| I | 學者日益 |
|---|---|
| MWDa | 爲□□□□ |
| MWDb | 爲學者日益 |
| WB | 爲學　日益 |

| 2 | 爲道者日臭 |
|---|---|
| MWDa | □□□□□ |
| MWDb | 聞道者日云 |
| WB | 爲道　日損 |

| 3 | 臭之或臭 |
|---|---|
| MWDa | □□□□ |
| MWDb | 云之有云 |
| WB | 損之又損 |

| 4 | 以至　亡爲也▬ |
|---|---|
| MWDa | □□□□□ |
| MWDb | 以至於无□ |
| WB | 以至於無爲 |

| 5 | 亡爲而亡不爲▬ |
|---|---|
| MWDa | □□□□□□ |
| MWDb | □□□□□□ |
| WB | 無爲而無不爲 |

..................................................

| | | |
|---|---|---|
| **MWDa** | 取天下也恒 | □□ |
| **MWDb** | 取天下　恒 | 无事 |
| **WB** | 取天下　常以無事 | |

| | |
|---|---|
| **MWDa** | □□□□□ |
| **MWDb** | 及亓有事也 |
| **WB** | 及其有事 |

| | |
|---|---|
| **MWDa** | □□□□□□□□ |
| **MWDb** | □□足以取天□□ |
| **WB** | 不足以取天下 |

### B:3 (Chapter 20, lines 1–7)

| | |
|---|---|
| 1 | 𢆶學亡悳 |
| **MWDa** | □□□□ |
| **MWDb** | 絕學无憂 |
| **WB** | 絕學無憂 |

| | |
|---|---|
| 2 | 唯　與可 |
| **MWDa** | 唯　與訶 |
| **MWDb** | 唯　與呵 |
| **WB** | 唯之與阿 |

| | |
|---|---|
| 3 | 相去幾可 |
| **MWDa** | 相去幾何 |
| **MWDb** | 相去幾何 |
| **WB** | 相去幾何 |

| | |
|---|---|
| 4 | 兯　㑱亞 |
| **MWDa** | 美　與惡 |
| **MWDb** | 美　與亞 |
| **WB** | 善之與惡 |

| | |
|---|---|
| 5 | 相去可若 |
| **MWDa** | 相去何若 |
| **MWDb** | 相去何若 |
| **WB** | 相去若何 |

| 6 | 人之所累 |
|---|---|
| MWDa | 人之□□ |
| MWDb | 人之所畏 |
| WB | 人之所畏 |

| 7 | 亦不可以不累＿人 |
|---|---|
| MWDa | 亦不□□□□　□ |
| MWDb | 亦不可以不畏　人 |
| WB | 　不可　不畏 |

## B:4 (Chapter 13)

| 1 | 㵾辱若纓 |
|---|---|
| MWDa | 龍辱若驚 |
| MWDb | 弄辱若驚 |
| WB | 寵辱若驚 |

| 2 | 貴大患若身 |
|---|---|
| MWDa | 貴大梡若身 |
| MWDb | 貴大患若身 |
| WB | 貴大患若身 |

| 3 | 可胃㵾辱 |
|---|---|
| MWDa | 苟胃龍辱若驚 |
| MWDb | 何胃弄辱若驚 |
| WB | 何謂寵辱若驚 |

| 4 | 㵾　爲下也 |
|---|---|
| MWDa | 龍之爲下 |
| MWDb | 弄之爲下也 |
| WB | 寵　爲下 |

| 5 | 尋之若纓 |
|---|---|
| MWDa | 得之若驚 |
| MWDb | 得之若驚 |
| WB | 得之若驚 |

6　　遊之若驚

MWDa　失□若驚

MWDb　失之若驚

WB　　失之若驚


7　　是胃龍辱＿驚

MWDa　是胃龍辱若驚

MWDb　是胃弄辱若驚

WB　　是謂寵辱若驚


8　　□□□□□若身

MWDa　何胃貴大梡若身

MWDb　何胃貴大患若身

WB　　何謂貴大患若身


9　　虐所以又大患者

MWDa　吾所以有大梡者

MWDb　吾所以有大患者

WB　　吾所以有大患者


10　　爲虐又身

MWDa　爲吾有身也

MWDb　爲吾有身也

WB　　爲吾有身


11　　返虐亡身　　或可□

MWDa　及吾无身　　有何梡

MWDb　及吾無身　　有何患

WB　　及吾無身吾有何患


12　　□□□□□爲天下

MWDa　故貴爲身於爲天下

MWDb　故貴爲身於爲天下

WB　　故貴以身　　爲天下


13　　若可以厇天下矣＿

MWDa　若可以迈天下矣

MWDb　若可以槀天下□

WB　　若可　寄天下

| 14 | 怘以身爲天下 |
|---|---|
| MWDa | 愛以身爲天下 |
| MWDb | 愛以身爲天下 |
| WB | 愛以身爲天下 |

| 15 | 若可以迭天下矣▬ |
|---|---|
| MWDa | 女可以寄天下 |
| MWDb | 女可以寄天下矣 |
| WB | 若可　詑天下 |

## B:5 (Chapter 41)

| 1 | 上士昏道堇能行於丌中 |
|---|---|
| MWDa | □□□□□□□□ |
| MWDb | 上□□道堇能行之 |
| WB | 上士聞道勤而行之 |

| 2 | 中士昏道若昏若亡 |
|---|---|
| MWDa | □□□□□□□ |
| MWDb | 中士聞道若存若亡 |
| WB | 中士聞道若存若亡 |

| 3 | 下士昏道大芺之 |
|---|---|
| MWDa | □□□□□□ |
| MWDb | 下士聞道大笑之 |
| WB | 下士聞道大笑之 |

| 4 | 弗大芺不足以爲道矣 |
|---|---|
| MWDa | □　□□□□□□ |
| MWDb | 弗　笑□□以爲道 |
| WB | 不　笑不足以爲道 |

| 5 | 是以建言又之▬ |
|---|---|
| MWDa | □□□□□□□ |
| MWDb | 是以建言有之曰 |
| WB | 故　建言有之 |

6 　明道女孛
MWDa 　□□□□
MWDb 　明道如費
WB 　明道若昧

7 　遲道女纈
MWDa 　□□□□
MWDb 　進道如退
WB 　進道若退

8 　□道若退
MWDa 　□□□□
MWDb 　夷道如纇
WB 　夷道若纇

9 　上惪女浴＿
MWDa 　□□□□
MWDb 　上德如浴
WB 　上德若谷

10 　大白女辱
MWDa 　□□□□
MWDb 　大白如辱
WB 　大白若辱

11 　㞷惪女不足
MWDa 　□□□□□
MWDb 　廣德如不足
WB 　廣德若不足

12 　建惪女□
MWDa 　□□□□
MWDb 　建德如□
WB 　建德若偷

13　　　　□貞女愈
MWDa　　□□□□
MWDb　　質□□□
WB　　　質眞若渝

14　　　　大方亡禺
MWDa　　□□□□
MWDb　　大方无禺
WB　　　大方無隅

15　　　　大器曼成
MWDa　　□□□□
MWDb　　大器免成
WB　　　大器晚成

16　　　　大音祇聖
MWDa　　□□□□
MWDb　　大音希聲
WB　　　大音希聲

17　　　　天象亡坓
MWDa　　□□□□
MWDb　　天象无刑
WB　　　大象無形

18　　　　道□□□
MWDa　　□□□□
MWDb　　道襃无名
WB　　　道隱無名

19　　　　　　□□□□□□
MWDa　　□□道善□□□□
MWDb　　夫唯道善始且善成
WB　　　夫唯道善貸且　成

| MWDa | 天下有始 |
| MWDb | 天下有始 |
| WB | 天下有始 |

| MWDa | 以爲天下母 |
| MWDb | 以爲天下母 |
| WB | 以爲天下母 |

| MWDa | 既得亓母以知亓□ |
| MWDb | 既得亓母以知其子 |
| WB | 既得其母以知其子 |

| MWDa | 　　　　　復守亓母沒身不殆 |
| MWDb | 既知亓子復守其母沒身不佁 |
| WB | 　　　　　復守其母沒身不殆 |

..........................................................

| 1 | 閟亓門 |
| MWDa | ·塞亓悶 |
| MWDb | 塞亓㙂 |
| WB | 塞其兌 |

| 2 | 賽亓㙂 |
| MWDa | 閉亓悶 |
| MWDb | 閉亓門 |
| WB | 閉其門 |

| 3 | 冬身不� |
| MWDa | 終身不堇 |
| MWDb | 冬身不堇 |
| WB | 終身不勤 |

| 4 | 啓亓㙂 |
| MWDa | 啓亓悶 |
| MWDb | 啓亓㙂 |
| WB | 開其兌 |

| | |
|---|---|
| 5 | 賽亓事 |
| MWDa | 濟亓事 |
| MWDb | 濟亓□ |
| WB | 濟其事 |

| | |
|---|---|
| 6 | 冬身不埮■ |
| MWDa | 終身□□ |
| MWDb | □□不棘 |
| WB | 終身不救 |

......................................................

| | |
|---|---|
| MWDa | □小曰□ |
| MWDb | 見小曰明 |
| WB | 見小曰明 |

| | |
|---|---|
| MWDa | 守柔曰強 |
| MWDb | 守□曰強 |
| WB | 守柔曰強 |

| | |
|---|---|
| MWDa | 用亓光復歸亓明 |
| MWDb | 用□□□□□□ |
| WB | 用其光復歸其明 |

| | |
|---|---|
| MWDa | 毋道身殃 |
| MWDb | □遺身央 |
| WB | 無遺身殃 |

| | |
|---|---|
| MWDa | 是胃襲常 |
| MWDb | 是胃□常 |
| WB | 是爲習常 |

## B:7 (Chapter 45)

| | |
|---|---|
| 1 | 大成若夬 |
| MWDa | 大成若缺 |
| MWDb | □□□□ |
| WB | 大成若缺 |

| | |
|---|---|
| 2 | 亓甬不幣＿ |
| MWDa | 亓用不幣 |
| MWDb | □□□□ |
| WB | 其用不弊 |
| | |
| 3 | 大涅若中 |
| MWDa | 大盈若溫 |
| MWDb | □盈如沖 |
| WB | 大盈若沖 |
| | |
| 4 | 亓甬不穿＿ |
| MWDa | 亓用不鄗 |
| MWDb | □□□□ |
| WB | 其用不窮 |
| | |
| 5 | 大攷若仳＿ |
| MWDa | 大直如詘 |
| MWDb | □□□□ |
| WB | 大直若屈 |
| | |
| 6 | 大成若詘＿ |
| MWDa | 大巧如拙 |
| MWDb | □巧如拙 |
| WB | 大巧若拙 |
| | |
| 7 | 大植若屈■ |
| MWDa | 大贏如炳 |
| MWDb | □□□絀 |
| WB | 大辯若訥 |
| | |
| 8 | 梟勲蒼＿ |
| MWDa | 趮勝寒 |
| MWDb | 趮朕寒 |
| WB | 躁勝寒 |

| 9 | 青勮然 |
|---|---|
| MWDa | 靚勝炅 |
| MWDb | □□□ |
| WB | 静勝熱 |

| 10 | 清清　　爲天下定■ |
|---|---|
| MWDa | 請靚可以爲天下正 |
| MWDb | □□□□□□□□ |
| WB | 清静　　爲天下定 |

## B:8 (Chapter 54)

| 1 | 善建者不枲 |
|---|---|
| MWDa | 善建者□撥 |
| MWDb | 善建者□□ |
| WB | 善建者不拔 |

| 2 | 善保者不兌 |
|---|---|
| MWDa | □□□□□ |
| MWDb | □□□□□ |
| WB | 善抱者不脫 |

| 3 | 子孫以兀祭祀不乇 |
|---|---|
| MWDa | 子孫以　祭祀□□ |
| MWDb | 子孫以　祭祀不絕 |
| WB | 子孫以　祭祀不輟 |

| 4 | 攸之　身兀悳乃𣊟 |
|---|---|
| MWDa | □□　□□□□□ |
| MWDb | 脩之　身亓德乃眞 |
| WB | 修之於身其德乃眞 |

| 5 | 攸之　㹔兀悳又舍 |
|---|---|
| MWDa | 攸□　□□□□餘 |
| MWDb | 脩之　家亓德有餘 |
| WB | 修之於家其德乃餘 |

| 6 | 攸之　昔亓悳乃長 |
|---|---|
| MWDa | 脩之　□□□□□ |
| MWDb | 脩之　鄉亓德乃長 |
| WB | 修之於鄉亓德乃長 |

| 7 | 攸之　邦亓悳乃奉 |
|---|---|
| MWDa | □□　□□□□□ |
| MWDb | 脩之　國亓德乃夆 |
| WB | 修之於國其德乃豐 |

| 8 | 攸之　天下□□□□ |
|---|---|
| MWDa | □□　□□□□□□ |
| MWDb | 脩之　天下亓德乃博 |
| WB | 修之於天下其德乃普 |

. . . . . . . . . . . . . . . . . . . . . . . . . . . . . . . . . . . . . . . . . . .

| **MWDa** | **以身□身** |
|---|---|
| **MWDb** | **以身觀身** |
| **WB** | **故以身觀身** |

. . . . . . . . . . . . . . . . . . . . . . . . . . . . . . . . . . . . . . . . . . .

| 9 | □□□豪 |
|---|---|
| MWDa | 以家觀家 |
| MWDb | 以家觀□ |
| WB | 以家觀家 |

| 10 | 以昔觀昔 |
|---|---|
| MWDa | 以鄉觀鄉 |
| WB | 以鄉觀鄉 |

| 11 | 以邦觀邦 |
|---|---|
| MWDa | 以邦觀邦 |
| MWDb | □□□國 |
| WB | 以國觀國 |

| 12 | 以天下觀天下 |
|---|---|
| MWDa | 以天□觀□□ |
| MWDb | 以天下觀天下 |
| WB | 以天下觀天下 |

| 13 | 虐可以智天□□□ |
|---|---|
| MWDa | □□□□□□□□□ |
| MWDb | 吾何□知天下之然茲 |
| WB | 吾何以知天下　然哉 |

| 14 | □□ |
|---|---|
| MWDa | □□ |
| MWDb | 以□ |
| WB | 以此 |

## C:1 (Chapters 17 and 18)

| 1 | 大上下智又之 |
|---|---|
| MWDa | 大上下知有之 |
| MWDb | 大上下知又□ |
| WB | 太上下知有之 |

| 2 | 丌即新　譽之 |
|---|---|
| MWDa | 其次親　譽之 |
| MWDb | 其□親　譽之 |
| WB | 其次親而譽之 |

| 3 | 丌旣愚之 |
|---|---|
| MWDa | 其次畏之 |
| MWDb | 亓次畏之 |
| WB | 其次畏之 |

| 4 | 丌即炙之 |
|---|---|
| MWDa | 其下母之 |
| MWDb | 亓下母之 |
| WB | 其次侮之 |

| 5 | 信不足安又不信 |
|---|---|
| MWDa | 信不足案有不信 |
| MWDb | 信不足安有不信 |
| WB | 信不足焉有不信焉 |

6 猷虖丌貴言也
MWDa □□其貴言也
MWDb 猷呵元貴言也
WB 悠兮其貴言

7 成事述玒
MWDa 成功遂事
MWDb 成功遂事
WB 功成事遂

8 而百眚　曰我自狀也
MWDa 而百省　胃我自然
MWDb 而百姓　胃我自然
WB 　百姓皆謂我自然

9 古大道發安又悬義
MWDa 故大道廢案有仁義
MWDb 故大道廢安有仁義
WB 　大道廢　有仁義

........................................................

**MWDa** 知快出案有大僞
**MWDb** 知慧出安有□□
**WB** 慧智出　有大僞

........................................................

10 六新不和安又孝孶
MWDa 六親不和案有畜茲
MWDb 六親不和安有孝茲
WB 六親不和　有孝慈

11 邦豪緒燮安又正臣■
MWDa 邦家閔乳案有貞臣
MWDb 國家閔凡安有貞臣
WB 國家昏亂　有忠臣

## C:2 (Chapter 35)

|  |  |
|---|---|
| 1 | 埶大象天下往 |
| MWDa | 執大象□□往 |
| MWDb | 執大象天下往 |
| WB | 執大象天下往 |

|  |  |
|---|---|
| 2 | 往而不害安坪大 |
| MWDa | 往而不害安平大 |
| MWDb | 往而不害安平大 |
| WB | 往而不害安平大 |

|  |  |
|---|---|
| 3 | 樂與餌伭客走 |
| MWDa | 樂與餌過格止 |
| MWDb | 樂與□過格止 |
| WB | 樂與餌過客止 |

|  |  |
|---|---|
| 4 | 古道□□□ |
| MWDa | 故道之出言也曰 |
| MWDb | 故道之出言也曰 |
| WB | 道之出口 |

|  |  |
|---|---|
| 5 | 淡可丌無味也 |
| MWDa | 談呵其无味也 |
| MWDb | 淡呵亓无味也 |
| WB | 淡乎其無味 |

|  |  |
|---|---|
| 6 | 見之不足見 |
| MWDa | □□不足見也 |
| MWDb | 視之不足見也 |
| WB | 視之不足見 |

|  |  |
|---|---|
| 7 | 聖之不足餾 |
| MWDa | 聽之不足聞也 |
| MWDb | 聽之不足聞也 |
| WB | 聽之不足聞 |

| 8 | 而不可既也 ■ |
|---|---|
| MWDa | 用之　不可既也 |
| MWDb | 用之　不可既也 |
| WB | 用之　不足既 |

## C:3 (Chapter 31)

| MWDa | 夫　兵者不祥之器□ |
|---|---|
| MWDb | 夫　兵者不祥之器也 |
| WB | 夫佳兵者不祥之器 |

| MWDa | 物或惡之 |
|---|---|
| MWDb | 物或亞□ |
| WB | 物或惡之 |

| MWDa | 故有欲者弗居 |
|---|---|
| MWDb | □□□□□□ |
| WB | 故有道者不處 |

.................................................................

| 1 | 君子居則貴左 |
|---|---|
| MWDa | 君子居則貴左 |
| MWDb | □子居則貴左 |
| WB | 君子居則貴左 |

| 2 | 甬兵則貴右 |
|---|---|
| MWDa | 用兵則貴右 |
| MWDb | 用兵則貴右 |
| WB | 用兵則貴右 |

.................................................................

| MWDa | 故兵者非君子之器也 |
|---|---|
| MWDb | 故兵者非君子之器 |
| WB | 　兵者不　祥之器 |

.................................................................

| 3 | 古曰兵者□□□□□ |
|---|---|
| MWDa | 　　□□不祥之器也 |
| MWDb | 　兵者不祥□器也 |
| WB | 　　非君子之器 |

| | |
|---|---|
| 4 | □寻已而甬之鋊纏爲上 |
| MWDa | 不得已而用之銛襲爲上 |
| MWDb | 不得已而用之銛慵爲上 |
| WB | 不得已而用之恬淡爲上 |

| | |
|---|---|
| 5 | 弗散也 |
| MWDa | 勿美也 |
| MWDb | 勿美也 |
| WB | 勝而不美 |

| | |
|---|---|
| 6 | 敔之　是樂殺人 |
| MWDa | 若美之　是樂殺人也 |
| MWDb | 若美之　是樂殺人也 |
| WB | 而美之者是樂殺人 |

| | |
|---|---|
| 7 | 夫樂□　　□□以尋志於天下 |
| MWDa | 夫樂殺人　不可以得志於天下矣 |
| MWDb | 夫樂殺人　不可以得志於天下矣 |
| WB | 夫樂殺人者則不可以得志於天下矣 |

| | |
|---|---|
| 8 | 古　吉事上左 |
| MWDa | 是以吉事上左 |
| MWDb | 是以吉事□□ |
| WB | 吉事尚左 |

| | |
|---|---|
| 9 | 喪事上右 |
| MWDa | 喪事上右 |
| MWDb | □□□□ |
| WB | 凶事尚右 |

| | |
|---|---|
| 10 | 是以支牲軍居左 |
| MWDa | 是以便將軍居左 |
| MWDb | 是以偏將軍居左 |
| WB | 偏將軍居左 |

| | |
|---|---|
| 11 | 上牲軍居右 |
| MWDa | 上將軍居右 |
| MWDb | 上將軍居右 |
| WB | 上將軍居右 |

| 12 | 言以堯豐居之也 |
|---|---|
| MWDa | 言以喪禮居之也 |
| MWDb | 言以喪禮居之也 |
| WB | 言以喪禮處之 |

| 13 | 古殺□　□則以忝悲位之 |
|---|---|
| MWDa | 　殺人　衆　以悲依立之 |
| MWDb | 　殺□　□　　□□□立之 |
| WB | 　殺人之衆　以哀悲泣之 |

| 14 | 戰勅則以堯豐居之■ |
|---|---|
| MWDa | 戰勝　以喪禮處之 |
| MWDb | 戰朕而以喪禮處之 |
| WB | 戰勝　以喪禮處之 |

## C:4 (Chapter 64, part 2)

| 1 | 爲之者敗之 |
|---|---|
| MWDa | □□□□□ |
| MWDb | 爲之者敗之 |
| WB | 爲　者敗之 |

| 2 | 埶之者遊之＿ |
|---|---|
| MWDa | □　□□□ |
| MWDb | 執　者失之 |
| WB | 執　者失之 |

| 3 | 　聖人無爲　古無敗也 |
|---|---|
| MWDa | □□□□□□也□无敗□ |
| MWDb | 是以即人无爲□□□□ |
| WB | 是以聖人無　爲故無敗 |

| 4 | 無埶　古□□□ |
|---|---|
| MWDa | 无執也故无失也 |
| MWDb | □□□□□□ |
| WB | 無執　故無失 |

| 5 | 斲冬若訂則無敗事壴＿ |
|---|---|
| MWDa | 民之從事也恒於亓　成事而敗之 |
| MWDb | 民之從事也恒於亓　成　而敗之 |
| WB | 民之從事　常於幾　成　而敗之 |

| 6 | 人之敗也亙於丌虐成　也敗之＿ |
|---|---|
| MWDa | 故　慎終若始則□□□□ |
| MWDb | 故曰慎冬若始則无敗事矣 |
| WB | 　慎終如始則無敗事 |

| 7 | 是以□人欲不欲　不貴㲅尋之貨 |
|---|---|
| MWDa | □□□□欲不欲而不貴難得之䐙 |
| MWDb | 是以耴人欲不欲而不貴難得之貨 |
| WB | 是以聖人欲不欲　不貴難得之貨 |

| 8 | 學不學　遝衆　之所迊＿ |
|---|---|
| MWDa | 學不學而復衆人之所過 |
| MWDb | 學不學　復衆人之所過 |
| WB | 學不學　復衆人之所過 |

| 9 | 是以能桶墓勿之自然而弗敢爲▪ |
|---|---|
| MWDa | 　能輔萬物之自□□弗敢爲 |
| MWDb | 　能輔萬物之自然而弗敢爲 |
| WB | 　以輔萬物之自然而不敢爲 |

# Appendix III

*Punctuation Marks and Determination of Chapter Divisions*

## *Laozi* A

1. *Chapter 19:* Chapter 19 begins at the top of a slip and ends with a "black square," which marks it as being distinct from the following lines (now chapter 66). However, in chapter 19, the copyist, for reasons that are not clear, placed a "black square" at the end of every two lines (2, 4, 6, 8, and 10). Chapter 19 is "complete," in that the Guodian "chapter" has the same number of lines that we find in this chapter in later editions. Moreover, it is clear that the first line of chapter 20—"Eliminate learning and you'll have no distress" (*juexue wuyou*, 絕學無憂)—which is sometimes thought to be the last line of chapter 19, is not part of this chapter.[1] The Guodian form of this chapter contains significant character variants, in that lines 1 and 3, which normally read "Eliminate Sageliness, get rid of knowledge" and "Eliminate humanity, get rid of righteousness," here seem to say "Eliminate knowledge, get rid of distinctions" and "Eliminate transformation, get rid of deliberation."

2. *Chapter 66:* Chapter 66 is also "complete." It is distinguished from chapter 19 by the black square at the end of chapter 19. No punctuation separates the end of chapter 66 from the start of chapter 46—the chapter that follows—but chapter 46 is clearly distinct in terms of ideas. The syntax of this version of chapter 66 is somewhat unique, so that these lines essentially say the same things that are said in the chapter in later editions, but in a different way.

3. *Chapter 46:* No punctuation separates the end of chapter 66 from the beginning of chapter 46, but chapter 46 is "self-contained" in terms of ideas ("Of vices, none is more onerous than . . . Of defects, none brings more sorrow than . . . ") and is clearly distinct in message from chapter 66. This version of chapter 46 omits the opening couplet of later editions—"When the world has the Way, ambling horses are used to fertilize fields. When the world lacks the

Way, war horses are reared in the suburbs"—the same couplet that is bracketed as a separate saying by punctuation, as we have noted, in Mawangdui copy A. Thus, this version of chapter 46 has only five lines.

4. *Chapter 30:* Punctuation separates the last line of chapter 46 from the first line of chapter 30, but the mark used is the "dash" or "hyphen" (▬). Still, in this case, since chapters 46 and 30 are clearly distinct in terms of ideas and message, this must indicate the end of a chapter. The Guodian version of chapter 30 consists of nine lines, omitting six or seven lines found in later editions, the lines normally translated: (1) "Such deeds easily rebound. In places where armies are stationed, thorns and brambles will grow"; (2) "He achieves his result, yet he abides with the result because he has no choice"; and (3) "When things reach their prime, they get old; We call this 'not the Way.' What is not the Way will come to an early end."

The other change made in later editions is that the final line in the Guodian version—"Such deeds are good and endure" (*qi shi hao chang,* 其事好長)—was changed slightly (*qi shi hao huan,* 其事好還—"Such deeds easily rebound") and was transposed to become line 3 in the chapter.

The punctuation marking the end of this "chapter," like chapter 46, is the short line (▬), not the "black square" (■), and it was incorrectly inserted, in my opinion, after the character 好 (*hao*) instead of after the character 長 (*chang*).[2] But it quite clearly marks the end of the chapter since, as mentioned, chapters 30 and 15 are distinct in terms of ideas and message.

5. *Chapter 15:* This version of chapter 15 is roughly the same as the one in later editions, but I suspect that the last three lines of the chapter—which are included in some form in all later editions—were understood at this time as constituting a separate saying. Lines 9 and 10 in the chapter are: "Natural and genuine were they! Like wood that hasn't been carved [*pu,* 樸,*p'ŭk]. Undifferentiated were they! Like muddy water [*zhuo,* 濁,*dŭk]." The final lines (11, 12, and 13) then read: "Who can be muddy, yet through tranquility gradually clear [*qing,* 清,*ts'ieŋ]? Who can be still, yet through motion gradually stir [*sheng,* 生,*sïeŋ]? The one who embraces this Way does not desire to be overly full [*ying,* 浧, *gieŋ]." The copyist ends line 11 with the black square (■) that normally indicates the end of a chapter, but clearly lines 11–13 form a rimed unit. My suspicion, therefore, is that chapter 15 was meant to end at the end of line 10— which is where the black square belongs—and that lines 11–13 follow chapter 15 because, like line 10, line 11 mentions "muddy water" (*zhuo,* 濁).

6. *Chapter 64, part 2:* No punctuation distinguishes the beginning of this chapter

from the end of chapter 15 (i.e., the line "The one who embraces this Way does
not desire to be overly full"), nor does punctuation distinguish the end of this
chapter from the first line in what follows—chapter 37. However, there is no
reason to look for connections between this group of lines and what precedes or
what follows, since this same set of lines—albeit with variations—is clearly set
off as a unit or "chapter" in *Laozi* C (C:4).

7. *Chapter 37*: We come to another chapter that is already "complete," in that
it contains the same number of lines as in later editions, and the wording is roughly
the same, though there are variants in lines 6 and 7 that are found in none of the
later editions. The end of the chapter is indicated by a "black square."

8. *Chapter 63*: This version of what we know as chapter 63 of the text has the
first three lines of the chapter and the last two lines of the chapter, conflates lines
4 and 13, and omits the rest (a total of nine lines). Line 4 normally reads: "Regard the small as large and the few as many [大小多少]," with line 13 reading
"Those who regard many things as easy will necessarily end up with many
difficulties [多易必多難]." The combination here reads "In affairs large or
small, the more things you take to be easy, the more difficulties there are bound
to be" [大小之多易必多難]. This "chapter" is set off from chapter 37, as
noted, by a black square and is distinguished from the lines that follow (= chapter 2) in the same way.

9. *Chapter 2*: Chapter 2 is "complete" and differs hardly at all from the Mawangdui form of the chapter. It is properly distinguished from what precedes and
what follows by the black squares that normally indicate the end of a chapter.

10. *Chapter 32*: Punctuation marks indicate that, at the time these copies were
made, this was regarded as two distinct chapters—lines 1–4 and 5–12—and at
first sight there is no apparent connection between these two sets of lines. However, lines 11–12—"The Way's presence in the world, Is like the relationship of
small valley streams to rivers and seas"—could serve as a model for what is said
in the opening lines: "The Way is constantly nameless. . . . Were marquises and
kings able to maintain it, The ten thousand things would submit to them on their
own." That is, in the ideal state, the people will naturally gravitate to the ruler in
the same way that streams eventually flow to the sea. Consequently, I remain
unsure of the significance of the black square at the end of line 4.

11. *Chapter 25*: This is another chapter that is almost word for word the same
as in later editions, though this version does contain some interesting character
variants. It is properly set off from what precedes and what follows by the punctuation marks that we expect (i.e., the black squares).

12. *Chapter 5* (middle lines only): The Guodian slips have only the middle four lines from chapter 5, which begin: "The space between heaven and earth—is it not like a bellows?" In later editions, four lines precede these four lines and two lines follow. But the marks that indicate chapter divisions set these lines off as standing alone. Still, it is important to remember that these lines, together with chapter 25, constitute unit 2 in *Laozi* A, and the mention of "heaven and earth" is consistent with the focus of chapter 25.

13. *Chapter 16, lines 1–6:* This begins at the top of a slip and ends with a black square before the slip ends. There is no way to know which "unit" of slips preceded or followed this slip in the original sequence. In later editions, chapter 16 contains twelve additional lines. The wording here varies from what we normally find at the start of this chapter, and there are different ways to understand the Guodian form of the text.

14. *Chapter 64, part 1:* This begins at the top of a slip: at the end of line 12—"Begins from under your foot"—the last line in the first half of the chapter—a small line (__) seems to indicate the end of the chapter, since these words have nothing in common with the chapter that follows.

15. *Chapter 56:* The integrity of these lines as a chapter is confirmed by punctuation marks at the beginning and end, properly by the "black square" at the end. The Guodian form of this chapter is almost word for word identical to later editions, though line 6, "files down the sharp edges" (*zuo qi rui,* 挫其銳) says something else. Exactly what it says is not yet clear.

16. *Chapter 57:* This chapter is distinguished from chapter 56 by the punctuation just noted; it ends, midway down the length of a slip, with the unique punctuation mark 乙 , which, as mentioned, is found only here and at the end of chapter 9. The content of this version of the chapter is essentially the same as in later editions, but there are some important variants to note and a change in the order of lines in the last part of the chapter.

17. *Chapter 55:* This begins at the top of a slip, the first chapter in the final "unit" of slips in *Laozi* A. Punctuation marking the end of the chapter follows the couplet "When things reach their prime they get old; This is called 'not the Way.'" Later editions follow this up with the words "What is not the Way will come to an early end." With the exception of this omission, the wording here is much the same as in the Mawangdui copies.

18. *Chapter 44:* This is yet another chapter that is essentially identical to later editions. "Chapter punctuation" (■) occurs at the end.

19. *Chapter 40*: This is a four-line chapter, as it is in later editions, the shortest of the eighty-one chapters in the *Laozi*. "Chapter punctuation" occurs at the end. There is some question about whether the last line in the Guodian version says what it normally does—"And Being comes from Non-being." The confusion arises because the copyist forgot to add the mark for repetition (=) after "Being" (*you*, 又) at the end of the previous line.

20. *Chapter 9*: Character variants in the third line will change the way this line is normally understood—"To pound it out and give it a point." Otherwise, this chapter is already the "chapter" that we know from later editions. As noted, like chapter 57, this chapter ends with the punctuation mark ㇄ , which appears to be a *pian* (section) marker.

**Laozi B**

1. *Chapter 59*: Chapter 59 begins at the top of a slip and ends with a black square; the content is the same as in later editions. There is a black square at the end of the fourth line, which seems to indicate this is actually two separate sayings. But the parallel structure of lines 4–7 make it clear that the correct punctuation mark would be the double lines (=) that indicate repetition: line 4 ends with the words *wu buke* (無不克), the same words that begin line 5.

2. *Chapter 48, lines 1–5:* These lines from chapter 48 are distinguished from the end of chapter 59 by the punctuation at the end of chapter 59 and by a change in the topic being discussed. Lines 4 and 5—"Until they reach the point where they do nothing at all" and "They do nothing, yet there is nothing left undone"—are both followed by the short stroke (＿), but it is not definite that the stroke at the end of line 5 in this case indicates the end of this "chapter." These lines from chapter 48 might have merged with the lines from chapter 20 that follow (lines 1–7), in which case the "dash" at the end of line 5 simply indicates the end of the first part of a chapter. Chapter 48 begins with the line "Those who toil at their studies increase day after day" (學者日益), while chapter 20 begins "Eliminate learning (or study) and you'll have no distress" (絕學無憂).

3. *Chapter 20, lines 1–7:* As already noted, these lines might be the second part of a "chapter" that began with the preceding lines from what is now the beginning of chapter 48. However, this could be a separate saying on "learning" or "study" that was put where it was because, like the preceding saying, it begins with a four-character line in which the key word is *xue* (學, study). Short-line

(▬) punctuation follows the *wei* (畏, fear) at the end of line 7, clearly indicating the end of the saying. But, as noted in the translation, I suspect that this punctuation mark is inserted one word too soon and should follow *wei ren* (畏 人, fear others).

4. *Chapter 13:* This chapter is complete, though there are some variant readings when we compare this form to those found in later editions. The chapter ends, appropriately, with a black square (▬), but it is set off from the preceding lines from chapter 20 by the "short line" (▬) punctuation. Since no black squares occur between the end of chapter 59 and the end of chapter 13, it could be argued that the lines we find here from chapters 48, 20, and 13 were at this time understood to constitute a unified "chapter." But that seems unlikely since chapter 13 is self-contained and distinct in terms of style and ideas from the preceding lines. The "short line" following *ru* (辱) in line 7 can be understood in several ways; my guess is that the copyist, with good reason, assumed the line ended with *ru* and inserted the mark before noting that *ru* was followed by *ying* (纓). The short line at the end of line 13 was apparently added to separate the parallel couplets formed by lines 12 and 13, and 14 and 15.

5. *Chapter 41:* The chapter begins at the top of a slip, and it appears to have ended near the bottom of a slip, possibly with the black square punctuation, but we cannot be sure of the ending since the slip in question is broken (slip 12, p. 8) with room for seven or eight characters after the break. Still, chapter 41 appears to have been complete, differing from later editions only in terms of character variants. There is a black square (▬) at the end of line 5 ("Therefore, as we find it in the fixed sayings"), setting up a run of fourteen rimed lines, most of them four-character lines. There is also a "dash" (▬) at the end of line 9, apparently highlighting a change in rime.

6. *Chapter 52, lines 5–10:* These six lines from the middle of chapter 52 begin at the top of a slip and end with a black square near the bottom of that same slip. There is no internal punctuation, and no connection in terms of ideas with the lines that follow. It seems very likely that the lines that now precede and follow these lines in chapter 52 were added to these from some other source.

7. *Chapter 45:* Punctuation, and changes in rime and meter, clearly indicate that what is now chapter 45 in the *Laozi* in the Guodian slips was understood to consist of two separate sayings. Lines 1–7 are set off from the lines that precede and follow by black squares (▬) indicating that this is a unit; lines 1–4 are two parallel couplets in four-character verse, both couplets beginning with the word *da* (大, great). Lines 5–7 continue in four-character, rimed verse, all three lines

beginning with the word "great." Lines 8–10 are also set off from what precedes
and what follows by black squares (although in the slip photographs, the square
at the end of line 10 is barely visible), and they are in three-character verse. The
ideas in these three lines seem completely unrelated to the preceding lines. Nonetheless, these lines remained in this position and came to be regarded as the final
lines of chapter 45 in later editions.

8. *Chapter 54:* The chapter begins after the black square at the end of what is
now chapter 45. We cannot be sure that a "black square" ended the chapter, since
the final slip is broken, and the final five or six characters in the chapter are missing. But the chapter seems to have been "complete," with the wording almost
exactly the same as in later editions.

## Laozi C

1. *Chapters 17 and 18:* Chapter 17 begins at the top of a slip, and the text is
continuous—without punctuation—until the end of chapter 18, where we find a
black square. Since what in later editions is chapter 18 here begins, as it does in
the Mawangdui copies, with the word *gu* (古 = 故, therefore), there is no reason
not to think that these lines were originally understood to constitute a unified
chapter.

2. *Chapter 35*: Chapter 35 begins at the top of a slip and ends with a black
square, which is close to the bottom of the next slip (though a new chapter could
have been started, had the copyist so desired). As with unit "C:1," there is no
internal punctuation, and the wording of the chapter is roughly the same as later
editions.

3. *Chapter 31*: This chapter also begins at the top of a slip, contains no internal
punctuation, and ends with a black square. Although the final slip is broken,
there would have been room for five or six characters after this punctuation.
Thus it appears that the copyist for bundle "C" preferred to begin all chapters at
the top of a slip, leaving blank space on a slip after the end of a chapter. This
version of chapter 31 omits the three lines with which this chapter begins in later
editions: "As for weapons—they are instruments of ill omen. And among things
there are those that hate them. Therefore, the one who has the Way, with them
does not dwell."

4. *Chapter 64, part 2:* As with the other chapters in *Laozi* C, this begins at the
top of a slip and ends with a black square. This punctuation occurs about a third
of the way down the final slip, and the rest of the slip is blank. However, in

contrast to the other "C" chapters, this chapter contains internal punctuation. There are short lines (__) marking internal divisions at the ends of lines 2 ("Those who hold on to it lose it"), 5 ("If you're as careful at the end as you were at the beginning, you'll have no disasters"), 6 ("As for people's disasters—they always ruin things when they're just about to complete them"), and 8 ("He learns how to unlearn and backs away from matters in which the masses go to excess").

# Notes

*Introduction*

1. There are three English translations of the *Laozi* based on these copies. The first was published by D. C. Lau as *Chinese Classics: Tao Te Ching* (Hong Kong: Chinese University Press, 1982). Then came my *Lao-tzu Te-tao ching: A New Translation Based on the Recently Discovered Ma-wang-tui Texts* (New York: Ballantine Books, 1989), followed by Victor Mair, trans., *Tao Te Ching: The Classic Book of Integrity and the Way* (New York: Bantam Books, 1990).

2. With one exception noted below, in part II of copy A.

3. The three exceptions are that chapter 24 occurs between chapters 21 and 22; chapter 40 is found between chapters 41 and 42; and chapters 80 and 81, in these versions, are placed between chapters 66 and 67.

4. Distinguishing it from the "Silk Manuscript *Laozi*" (*boshu Laozi*, 帛書老子)—meaning the Mawangdui copies.

5. Confucius lived from 551 to 479 B.C.

6. For readers unfamiliar with this biography, I have provided a translation—with comments and notes—as an appendix to this book (appendix I).

7. This group included people like Liang Qichao (梁啓超), Gu Jiegang (顧頡剛), Ma Xulun (馬敍倫), and Gao Heng (高亨). Most of these articles can be found in volume 4 of Luo Genze [羅根澤], ed., *Gushi bian* [古史辨] (Shanghai: Guji, 1982). Wing-tsit Chan provides a good summary of the arguments made in those articles and the evidence used for support (*The Way of Lao Tzu* [Indianapolis: Bobbs-Merrill, 1963], pp. 35–91).

8. Critical, in the view of Liang Qichao, was the fact that many terms and phrases in the *Laozi* make sense only in the context of the "Warring States" period: (1) "marquises and kings" (*houwang*, 侯王) in chapters 32, 37, and 39; (2) "kings and dukes" (*wanggong*, 王公), in chapter 42; (3) "the ruler of ten thousand chariots" (*wansheng zhi zhu*, 萬乘之主) in chapter 26; and (4) the titles "lieutenant general" (*pian jiangjun*, 偏將軍) and "supreme general" (*shang jiangjun*, 上將軍) in

chapter 31. On this, see, for example, my article "The Ma-wang-tui Manuscripts of the *Lao-tzu* and the Problem of Dating the Text," *Chinese Culture* 20:2 (June 1979): 8–12.

9. Perhaps the most popular view was that it was written by the second "Dan" mentioned in Sima Qian's biography, the Dan who met with Duke Xian of Qin in 374 B.C.

10. D. C. Lau, *Lao Tzu: Tao Te Ching* (Middlesex, UK: Penguin Books, 1963).

11. Ibid., p. 172. For Appendix 2, see pp. 163–174.

12. Ibid., p. 166.

13. Ibid., p. 174.

14. See A. C. Graham, *Disputers of the Tao: Philosophical Argument in Ancient China* (La Salle, IL: Open Court, 1989), p. 216.

15. Chen Guying [朝躬萊], "*Huangdi sijing" jinzhu jinyi* [《黃帝四經》今註今譯] (Taibei: Commercial Press, 1995), p. 33.

16. Li Xueqin, "Shenlun *Laozi* de niandai" [申論《老子》的年代], *Daojia wenhua yanjiu* [道家文化研究] 6 (1995): 72–79. Li argues (1) that the "Old Peng" mentioned in *Analects* 7:1 refers to Laozi; and (2) that the line "Repay resentment with kindness" cited in *Analects* 14:34 is quoted from chapter 63 of the *Laozi*. More is said about this below. "Huang-Lao" was a type of philosophy promoted in China during late Warring States and early Han dynasty times (that is, from roughly 400 to 100 B.C.). It was a syncretistic approach to statecraft, combining the cosmological views of the Daoists and the Yin-Yang thinkers with the political views of the Legalists and the Confucians. Little was known of this philosophical "school" before the textual find at Mawangdui in 1973. For a translation and study of the relevant sources found there, see Robin D. S. Yates, *Five Lost Classics: Tao, Huang-Lao, and Yin-Yang in Han China* (New York: Ballantine Books, 1997).

17. My main source here is Liu Zuxin [劉祖信], "Jingmen Guodian yihao mu gailun" [荆門郭店一號墓概論] (paper presented at the international conference on the "Guodian *Laozi*," May 1998). However, most of this information can be found in the site report published in Hubeisheng Jingmenshi bowuguan [胡北省荆門市博物館], "Jingmen Guodian yihao Chumu" [荆門郭店一號楚墓], *Wenwu* [文物] (July 1997): 35–48. A "group" of tombs consists of one large tomb around which smaller mounds are arrayed. "Chu tomb no. 1" is part of group 1.

18. Peng Hao (彭浩) noted this at the "Guodian *Laozi*" conference, May 1998. Most of the bamboo slips at the site were found floating in water. All the slips were originally stored in the "head box" of the coffin.

19. Hubeisheng Jingmenshi bowuguan, "Jingmen Guodian yihao Chumu," pp. 35–48, see especially pp. 46 and 47.

20. Ibid., p. 47. A complete inventory of the items found in the tomb—articles made of bronze, lacquer, jade, etc.—is listed on pp. 36–46. These items include a rare seven-string wooden lute.

21. See Li Xueqin, "Jingmen Guodian Chujian zhongde *Zi Si zi*" [荆門郭店楚簡中的《子思子》], *Wenwu tiandi* (Cultural Relics World) 2 (1998): 28–30.

22. For more information on the *qiance*, see Peng Hao, "Zhanguo shiqi de qiance" [戰國時期的遣策], in Li Xueqin, ed., *Jianbo yanjiu* [簡帛研究] (Beijing: Falu chubanshe, 1996), 2: 48–55.

23. Two of the texts do in fact have titles—"Ziyi" and "Wuxing." In all other cases, titles were assigned using either the opening words of the text or the main theme of the text as its title.

24. By now everyone seems to agree that this was included in *Laozi* C, but it is treated as a separate text in Hubeisheng Jingmenshi bowuguan [湖北省荆門市博物管], ed., *Guodian Chumu zhujian* [郭店楚墓竹簡] (Beijing: Wenwu Press, 1998).

25. Tang (唐) and Yu (虞) are the reign titles associated with the supposed early rulers Yao (堯, r. 2356–2256 B.C.) and Shun (舜, r. 2255–2205 B.C.).

26. Li Xueqin, "Jingmen Guodian Chujian."

27. Ibid., p. 29.

28. They were both written on slips that are 32.5 cm long, "cornered" at the top edge, with a cord separation of 12.8–13 cm. Note that the copy of the "Wuxing" found at Mawangdui in 1973 has both the *jing* and the *zhuan*—the "canon" and the "commentary"—but the Guodian copy has only the *jing*.

29. Cui Renyi (崔仁義) has suggested that since it is unlikely that "Mu Lugong wen Zi Si zi" would have been written during his lifetime, if all the texts found at Guodian were copied at the same time, the earliest date at which these *Laozi* materials were written would be 377 B.C. However, as he correctly notes, that does not mean that these sayings had not been "composed" before that time. See Cui Renyi, "Shilun Jingmen zhujian *Laozi* de niandai" [試論荆門竹簡《老子》的年代], *Jingmen daxue xuebao* [荆門大學學報] 2 (1997): 38–42.

30. That is, 32.5 cm long and cornered at the top.

31. The ideas on "inborn nature" (*xing,* 性) and the development of virtue in "Xing zi ming chu" and "Liu de" are quite sophisticated. And in the latter selection (Jingmenshi bowuguan, *Guodian Chumu zhujian*, p. 188), mention is made of a matter that Mencius later debated—the claim that "humanity is internal" while "righteousness is external" (仁內也, 義外也). This position found advocates in Gao zi (告子) and Meng Ji zi (孟季子), but Mencius himself rejected the view (see *Mencius*, 6A4). Li Xueqin has argued that Mencius might have seen and read all these texts ("Montgomery Fellow Lecture" presented at Dartmouth College, October 22, 1998). It is true that in 4A4 and 4A12 in the *Mencius*, he uses a phrase that is prominent in "Cheng Zhi wenzhi": *qiuzhi yu ji* (求之于己) or *qiu zhu ji* (求諸己)—"seek for it inside yourself."

32. In the Guodian materials only four chapters are in the same sequence as in later editions: 56 is followed by 57, and 17 is followed by 18 (in *Laozi* C).

33. In Peng Hao's initial transcription, units 4 and 5 are reversed. We hope that further research, combined with closer analysis of the original slips, will clarify this matter since it is an issue of some importance if we are to understand the exact nature of each of these bundles.

34. Some will wonder whether this order corresponds to those we might infer from the "Jie *Lao*" (解老) and "Yu *Lao*" (喻老) chapters in the *Han Feizi* (韓非子), or the "Daoying" (道應) chapter in the *Huainanzi* (淮南子). The answer is no. The sequence of chapters from which lines are cited in the "Jie *Lao*" chapter is: 38, 58, 59, 60, 46, 14, 1, 50, 67, 53, and 54. In the "Yu *Lao*" chapter, the order is: 46, 54, 26, 36, 63, 64, 52, 71, 64, 47, 41, 33, and 27. Without citing the entire list from the *Huainanzi*, the order there is: 2, 56, 70, 57, 9, 28, 10, 4, 73, 74, 28, 52, and so on.

35. Wang Bo, "Guodian *Laozi* weishenma you sanzu?" [郭店《老子》爲什麼有三組?] (paper presented at the international conference on the "Guodian *Laozi*," May 1998).

36. I have done further work on unit 1 in *Laozi* A, and my research confirms Wang Bo's thesis. In fact, the first chapter—chapter 19—sets out an agenda for the Daoist ruler, with the themes of that chapter—that the good ruler "eliminates knowledge" and does not try to "transform the people," since if he "does nothing" (*wuwei*) they will transform on their own, that the good ruler values the "simple" and "genuine" (*pu*, 樸), and is "selfless" and "has few desires"—developed in the subsequent materials found in the unit. My results will be published as "The Ruler's Agenda: A Proposed Reading of Section One in Document A of the Guodian *Laozi*" [Zhiguo dagang—shidu Guodian *Laozi* jiazu de diyi bufen, 治國大剛——試讀郭店《老子》甲組的第一部分], *Daojia wenhua yanjiu* 17 (1999): 144–88. Chapter 57, the final chapter in unit 4 of *Laozi* A, in some ways seems to wrap up these thoughts on the Daoist ruler. Hence, I suspect that units 1 and 4 originally formed one of two *pian* (篇, sections) in *Laozi* A.

37. In Peng Hao's initial transcription, units 1 and 2 are reversed. Thus, he would have *Laozi* B begin with chapter 41.

38. See their "Explanation," in *Guodian Chumu zhujian*, p. 125.

39. Again the sequence in *Guodian Chumu zhujian* varies slightly from Peng Hao's original order; Peng thought *Laozi* C began with chapter 35.

40. Xing Wen (邢文) argues, for example, that the "logical" sequence of themes and ideas in *Laozi* C implies that the original arrangement was the first part of "Taiyi shengshui" (slips 1–8), followed by the second part of "Taiyi shengshui" (slips 9–13), with the chapters from the *Laozi* then at the end, in the sequence 17–18, 35, 31, and 64. See his article "Lun Guodian *Laozi* yu jinben *Laozi* bu zhu yixi—Chujian 'Taiyi shengshui' ji qi yiyi" [論郭店《老子》與今本《老子》不屬一系——楚簡《太一生水》及其意義], *Zhongguo zhexue*, no. 20 (October 1998): 165–86. Cui Renyi, on the other hand, has the following order in *Laozi* C (his *Laozi* A): "Taiyi shengshui," chapters 17–18, 35, 31, and 64. His arrangements of *Laozi* A

and B are as follows: *Laozi* A (his *Laozi* C)—chapters 25, 5, 16, 37, 63, 2, 32, 64 (part 1), 56, 57, 19, 66, 46, 30, 15, 64 (part 2), 55, 44, 40, and 9; *Laozi* B—chapters 41, 52, 45, 54, 59, 48, 20, and 13 (Cui Renyi, "Shilun Jingmen zhujian *Laozi* de niandai").

41. From Liu Xin, "Qilue" [七略], as cited in Xie Shouhao [謝守灝], *Hunyuan shengji* [混元聖紀] (completed in 1132). This is CT 770 (text no. 770) in *Zhengtong daozang* [正統道藏] (Taibei: Yiwen yinshuguan, 1977), 30: 23758, top and bottom.

42. For more on different ways for dividing the text, see my article "On the Chapter Divisions in the *Lao-tzu*," *Bulletin of the School of Oriental and African Studies* 45:3 (1982): 501–24.

43. See line 58 in the photographs of the slips published in Guojia wenwuju guwenxian yanjiushi, ed., *Mawangdui Hanmu boshu* [馬王堆漢墓帛書] (Beijing: Wenwu Press, 1981), vol. 1.

44. Cui Renyi was the first to suggest that these might be *pian* markers ("Shilun Jingmen zhujian *Laozi* de niandai," pp. 40–41). Peng Hao noted that this mark resembles the character 以 (*yi*), as it was written in Eastern Zhou times, though the meaning appears to be that of 止 (*zhi*, to stop, i.e., the end) ("Guanyu Guodian Chujian *Laozi* zhengli gongzuo de jidian shuoming" [關于郭店楚簡《老子》整理工作的几點說明] [paper presented at the international conference on the "Guodian *Laozi*," May 1998]). Donald Harper, on the other hand, in remarks at that conference suggested that it might be a stylized 乙 (*yi*), noting that Chen Mengjia (陳夢家) had drawn attention to the use of this character for punctuation, and that it was often written to look like a "hook" (∠). (For more on this point, see Gao Dalun [高大倫], "Shi jiandu wenzi zhongde jizhong fuhao" [釋簡牘文字中的幾種符號], in *Qin Han jiandu lunwenji* [秦漢簡牘論文集] [Gansu: Gansu renmin chubanshe, 1989], pp. 291–301.) The end of a text is marked in a number of ways in the other materials found at Guodian. In some cases, the final mark is a "hook" (∠), which is sometimes put in the center of the slip and other times off to the right side. In other cases, a black line (▬) has been drawn across the entire slip at the end (as in "Mu Lugong" and "Tang Yu zhi dao").

45. Wang Bo, "Guodian *Laozi* weishenma you sanzu?"

46. Things like continuation of rime or continuity of ideas. The end of chapter 66 is not distinguished from the beginning of chapter 46 by punctuation. Still, it is clear that chapter 46 is a self-contained passage based on the ideas discussed and the uniform syntactical pattern.

47. See below for more on this chapter, which contains important variants.

48. Since 300 B.C. is the approximate date that the slips were put into the ground; we do not know when they were made. See the conclusion below.

49. It is also possible that the initial lines of chapters 48 and 20 were regarded as a single "chapter" in the Guodian slips. In both cases the focus is on the detrimental effects of "learning." See appendix III.

50. Note that this seems to confirm D. C. Lau's thesis about this particular chapter.

51. Recall that the initial four lines in chapter 52 are also distinguished by punctuation from the middle lines of copy A of the Mawangdui manuscripts. Peng Hao has argued that the *final* four lines in the chapter are also set off from the middle lines of the chapter in copy A (in his "Guodian Chujian *Laozi* de niandai ji fenzhang"). But the poor state of the silk at this point in the text does not allow us to confirm such punctuation (·).

52. *You* (憂, distress) is not an exact rime, however, with *pu* (樸, genuine) and *yu* (欲, desires). The latter were both "*hou*" (侯) group words, while *you* was in the "*you*" (幽) group.

53. See *Guodian Chumu zhujian*, p. 113, notes 1–4.

54. Also note that two of the chapters from the *Laozi* included in these three bundles could certainly be read as Confucian—chapters 54 (B:8) and 31 (C:3).

55. See Michael La Fargue, *The Tao of the Tao Te Ching* (Albany: State University of New York Press, 1992), especially pp. 196–99.

56. Another intriguing possibility presents itself when we read the text called "Liu de" (Six Virtues); see *Guodian Chumu zhujian*, p. 187. The first four of the six virtues discussed are *sheng* (聖), *zhi* (智), *ren* (仁), and *yi* (義), the exact things to be rejected in the opening lines of this chapter in later editions. Were later editions of the *Laozi* revised with "Liu de" in mind?

57. Which is how it is understood in "Cheng Zhi wenzhi" (*Guodian Chumu zhujian*, p. 168).

58. Note that the character 慮 is understood to be *lu* (慮) in the line "欲生於性, 慮生於欲" (desires stem from our natures, and calculation/deliberation stems from our desires), in "Collected Sayings, Part II" (*Guodian Chumu zhujian*, p. 203).

59. And throughout the "Liu de" and "Zun deyi" selections.

60. In other words, I understand *hua* in the sense of *jiaohua* (教化) and *lu* in the sense of *lushi* (慮事).

61. One good reason for seeing the Guodian reading as the earliest reading is that Confucians would say that "filial piety" and "compassion" are virtues that *require* "transformation through education" (*jiaohua*, 教化).

62. For more on the significant role this chapter plays in unit 1 of *Laozi* A, see my forthcoming article "The Ruler's Agenda."

63. For the additional lines, see Henricks, *Lao-tzu Te-tao ching*, p. 246.

64. This line does not occur in all later editions. See Henricks, *Lao-tzu Te-tao ching*, p. 246.

65. Presumably they make the same point that success comes by "stopping in time."

66. Punctuation in the last line of chapter 30 on the Guodian slips seems to indicate that the final line should be *qi shi hao* (其事好), not *qi shi hao chang* (其事好長). But I suspect this punctuation was inserted one character too soon. See my notes to the translation of this chapter below.

67. Paul Thompson noted this possibility—that the error resulted from "eye skip"—at the "Guodian *Laozi*" conference, May 1998.

68. This passage is translated by Lau as "Someone said, 'Repay injury with a good turn [報怨以德]. What do you think of this saying?' The Master said, 'What, then, do you repay a good turn with? You repay an injury with straightness, but you repay a good turn with a good turn'" (D. C. Lau, *Confucius: The Analects* [Middlesex, UK: Penguin Books], p. 129).

69. The ten *"wuwei"* chapters are 2, 3, 10, 37, 38, 43, 48, 57, 63, and 64; *"wushi"* occurs in chapters 57 and 63.

70. Harold Roth includes "The Way of Heaven" (*tian zhi dao*, 天之道) in his list of "Technical Terms of Huang-Lao Philosophy" ("What Is Huang-Lao?" [paper presented at the annual meeting of the Association for Asian Studies, 1991]).

71. Xing Wen, "Lun Guodian *Laozi* yu jinben *Laozi* bu zhu yixi."

72. The *"chizi"* is mentioned in chapter 55, which is included in *Laozi* A.

73. Lau, *Lao Tzu: Tao Te Ching*, p. 172: "the clue to editing lies often in the use of connectives like *ku* (therefore, thus) and *shih yi* (hence)."

74. Another theme that does not show up in this selection of chapters is the "I alone" theme in the second part of chapter 20 ("The masses do this. . . . I alone do this") and elsewhere in later editions.

75. Cui Renyi, "Shitan Jingmen zhujian *Laozi* de niandai," especially p. 41.

76. I take issue with this conclusion. Han Feizi seems to select chapters, or portions of chapters, on which he will comment completely at random; the order he follows should not be taken as indicating the order of chapters in the version of the *Laozi* that he was using. The important point, however, is that he is clearly citing from a "book" that he knew as the *Laozi*.

77. Li Xueqin, "Jingmen Guodian Chujian suojian Guanyin yishuo" [荆門郭店楚簡所見關尹遺說], *Zhongguo wenwubao* [中國文物報], April 8, 1998.

78. Translated by A. C. Graham, *Chuang Tzu: The Inner Chapters* (London: George Allen & Unwin, 1981), pp. 281–82.

79. See appendix I for a translation of Sima Qian's biography of Laozi.

80. Guo Yi, "Cong Guodian Chujian *Laozi* kan *Laozi* qiren qishu" [從郭店楚簡《老子》看老子其人其書], *Zhexue yanjiu* [哲學研究, Philosophical Research] (July 1998): 47–55.

81. Ibid., pp. 48–49.

82. Ibid., pp. 53–55.

83. Who, Guo suggests, is actually the person who served as the archivist in Zhou—not Li Er—and the Dan who saw the Zhou in decline and left was also this second Dan: He fled to the state of Qin, where he met with Duke Xian, as our sources all tell us. Taking refuge in Qin, he proceeded to develop Legalist thought. This is all possible. But the evidence we have can neither prove nor disprove this thesis.

84. Xing Wen, "Lun Guodian *Laoʒi* yu jinben *Laoʒi* bu zhu yixi."

85. Recall that the chapters in the *Laoʒi* in which the Dao is equated with the "One"—chapters 10, 22, 39, and 42—are not found on the Guodian slips.

86. As Harold Roth has pointed out, "even a cursory attempt at textual criticism comparing the two parallel versions of chapter 64, lines 10–18 in the received *Lao Tʒu* found in bundle A, verse 6 and C verse 5 clearly indicates that they could not be taken from each other nor could they have had a common source" ("Some Methodological Issues in the Study of the Kuo Tien *Lao Tʒu* Parallels" [paper presented at the international conference on the "Guodian *Laoʒi*," May 1998], p. 5). This is one of the reasons that Roth—and I agree with him on this—suspects that "the three bundles of bamboo strips that contain the Kuo Tien *Lao Tʒu* material did not even come from the same source" (ibid., p. 4).

87. This might also explain why there is a blank space left on the slip between the end of chapter 2 (A:9) and the beginning of chapter 32 (A:10); that is, the copyist changed to another source for the text of chapter 32. *Dao* is again written 𧗞 in "Liu de" and "Collected Sayings, Part I," while in "Collected Sayings, Part II," the character used is 衛. Another significant variation is that in *Laoʒi* A and *Laoʒi* B the negative "without" is consistently written as 亡 (*wang*), as it is in the Shang oracle bones, while in *Laoʒi* C, the more familiar character 無 (*wu*) is used. The significance of these changes must be explored.

88. By "complete" text, I mean one containing the eighty-one chapters in current editions in terms of "content"; it need not be divided into chapters. In my view, the Mawangdui copies are "complete" versions of the *Laoʒi*.

89. Copy A appears to have been made before the reign of Han Gaozu, Liu Bang (劉邦, r. 206–194 B.C.) since it does not avoid the taboo on his personal name (*bang*, state). Copy B does avoid this taboo—changing all "*bang*s" in the text to *guo*s (國), and was probably made *during* the reign of Liu Bang. (See, for example, Henricks, *Lao-tʒu Te-tao ching*, p. xv.)

90. The high quality of the calligraphy on the slips suggests that the latter is true; these were not done in a "slap-dash" fashion to be put into a tomb. Sarah Allan has suggested to me that these texts might well have belonged to the teacher of the deceased.

91. Perhaps the clearest evidence we have demonstrating that this was the case occurs in chapter 59 (B:1), where the copyist repeated the words *shiyi ʒao* before he finished the line—*shiyi ʒao, shiyi ʒaobei* (是以早, 是以早備). I believe that the same is true of the Mawangdui copies of the *Laoʒi*. Although it is commonly argued that the "phonetic loans" we find in these copies are the result of unlearned scribes taking oral dictation, I am convinced that the scribes who wrote them were "looking at" previous copies. Two cases should make this clear. (1) In chapter 27 (in copy B), line 3 reads: "The good counter doesn't use tallies or chips," then line 4 begins "The good *counter*, closer of doors" (Henricks, *Lao-tʒu Te-tao ching*, pp. 240–41). The

character 數 (*shu*, counter) was written down but then blotted out when the scribe realized he was mistakenly repeating the previous line. Line 4 ought to begin: "The good closer of doors." (2) The other example is in chapter 7 (again in copy B). Here the line "He puts himself in the background yet finds himself in the foreground" should be followed by "Puts self-concern out of his mind, yet his self-concern is preserved." But, having started the second line correctly, the scribe mistakenly ended the line with the end of the previous line—"Puts self-concern out of his mind, *yet finds himself in the foreground*" (ibid., pp. 200–201).

92. That is, when were these sayings first formulated as ideas and words and spoken, so that they could be memorized and start to circulate orally? The work of Liu Xiaogan (劉笑敢), in which he notes that the syntactic patterns of rimed parts of the *Laozi* often match those of the *Shi* (詩, Book of Songs), might suggest that such sayings were formulated as early as the "Spring and Autumn" period (722–481 B.C.). (See Liu's article, "*Laozi* zaoqi shuo zhi xin zheng" [《老子》 早期說之 新證], *Daojia wenhua yanjiu* 4 (1994): 419–37.)

*Translator notes*

1. William G. Boltz, "The Study of Early Chinese Manuscripts: Methodological Preliminaries" (paper presented at the international conference on the "Guodian *Laozi*," May 1998), p. 1. He elaborates, "Manuscripts should be transcribed so as to reveal the exact form of what is written as precisely and unambiguously as possible without introducing any interpolations, alterations or other extraneous material based on assumptions, biases or subjective decisions of the scholar-transcriber or of anyone else."

2. Wang Bi often quotes the text in his commentary, and in many places his citations do not correspond to what we now find in the text that circulates with his commentary attached. For the evidence on this, see Shima Kunio [島 邦 男], *Rōshi kōsei* [老子校正] (Tokyo: Kyūko shoin, 1973); Rudolf G. Wagner, "The Wang Bi Recension of the *Laozi*," *Early China* 14 (1989): 27–54; and William G. Boltz, "The Lao tʒu Text That Wang Pi and Ho-shang Kung Never Saw," *Bulletin of the School of Oriental and African Studies* 48.3 (1985): 493–501.

Laozi *A*

1. *Guodian Chumu ʒhujian*, p. 3, slips 1–2.

2. My reading of 或命之或虎豆 would be 或令之有所屬, reading the last two characters as phonetic loans. Qiu Xigui (*Guodian Chumu ʒhujian*, pp. 113–14 n 5), proposes a different reading: 或命之或呼屬 ("Some people name them, others note the categories to which they belong"[?]) The reconstructed archaic pronunciations of the relevant words are: (1) *hu* (乎 or 呼, *ɦag), (2) *suo* (所, *sïag),

(3) *dou* (豆, \*dug), and (4) *shu* (屬, \*dhiuk). *Hu* and *suo* were both *yu* (魚) group words in terms of rime, while *dou* and *shu* were both *hou* (侯) group words.

3. *Guodian Chumu ʒhujian*, p. 113 n 3. He argues that the phonetic element in the character 虘—which he transcribes as 慮—is *qie* (且, \*tsʻiăg), which would make this, in terms of archaic pronunciation, a phonetic loan for *ʒha* (\*tsăg). On the character 慮, note that this character is found again in chapter 18 (*Laoʒi* C, passage 1), where it is understood to mean *hua* (化); it is also used for *hua* (化) in chapter 37 in copy A of the Mawangdui manuscripts. The archaic pronunciation of *hua* (化) was \*fiuăr while that of *wei* (爲) was \*fiiuar.

4. It is also transcribed as *shi* (使) in "Collected Sayings, IV," for which see *Guodian Chumu ʒhujian*, p. 217, and throughout the selections "Liu de" and "Zun deyi."

5. Ding Yuanzhi (丁原植) agrees with this reading and argues that the character *wen* (文) in this place in the Mawangdui copies developed from writing *shi* (史) incorrectly (in *Guodian ʒhujian "Laoʒi" shixi yu yanjiu* [郭店竹簡《老子》釋析與研究] [Taibei: Wanjuanlou, 1998], p. 11).

6. *Guodian Chumu ʒhujian*, p. 3, slips 2–5.

7. Henricks, *Lao-tʒu: Te-tao ching*, p. 154.

8. *Guodian Chumu ʒhujian*, p. 3, slips 5–6.

9. Reading *hua* (化, \*huăr) as a phonetic loan for *guo* (禍, \*fiuar).

10. See Henricks, *Lao-tʒu: Te-tao ching*, pp. 114–15.

11. *Guodian Chumu ʒhujian*, p. 3, slips 6–8.

12. The last line is 丌事好 ▄. But I suspect that the *chang* (長) that seems to begin the following passage—chapter 15 in current editions—actually belongs at the end of this line. The copyist has punctuated the text one character early. For evidence, I offer three pieces of evidence: (1) This passage ends with a series of four-character phrases. It makes no sense, then, that the final line would consist of only three characters. (2) *Chang* (長,\*dıaŋ) rimes with the last character of the preceding line *qiang* (強,\*gıaŋ). (3) In no other case does chapter 15 of the *Laoʒi* begin with the word *chang*. Note that the final word in line 7—矜 (*jin*), here written 猻—might have marked a phonetic transition to the final two lines. Xu Shen (許慎), in the *Shuowen jieʒi* (說文解字), claims that the "phonetic" of *jin* was *ling* (令, \*lıeŋ). See Xu Shen [許慎], comp., *Shuowen jieʒi ʒhu* [說文解字注], annotated by Duan Yucai [段玉裁] (repr. Shanghai: Guji, 1981), 14A.36b, p. 719.

13. The negatives *wu* (毋) and *wu* (勿) are never used in the Guodian *Laoʒi* documents.

14. *Guodian Chumu ʒhujian*, p. 3, slips 8–10.

15. For the arguments for moving the character *chang* (長) from the head of this passage to the end of the previous one, see note 12 above.

16. Understanding *fei* (非, \*pıuər) and *ni* (溺, \*nög) as phonetic loans for *wei* (微, \*mıuər) and *miao* (妙, \*mıɔg). The final character in this line is normally *da* 達, and the Guodian graph is understood to be *da* in the Wenwu transcription. However, as

Ikeda has already noted ("Biji," n 38) the Guodian graph is exactly the same as that found on "Baoshan slip 137," a graph read as *ʒao* 造 (see Zhang Shouzhong [張守中], *Baoshan Chujian wenʒibian* [包山楚簡文字編] [Beijing: Wenwu Press, 1996], p. 22). Moreover, the Guodian graph does not correspond to the version of *da* 達 preserved by Xia Song [夏竦] in his *Guwen sisheng yun* [古文四聲韻] (5.12b, 224:498). And, *ʒao* (\*dzɔg) would have rimed with *miao* (\*miɔg) in the line, providing internal rime; this is not true of *da* (\*dat).

17. *Zhi* (志) is commonly used for *shi* (識) in the Mawangdui copies as well.

18. Reading *ye* (夜 , \*ḍiăg) as a phonetic loan for *yu* (豫, \*ḍiag).

19. 罖 is used for *lin* (鄰) in copy B of the Mawangdui manuscripts as well.

20. The archaic pronunciations of *ʒhu* (竺) and *shu* (孰) were \*tiok and \*dhiok, respectively. *Ci* (束), here used for *jing* (靜, \*dzieŋ), was pronounced \*ts'ieg in antiquity.

21. See Shima Kunio, *Rōshi kōsei*, p. 82.

22. The word *song* (頌, \*giuŋ) could be read as a phonetic loan for *rong* (容, \*giuŋ), but as Tomohisa Ikeda [池田知也] has pointed out, in the *Shuowen jieʒi* (9A.2b, p. 416), the character 額 is noted as the "large seal" (*ʒhouwen*, 籀文) form of *song* ("Jingmenshi bowuguan *Guodian Chumu ʒhujian* biji" [荊門市博物館《郭店楚墓竹簡》筆記] [paper presented at the international conference on the "Guodian *Laoʒi*," May 1998], n 40) [hereafter cited as "Biji"]. From this it seems likely that *rong* was derived from *song*.

23. Copy B of the Mawangdui manuscripts omits the next to last line; in copy A, the line reads "It is precisely because he does not wish [to be full]."

24. *Guodian Chumu ʒhujian*, pp. 3–4, slips 10–13. The first half of what is now chapter 64 constitutes a distinct passage: see A:14. Passage C:4 provides a second, and different, version of this passage.

25. Literally, "Those who hold on to it *yuan* (遠) it—that is, "put it at a distance" or "find themselves separated from it." But I suspect this 遠 is a mistake for 遊, the character used in line 4. Qiu Xigui (*Guodian Chumu ʒhujian*, p. 114 n 28) points out that the latter character is commonly used for *shi* (失, to lose) in Chu script.

26. *Guodian Chumu ʒhujian*, p. 4, slips 13–14.

27. For 愚 as phonetic loan for 化, see the notes to passage A:1 note 3 above.

28. The character *ʒu* (足) is omitted on the Guodian slips, but this must be a mistake. On *ci* (束) as phonetic loan for *jing* (靜), see note 20 above.

29. *Guodian Chumu ʒhujian*, p. 4, slips 14–15.

30. Henricks, *Lao-tʒu Te-tao ching*, p. 148.

31. For the relevance of this line to the issue of dating the text, see the introduction.

32. *Guodian Chumu ʒhujian*, p. 4, slips 15–18.

33. Although "sound" (*sheng*, 聲) is commonly used as a phonetic loan for "sage" (*sheng*, 聖) in copy A of the Mawangdui manuscripts, here we find the reverse.

34. As for the character 冂, here read as *shi* (始): This may be a phonetic loan

since the archaic pronunciation of *si* (司) was \*siəg while *shi* (始) was read as \*thiəg. Another explanation is that the graphs 司 and 台 were virtually indistinguishable in archaic script.

35. *Guodian Chumu zhujian*, p. 4, slips 18–20.

36. Where other editions have the word "small" (*xiao*, 小), the character here is 妻 (*qi*, wife). The Wenwu editors suggest that this should be read as *wei* (微, \*miuər, subtle); but, in agreement with Li Ling, I prefer to read this as *xi* (細, \*ser, trivial or unimportant) (Li Ling [李零], "Du Guodian Chujian *Laozi*" [讀郭店楚簡《老子》] [paper presented at the international conference on the "Guodian *Laozi*," May 1998]). The archaic pronunciation of *qi* (妻) was \*ts'er. It could also be read as a phonetic loan for *di* (底, \*ter, low or lowly).

37. 坓 is the way "earth" (*di*, 地) was written in Chu script. See, for example, Teng Rensheng, *Chuxi jianbo wenzibian*, pp. 963–64.

38. For reading *ci* (詞) as *shi* (始), see note 34 above. *Zhe* (折, \*tiat, break) is a phonetic loan for *zhi* (制, \*tiad, to regulate or put into order).

39. Note that lines 1 to 4 seem to be self-contained in terms of the rime (the final word in line 2 [*chen*, 臣, \*ghien, subject] rimes with the final word in line 4 [*bin*, 賓, \*pien, submit as a guest]).

40. *Guodian Chumu zhujian*, pp. 4–5, slips 21–23.

41. Reading 敆 as *ji* (寂) and 繆 as *mu* (穆). These would have rimed: \*dzök and \*miok.

42. For more on the distinction between how we "refer" to something, or its "style" (*zi*, 字) and its "name" (*ming*, 名), see the translation of "Taiyi shengshui" part I, C:5, and the introductory "note."

43. The character translated as "realm" is 國 (*guo*), which we would normally translate as "state," but that makes no sense, since this is something that embraces heaven, earth, the Way, and the king. I suggest, therefore, that we read this as *yu* (域), the same word that is used in B:1 (chapter 59) below. If the author's intention was to say "state," he would have used the character *bang* (邦). Note that in the Mawangdui manuscripts, where *bang* in copy A is always changed to *guo* in copy B, the original in copy A in chapters 25 and 59 is *guo*, a sure indication that there was a distinction between *bang* and *guo* (or *yu*). In addition, it must be that *yu* meant something larger, more all-embracing than "state." The use of *yu* (域) in song 303 in the *Songs* might be relevant here. Karlgren's translation of the pertinent lines reads: "Of old, God gave the appointment to the martial T'ang; he regulated and set boundaries [*zhengyu*, 正域] for those four quarters" (Bernhard Karlgren, *The Book of Odes* [Stockholm: Museum of Far Eastern Antiquities, 1950], p. 263). Thus *yu* means "bounded space," but that could include all space that is known.

44. Qiu Xigui's note 51, in *Guodian Chumu zhujian*, p. 116.

45. Ibid., p. 153 n 47, reading the left side of the character as the phonetic element instead of the radical.

46. In this way, the second and fourth characters in the line—狀 (*zhuang*, *dzïaŋ) and 成 (*cheng*, *dhieŋ)—would have rimed.

47. *Guodian Chumu zhujian*, p. 217.

48. Ibid., p. 219 n 17.

49. Xia Song [夏竦], ed., *Guwen sisheng yun* [古文四聲韻], p. 1.31b, in the *Siku quanshu* [四庫全書] edition (repr. Shanghai: Guji, 1987), 224:432.

50. *Guodian Chumu zhujian*, p. 5, slip 23.

51. At the "Guodian *Laozi*" conference, Donald Harper suggested that the character 籊, in the expression 囵籊 (bellows) might be a variant writing of 管 (*guan*, pipe), in which case it should not be read as *yue* (籥) (as it is read in the Wenwu transcription). This makes good sense given the phonetic element of the character in question; also, lines 1 and 2 would then presumably rime (*kăn and *kuan, respectively).

52. Lau, *Lao Tzu: Tao Te Ching*, p. 166.

53. See Shima Kunio, *Rōshi kōsei*, p. 62.

54. Henricks, *Lao-tzu Te-tao ching*, p. 196.

55. *Guodian Chumu zhujian*, p. 5, slip 24.

56. Reading 篙 as the *du* (篤) that is found here in later editions. These two characters were used interchangeably in ancient texts. The character 篙 is defined as *hou* (厚) in the *Shuowen jiezi* (in the *Shuowen jiezi zhu*, 5.29a, p. 229).

57. See, for example, Zhang Xuan [張瑄], *The Etymologies of 3000 Chinese Characters in Common Usage* (Hong Kong: Hong Kong University Press, 1968), pp. 305 and 416.

58. It is also preferred over *heng* on phonological grounds. Lines 2 and 4 rimed, and lines 1 and 3, if we read this word as *ji*, would have been phonologically close: 極 (*kɪak), 作 (*tsak), and 篙 (*tok), 復 (*bɪuak).

59. Ikeda, "Biji," n 134.

60. It is possible that *xu* and *ju* are both phonetic loans for other characters or different ways of writing other characters. This is something that awaits further research. The right side of 須 (*xu*), for example, differed little from the character 見 (the right side of *guan*) in ancient Chu script as we can see from the samples in Teng Rensheng, *Chuxi jianbo wenzibian* (pp. 701 and 707). Thus *xu* might be an ancient way of writing "look at" or "see." Also, *ju* and *wu* were phonetically close in archaic terms, pronounced *kiag and *ŋag respectively. But the character that is always used for *wu* (I), on the Guodian slips is 虗.

61. Wang Bo made this proposal at the "Guodian *Laozi*" conference. Another possibility is raised by Ikeda in "Biji" (n 137): to translate (my choice of wording, not his) this as "The Way of Heaven [generates things] in multiple numbers."

62. See the samples in Teng Rensheng, *Chuxi jianbo wenzibian*, pp. 15 and 787. See also *Guodian Chumu zhujian*, p. 115 n 45, on the confusion in the slips in the use of the characters *fu*, *tian*, and *er* (而). All three characters looked much the same at this time.

63. Note that both characters—啬 in chapter 25 and 道 (*dao*) in this line—are in later editions, including that represented by the Mawangdui copies, replaced by the character 物 (*wu*, thing). This suggests that they stand for the same word (William Boltz first made this suggestion), and "form," in both cases, makes better sense than the "Way."

64. Henricks, *Lao-tzu Te-tao ching*, p. 218.

65. *Guodian Chumu zhujian*, p. 5, slips 25–27.

66. "Fragile" is 霢, which the Wenwu editors read as a phonetic loan for 脆 (*cui*, brittle), the character found here in later editions. But there seems no reason not to see this as 毳 (*cui*), which refers to "very fine hair."

67. The character translated "begins" is written as 甲 (*jia*) on the Guodian slips. Ikeda thinks that this transcription is wrong and that the character is actually 己 (*ji*), which would then stand for 起 (*qi*, begins) (Ikeda, "Biji," n 146). It is true that the characters 甲 and 己 looked a lot alike in Chu script (for samples of each, see Teng Rensheng, *Chuxi jianbo wenzibian*, pp. 1054 and 1064), but the Guodian character is clearly 甲. I suspect the copyist meant to write 起 or possibly 作 (*zuo*)—since the right side of 作 *also* looked a lot like 甲 [ibid., p. 661)—but wrote 甲 by mistake.

68. Actually copy B has *baiqian zhi gao* (百千之高), but, if Gao Ming (高明) is right, this 千 (*qian*) should be read as 刃 (*ren*) (*Boshu Laozi jiaozhu* [帛書老子校注] [Beijing: Zhonghua shuju, 1996], pp. 136–37).

69. See Shima Kunio, *Rōshi kōsei*, p. 188.

70. In his study of the poetical parts of the *Laozi*, Karlgren noted that lines 1, 2, and 5 in this chapter rime, as do lines 3, 4, and 6. The finals in lines 10 and 12 are 土 (*tu*, *t'ag) and 下 (*xia*, *ħăg). See his "The Poetical Parts of Lao-Tsï," *Göteborgs Högskolas Årsskrift* 38: 3 (1932): 3–45.

71. *Guodian Chumu zhujian*, p. 5, slips 27–29.

72. Ikeda, "Biji," n 152.

73. *Guodian Chumu zhujian*, p. 5, slips 29–32.

74. As others have already noted (Chen Guying, Xu Kangsheng), the Guodian and Mawangdui copies of the *Laozi*, like the Xiang'er and Heshanggong recensions, have 法物 (*fawu*, exemplary things, i.e., beautiful and valuable things) in this line, while other editions have 法令 (*faling*, laws). It seems clear that *fawu* was the earliest reading. Gao Ming (*Boshu Laozi jiaozhu*, p. 106) cites the Heshanggong commentary on this: "'Exemplary things,' means 'good things.' When precious items are produced and displayed, then farming affairs are neglected and hunger and cold both arise."

75. *Pin* and *hun* were both *wenbu* (文部) in terms of rime; *pan* was a *yuanbu* (元部) word.

76. This is also the way Peng Hao read this character in his initial transcription.

77. My thanks to Xing Wen for bringing this connection to my attention.

78. But lines 1 and 2 could both allude to the "Militarists" or "Strategists" (*bingjia*,

兵家). *Zheng* (正, upright and correct) and *qi* (奇, irregular methods), in the vocabulary of the Militarists, referred to different types of troop deployment. On this point see D. C. Lau and Roger T. Ames, trans., *Sun Pin: The Art of Warfare* (New York: Ballantine Books, 1996), pp. 253–56. The title of chapter 31 of the *Sun Pin bingfa* is "Qizheng" (奇正, Straightforward and Surprise Operations).

79. See Shima Kunio, *Rōshi kōsei*, p. 174. But note that Mawangdui copy A (the text is missing for copy B) agrees with the Guodian reading.

80. The Xiang'er lineage is an exception. There the order is 11, 10, 12, and 13. See Shima Kunio, *Rōshi kōsei*, p. 175.

81. Literally, the last line reads "I desire not to desire, and the people on their own are genuine and natural [*pu*]." But such people would be content with "the simple and unadorned" and have no desire for "exemplary things." I suspect that lines 10 to 13 were also originally eight-character lines. Line 13 still is in the Guodian and Mawangdui versions, and so is line 10 in Mawangdui copy A. In addition, note that there is internal rime in each of these lines: line 10—*shi* (事) and *fu* (富); line 11—*wei* (爲) and *hua* (化); line 12—*jing* (靜) and *zheng* (正); and line 13—*yu* (欲) and *pu* (樸).

82. *Guodian Chumu zhujian*, pp. 5–6, slips 33–35.

83. The Wenwu editors read the final character here—惪—as 憂 (*you*, anxious or sad). But, like Ikeda ("Biji," n 180), I believe the right word here would be 嗄 (*sha*, *săg), in part because this is probably meant to rime with the word 呼 (*hu*, *ɦag, scream).

84. In the Wenwu transcription this character appears as 羕 (*yang*), which is then understood as a phonetic loan for the character normally found in this place—祥 (*xiang*). Since 祥 (*xiang*) means "good fortune," while to "increase your life" or attempt to "add on to life" (益生) is seen as the wrong thing to do in Daoism, Ikeda suggests that the correct word here should be 殃 (*yang*, misfortune or calamity), and he finds support for reading *xiang* as a phonetic loan for *yang* (Ikeda, "Biji," n 184). But in his commentary to the *Shuowen jiezi*, Duan Yucai says that, broadly speaking, "disaster is also referred to as *xiang*" (災亦謂之祥; *Shuowen jiezi zhu*, 1A.5a, p. 3).

85. Note that lines 10 to 13 all rime—常 (*dhiaŋ), 明 (*mɪăŋ), 祥 (*ġiaŋ), and 強 (*gɪaŋ)—but the rime changes for lines 14 and 15 (老 [*lao*, *log] and 道 [*dao*, *dog]).

86. See Shima Kunio, *Rōshi kōsei*, p. 170, for the main variations by lineage.

87. For various forms of this line, see ibid. It appears as though the original Wang Bi and Xiang'er recensions also had the line in this form.

88. For the identification as *ran*, see *Guodian Chumu zhujian*, p. 116 n 71. This line needs a grammatical connective, and *ran* would serve that purpose, but then there would be no subject for the verb 怒 (*nu*, gets firm/stiff). I suspect that the connective 而 (*er*), which is found where it belongs, right before *juan nu*, in all later editions, was omitted by the copyist for the sake of balance within the line; without the *er*,

line 6 becomes an eight-character line in which characters 4 and 8— 戊 (*wu*, \*mug) and 怒 (*nu*, \*nag)—though they do not rime, were phonologically close. On the identification of 旸 as 陽 (*yang*)—*yang* is written without the radical in "Taiyi shengshui" (*Guodian Chumu zhujian*, p. 13, slip 2), and in the present case I suspect that 上 (*shang*) has replaced 日 (*ri*) as the top part of the character. (For the writing of *shang* [上] in this way, see *Shuowen jiezi zhu*, 1A.3a, p. 2). Teng Rensheng shows that 易 (*yang*) was sometimes written with an additional element on top, an element that could be mistaken for 上 (*shang*), but which would probably be transcribed as 止 (*zhi*) (*Chuxi jianbo wenzibian*, p. 738). So the copyist might be writing that form of *yang*, omitting, however, the element 日 (*ri*).

89. *Guodian Chumu zhujian*, p. 6, slips 25–27.

90. The "Therefore" is also omitted from the start of line 4 in the Heshanggong lineage, and the Xiang'er lineage maintains the "Therefore" at the start of line 6. (See Shima Kunio, *Rōshi kōsei*, p. 148.)

91. The archaic pronunciations of *zhi, dai*, and *jiu* were, respectively, \*tiəg, \*dəg, and \*giog.

92. *Guodian Chumu zhujian*, p. 6, slip 37.

93. The omission of the particle 之 (*zhi*) must be a mistake.

94. Lines 1 and 2 rime—動 (\*duŋ) and 用 (\*diuŋ)—and the word for "non-being" at the end of line 4— 亡 (*wang*, \*mɪaŋ)—probably sounded better in this context than its later replacement 無 (*wu*, \*mɪuag).

95. *Guodian Chumu zhujian*, p. 117 n 75.

96. Chen Guying, "Chu du jianben *Laozi*" [初讀簡本 《老子》] (paper presented at the international conference on the "Guodian *Laozi*," May 1998), p. 2. Chen raises this issue and goes into it in some detail in his recently published *Laozi jinzhu jinyi* (Taibei: Commercial Press, 1997), pp. 205–8. Related to this, Chen understands *wu* and *you* as nouns in lines 3 and 4 of chapter 1 of the *Laozi*: 無, 名天地之始 and 有, 名萬物之母 (*Laozi jinzhu jinyi*, pp. 47–52).

97. *Guodian Chumu zhujian*, p. 6, slips 37–39.

98. In the Guodian version the two exceptions to this are lines 4 and 7. Line 4 has five characters, but the final 也 (*ye*) could be omitted and is probably added to mark the metaphorical relationship of lines 1 to 4 to what follows in lines 5 to 8. Line 7 has only three characters, but I suspect the connective 而 (*er*) has been incorrectly left out. The rime words are "maintain" (\*pog), "safeguard" (\*thiog), "disaster" (\*kog), and "Way" (\*dog). There is also internal rime in line 9 with the characters in the second and fourth positions: 攻述 (\*diuət) 身退 (\*t'uəd).

99. *Guodian Chumu zhujian*, p. 117 n 76. Note that the Mawangdui copies both have 植 in this location.

100. At the "Guodian *Laozi*" conference, William Boltz and I spent some time discussing these lines, and he suggested that the later form of this line probably came about when someone wrote 允 (*yun*) as 兒 (*dui*), something easy to do. Following this, the change was made from 湍 to 揣, and 允 to 銳.

101. From Li Kang [李康], "Yunming lun" [運命論, Essay on Fate), as cited in Yan Kejun [嚴可均], ed., *Quan shanggu sandai Qin Han sanguo liuchao wen* [全上古三代秦漢三國六朝文] (Taibei: Zhongwen chubanshe, 1972), 2:1295.

## Laozi *B*

1. *Guodian Chumu Laozi*, p. 7, slips 1–3.

2. For the end of line 2 and the start of line 3, the copyist incorrectly wrote: 夫售嗇是以曻是以曻備. The original was probably: 夫售嗇是以曻＝備＝.

3. There is a full stop punctuation mark (■) at the end of this line, which normally signals the end of a passage or chapter. Here, this clearly ought to be "＝," the sign that means "repetition"; in fact the last three words should be repeated (i.e., the line should end with 亡＝不＝克＝).

4. As it was in line 1 in chapter 16 (A:13), the character 互 here must be a mistake for the right side of the character 極 (*ji*). If the "sense" of the line does not affirm that, the rime scheme certainly does.

5. Chen Guying, following the arguments of Yao Nai (姚鼐), had read "submit" here to mean "prepare" (*bei*), the word that we find in the Guodian slips. See his *Laozi zhuyi ji pingjie* [《老子》註譯及評介] (Hong Kong: Zhonghua shuju, 1987), p. 296.

6. In the "Collected Sayings, Part III," *bei* stands for *fu* on p. 212, while on p. 211, where what *is* intended is the word *bei* ("prepare"), the character 備 (*bei*) is written without the radical *ren* (i.e., 甫).

7. On the meaning of *yu* (域) as "realm" or "the entire, known world," see note 43 in *Laozi* A.

8. 深根 (*thiemkən*), 固柢 (*kagter*), 長生 (*dɪaŋsïen*), and 舊視 (*gɪogdhɪer*).

9. 舊 for 久 is a common substitution in the Guodian slips. The Wenwu editors seem to understand it as a "phonetic loan," but that may not be necessary. The two words could be used interchangeably in ancient texts.

10. *Guodian Chumu zhujian*, p. 7, slips 3 and 4.

11. See Gao Ming, "Boshu *Laozi* jiayiben yu jinben *Laozi* kanjiao zhaji" [帛書《老子》甲乙本與今本《老子》勘校札記], in Wenwu bianji weiyuanhui [文物編輯委員會], ed., *Wenwu ziliao congkan* [文物資料叢刊] (Beijing: Wenwu Press, 1978), 2: 209–21; see also idem, *Boshu Laozi jiaozhu*, pp. 54–57.

12. As I pointed out in my 1981 article, "The Philosophy of Lao-tzu Based on the Ma-wang-tui Texts: Some Preliminary Observations," *Bulletin of the Society for the Study of Chinese Religions* 9 (October 1981): 60–61.

13. *Guodian Chumu Laozi*, p. 7, slips 4 and 5.

14. Xu Kangsheng [許抗生], "Chudu Guodian zhujian *Laozi*" [初讀郭店竹簡《老子》] (paper presented at the international conference on the "Guodian *Laozi*," May 1998), p. 2.

15. *Guodian Chumu Laozi*, p. 118.

16. The text in copy A is missing at this point, but the general assumption seems to be that A and B were the same.

17. Xu Kangsheng makes this point in "Chudu Guodian zhujian *Laozi*." So does Gao Ming in *Boshu Laozi jiaozhu*, pp. 317–18.

18. Henricks, *Lao-tzu Te-tao ching*, p. 226. The "I alone" refrain in these lines is very reminiscent of the *Chuci* tradition.

19. *Guodian Chumu zhujian*, p. 7, slips 5–8.

20. The one granting the favor is clearly in the higher position.

21. Note that, in place of the character 若 (*ruo*, like), the scribe has inserted a small line after the character 辱 (*ru*). Since line 1 is herein being repeated, clearly the *ruo* ought to be there. Qiu Xigui suggests that the punctuation mark here—the same short line (▬) that elsewhere marks the end of a section in a chapter—might indicate that a character has been omitted (*Guodian Chumu zhujian*, p. 119 n 7). I can think of at least two other explanations. The first is that here, as it does in passage B:1 (chapter 59), this line is used to mark "repetition," something normally indicated by "=." If this is so, the character repeated is 辱 (*ru*), with the second *ru* being a phonetic loan for *ruo* (若). Though *ru* and *ruo* were not exact homophones, the difference in sound was not very great (*ru* [辱], was *niuk, and *ruo* [若] was *niak). The other possibility is that the scribe, thinking this line would respond directly to line 3, assumed it would simply say *shi wei chongju* (是謂寵辱, "This is why I say 'Favor is really disgrace'") *period*. But having marked the end of the line (▬), he then discovered that there were two more characters to write.

22. Since the author discusses nothing but "favor" when he asks "What do I mean by *chongru*?" it is possible to read the phrase *chongru* to mean only the former—"favor."

23. See Shima Kunio, *Rōshi kōsei*, p. 78.

24. Ibid. In addition, for a good discussion of these variants and the commentaries on these opening lines, see Gao Ming's *Boshu Laozi jiaozhu*, pp. 276–78.

25. See Shima Kunio, *Rōshi kōsei*, p. 78.

26. Henricks, *Lao-tzu: Te-tao ching*, pp. 212–13.

27. A. C. Graham, trans., *Chuang Tzu: The Inner Chapters* (London: George Allen & Unwin, 1981), p. 224.

28. *Guodian Chumu zhujian*, pp. 7–8, slips 9–12.

29. The final words in lines 1 and 2 were close to riming (*zhong*, 中, *tioŋ; and *wang*, 亡, *mıaŋ), as were the final words in lines 3 and 4 (*xiao*, 笑, *sıɔg; and *dao*, 道, *dog). In later editions, where the word at the end of line 1 is *xing* (行, *ɦăŋ, to put into practice), the riming of lines 1 and 2 is clearer to see. It is tempting to think that, in the original form of these lines, lines 1 to 4 were all eight-character lines. Lines 1 and 2 still are in most later editions, and line 4 could easily be an eight-character line in the Guodian slips by dropping either the *da* (大) or the *yi* (矣); the rhythm of the line suggests a reading of "*fu da xiao* (*sıɔg), *bu zu yi wei dao* (*dog)."

Line 3 was in fact written as an eight-character line in a number of cases where the final four words were *da er xiao zhi* (大而笑之). (On this point, see Jiang Xichang [蔣錫昌], *Laozi jiaogu* [老子校詁] [Taibei: Minglun chubanshe, 1971], p. 270.)

30. The *Shuowen jiezi zhu* notes that the *guwen* character 遟 (*chi*, slow) was read as 夷 (*yi*, level or even). See *Guodian Chumu zhujian*, p. 119 n 12. In the Wenwu transcription characters 3 and 4 in this line are shown to be missing. However, the characters 女繢 appear on "fragment 20" in the appendix, "Fragments of Slips" (*Guodian Chumu zhujian*, p. 108), and Li Jiahao (correctly, I think) suggests that this fragment belongs at the end of slip 10 in copy B (Li Jiahao [李家浩], "Du *Guodian Chumu zhujian* yiyi" [讀《郭店楚墓竹簡》遺議], *Zhongguo zhexue* [中國哲學], no. 20 (October 1998): 339–58). *Hui* (繢, *huəd) would be a phonetic loan for the more common *lei* (纇, *lıuəd).

31. The third character in this line remains unidentified. But Qiu Xigui (*Guodian Chumu zhujian*, p. 119 n 15) suggests that it might be a variant writing of 祇 (*qi*), which he believes was a phonetic loan for 希 (*xi*, rarefied), the word used here in later editions.

32. This reading is unattested elsewhere.

33. Suggested to me by Sarah Allan.

34. Ikeda ("Biji," n 235) shows that books with similar titles are cited in other sources; "Fayan" (法言) (in the *Zhuangzi*), "Yiyan" (逸言) (in the *Heguanzi*), and "Yinyan" (隱言) (in the *Guiguzi*). D. C. Lau translates this line: "Hence the *Chien yen* has it" (*Lao Tzu: Tao Te Ching*, p. 102).

35. With the exception of the Fu Yi edition (see Shima Kunio, *Rōshi kōsei*, p. 142).

36. Assuming that the last words in lines 18 and 19 were *ming* (名) and *cheng* (成) as they are in later editions.

37. *Guodian Chumu zhujian*, p. 8, slip 13.

38. Ibid., p. 119 n 19.

39. Henricks, *Lao-tzu Te-tao ching*, p. 126.

40. Ibid.

41. In later editions of the *Laozi*, what is now chapter 8 was probably constituted in the same way. That is, the beginning and end of the chapter are a unified saying, while the middle part of the chapter constitutes a separate saying, which is only vaguely connected with the beginning and end. In that case, the common concern is with things that are "good" (*shan*, 善). (See Henricks, *Lao-tzu Te-tao ching*, p. 202.)

42. *Guodian Chumu zhujian*, p. 8, slip 13.

43. Reading 佀 as *zhuo* (拙).

44. Reading *chu* (詘, bend or yield) as *chu* (絀, decrease or retreat).

45. As in Mawangdui copy A. Although some might conclude that *da cheng* at the start of this line must be a mistake since line 1 already began in that way, I do not see this as a problem. Line 1 requires line 2 and rimes with it; the same is true with lines 3 and 4. Lines 5 to 7 form a new, distinct unit, in which the final characters share the

phonetic element *chu* (出). However, *cheng* might have been changed to *ying* (贏) in Mawangdui copy A to clarify the distinction. Note that *cheng* and *ying* are semantically and phonetically similar; in archaic Chinese, *cheng* was pronounced *dhieŋ, while *ying* was pronounced *dieŋ.

46. The final word in line 9(2) in Mawangdui copy A, *jiong* (炅, *kiweng), clearly rimed with the *ding* in line 10(3). In lines 8 (1) and 9 (2), 桌 could be read as *zao* (燥, hot and dry) instead of *zao* (躁, activity), and *qing* (青) could be read as *qing* (清, cool) instead of *jing* (靜, tranquil). These are the readings preferred in the Wenwu transcription. But surely the author was saying something more profound than "heat conquers cold, and cold conquers heat." The Wenwu editors also believe that the author meant *re* (熱, hot) when writing *ran*, but I see no reason for making this change. *Re* (*niat) would have rimed neither with *cang* nor *ding*, and from the "Taiyi shengshui" selection in *Laozi* C, it is clear that *cang* (蒼 = 滄) and *ran* were the words used to mean "cold and hot" in the Guodian slips, whenever or wherever these slips were written. Later, they were changed to *han* (寒) and *re* (熱), the pair used in current editions.

47. *Guodian Chumu zhujian*, p. 8, slips 15–18.

48. This way of writing the character 拔 (*ba*)—朵—is attested in Xia Song, *Guwen sisheng yun* (5.13b), where his source is a "*gu Laozi*" (ancient edition of the *Laozi*).

49. The character 屯 (*tun*) should be changed to 乇 (*tuo*) at the end of this line in the transcription (*Guodian Chumu zhujian*, p. 118). *Tuo* was presumably a phonetic loan for *chuo* (輟). Thus, lines 1 to 3 rimed: 拔 (*bǎt), 脫 (*duat), and 輟 (*truat).

50. Translated by Wing-tsit Chan, *A Sourcebook in Chinese Philosophy* (Princeton: Princeton University Press, 1963), p. 86. The "Great Learning" (*daxue*, 大學), has been attributed to the grandson of Confucius, Zi Si.

51. In most editions "widespread" is *pu* (普), but it is *bo* (博) in Mawangdui copy B. Of these two, *pu* (*p'ag) gives us the better rime with the *xia* of *tianxia* (天下, *hǎg); the archaic pronunciation of *bo* was *pak.

52. There is space for about five characters at the end of the slip. Ikeda ("Biji," n 261) suggests the following reading: 虐可以智天[下然哉。以此]; but it could also have been [下之然。以此]. The parallel with line 4 in chapter 57 suggests that the missing characters were 下之然也夫. But, as noted, that would mean the chapter ended with an unanswered question.

## Laozi *C*

1. *Guodian Chumu zhujian*, p. 9, slips 1–3.

2. In his *Guwen sishengyun*, Xia Song noted that *wu* (侮) was written 炙 in a *guwen* edition of the *Xiaojing* [孝經, Classic of Filial Piety) (*Guwen sishengyun*, 3.10a; 224:456).

3. Lines 1 and 4 also rimed (又, *ɦɪuəg, and 侮, *mɪuəg); not so, the final words in lines 2 and 3—*yu* (譽, *ĝiag) and *wei* (畏, *·ɪuər).

4. Zhou Fagao's reconstructions are: 廢 *pjwar, 義 *ngia; 和 *gwa, 慈 *dzjiəγ; 亂 *lwan, and 臣 *djien (*Hanzi gujin yinhui* [漢字古今音彙, A Pronouncing Dictionary of Chinese Characters] [Hong Kong: Chinese University of Hong Kong, 1973]).

5. *Guodian Chumu zhujian*, p. 9, slips 4–5.

6. If we omit, for this purpose, the grammatical *er* (而) in line 2.

7. Either 用之不可既 or 用之不足既.

8. This is indicated by the grammatical particle *ye* (也) at the end of lines 5 and 8. Also, line 8 may have rimed with line 5: 味 (*mɪuəd/mɪuəi) and 既 (*kɪar/kɪəi).

9. *Guodian Chumu zhujian*, p. 9, slips 6–10.

10. In most later editions, the phrase I have translated "dignified and reverent" is *tiandan* (恬淡, *dām dam). But for *dan*, the Guodian slips have the character 纏, a character that, like the Mawangdui characters 襲 and 懥, appears to use *long* (龍, *lɪuŋ) as the phonetic. It seems unlikely that any of these could have been a phonetic loan for *dan*, which means "poor," "weak," or "lacking in flavor." I suspect the intended word here is *gong* (龔, *kɪuŋ), which means "reverent." The Guodian character, without the "silk" radical, is catalogued in Teng Rensheng, *Chuxi jianbo wenzi bian* (p. 204), where he identifies it with the character 龔 (*gong*).

11. The negative *fu* (弗) must be read here as an imperative; the Mawangdui copies have the correct negative—*wu* (勿). Note that this could mean that the string of *fu*'s in chapter 30 (A:4, lines 5–7) should also be read as imperatives.

12. My guess is that the three missing characters here were 殺 and 不可.

13. The word "fine" (*jia*, 佳) is omitted in the Mawangdui copies. See Henricks, *Lao-tzu Te-tao ching*, p. 248.

14. Ibid.

15. *Guodian Chumu zhujian*, p. 10, slips 11–14.

16. In the Wenwu transcription, the character 虙 is understood as a phonetic loan for *qie* (且), which I would here read as *jiang* (將, to be about to). For this grammatical use of the particle *qie*, see Pei Xuehai [裴學海], *Gushu xuzi jishi* [古書虛字集釋] (Taibei: Guangwen shuju, 1971), p. 655.

17. There, *shigu* (是故); here, *shiyi* (是以).

18. In passage A:6, the line ends "yet he *cannot* do it" (*er fu neng wei*, 而弗能爲).

19. *Guodian Chumu zhujian*, p. 13, slips 1–8, 10–12.

20. See *Guodian Chumu zhujian*, p. 125.

21. *Shenming* (神明)—which I have translated "the gods above and below"—as A. C. Graham noted in his work on the *Heguanzi* (鶡冠子), "is a pair of concepts which has always resisted English translation" (Graham, "A Neglected Pre-Han Philosophical Text: *Ho-kuan-tzu*," *Bulletin of the School of Oriental and African*

*Studies* 52.3 [1989]: 515). He went on to note, "In *Ho-kuan-tzu* they are the active and passive sides of the unifying intelligence which exceeds a piecemeal acquaintance with things; as rough equivalents we choose 'clairvoyant' and 'illumined.'" But in the present selection, *shenming*, while it surely refers to a pair, must be something with cosmological standing. So I agree with Xing Wen in reading *shenming* as *shenqi* (神祇, the gods above and below, or the gods of heaven and earth). (See Xing Wen, "Lun Guodian *Laozi* yu jinben *Laozi* bu zhu yixi," pp. 1–4.) Cosmologically speaking, the pair we might expect in this place is the "sun and the moon," but I can find no support for reading *shenming* in that way. Note that all features of the cosmos, beginning with heaven and earth, are presented as binary oppositions.

22. See *Guodian Chumu zhujian*, p. 126 n 12. The Wenwu editors suggest reading *ji* (忌, taboo) as *ji* (紀, initial thread); Qiu Xigui feels the correct reading is *ji* (己, self), but that seems awkward to me: "it considers itself." Note the connection here with chapter 14 of the *Laozi*, where, having described the Dao as something that cannot be perceived, the author ends with the words "This is called the initial thread of the Way" (是謂道紀).

23. A color photograph of the painting can be found in Fu Juyou [傅舉有] and Chen Songchang [陳松長], ed., *Mawangdui Hanmu wenwu* [馬王堆漢墓文物] (Hunan: Hunan Publishing Co., 1992), p. 35. Curiously, the first article to provide a photograph of this painting (in black and white) and briefly discuss its contents was published in 1986, thirteen years after the painting was found at Mawangdui: Zhou Shirong [周世榮], "Mawangdui Hanmu zhong de renwu tuxiang ji qi minzu tedian chutan" [馬王堆漢墓中的人物圖像及其民族特點初探], *Wenwu yanjiucongkan* [文物研究叢刊] 2 (December 1986): 71–77.

24. On this point see my article, "The Three-Bodied Shun and the Completion of Creation," *Bulletin of the School of Oriental and African Studies* 59.2 (1996): 268–95.

25. Ge Zhaoguang, "Zhongmiao zhi men—Beiji yu Taiyi, Dao, Taiji" [眾妙之門——北極與太一, 道, 太極], *Zhongguo wenhua* [中國文化] 3 (1990): 46–65.

26. Henricks, *Lao-tzu Te-tao ching*, p. 106.

27. Cui Renyi, "Jingmen Chumu chutude zhujian *Laozi* chutan" [荊門楚墓出土的竹簡《老子》初探], *Jingmen shehui kexue* [荊門社會科學], no. 5 (1997): 31–35.

28. Li Xueqin, "Jingmen Guodian Chujian suojian Guanyin yishuo."

29. In her remarks at the international conference on the "Guodian *Laozi*," May 1998.

30. Zhu Bin [朱彬], "Liji xunzuan" [禮記訓纂], in the *Sibu beiyao* [四部備要] edition (repr. Shanghai: Zhonghua shuju, 1927–35; Taibei: Zhonghua shuju, 1966), 9.12a.

31. "Great Music" [*da yue*, 大樂], in Lu Buwei [呂不韋], *Lushi chunqiu* [呂氏

春秋], in the *Sibu beiyao* edition (repr. Shanghai: Zhonghua shuju, 1927–35; Taibei: Zhonghua shuju, 1982), 5.3a.

32. Ibid., 5.3ab.

33. *Guodian Chumu zhujian*, p. 13, slips 9, 13, and 14.

34. Following Qiu Xigui (*Guodian Chumu zhujian*, p. 126 n 15) in reading *que* (雀, sparrow) as a phonetic loan for *xue* (削, slice off or cut into). It might also be read as *que* (摧, to strike).

35. Liu An [劉安], comp., *Huainanzi*, in the *Sibu beiyao* edition (repr. Shanghai: Zhonghua shuju, 1927–35; Taibei: Zhonghua shuju, 1987), 3.1ab.

36. See Sarah Allan, *The Shape of the Turtle: Myth, Art, and Cosmos in Early China* (Albany: SUNY Press, 1991), pp. 74–111.

37. See, for example, chapter 76 or chapter 43: "The softest, most pliable thing in the world [i.e., water] runs roughshod over the firmest thing in the world [i.e., rock]" (Henricks, *Lao-tzu Te-tao ching*, p. 108).

38. Henricks, *Lao-tzu Te-tao ching*, p. 132.

39. If the words on slip 9 allude to the myth of Gonggong, the character *que* (雀, sparrow) might better be read as a phonetic loan for *que* (摧, to strike): "One who strikes or severs what is already complete in order to better his life."

40. One final thought on this matter. We might connect the three slips if we approach the problem in the following way. As a result of Gonggong's action, the sky is no longer "level"; it slants up in the southeast and down in the northwest. The same is true of the earth—it is no longer "level"; it slants up in the northwest and down in the southeast. Were one's goal to make the two level again, one would have to "slice off" that part of the sky that dips down too low (i.e., the portion in the northwest), "adding it on" to the other end of the sky, then do the same with the earth, cutting off the part that now sticks up too high (the northwestern part). In other words, we would translate the words *qixia gao yi qiang* (其下高以強) not as "what is below it is high and firm" or "what is below it is high as the result of violence" but as "to make high the part that is low would require the use of force." The author's point at the end would then be the good Daoist point that both things (heaven and earth) are already "balanced," while not being level, so it is best to leave them alone. That is, with both things, there is a deficiency at one end but a surplus at the other. Understood in this way, slip 9 would indeed lead directly into slips 13 and 14, and the saying as a whole might be related to chapter 77 in the *Laozi*, which begins with the words: "The Way of Heaven is like the flexing of a bow. The high it presses down; the low it raises up. From those with a surplus it takes away; to those without enough it adds on. Therefore the Way of Heaven is to reduce the excessive and increase the insufficient" (Henricks, *Lao-tzu Te-tao ching*, p. 180). The problem here is: Can *gao yi qiang* be read in this way? We will have to see what others make of this passage before we decide.

1. Translated from *Shiji* 63 (repr. Beijing: Zhonghua shuju, 1959), 7:2139–43. This has been translated into English a number of times. Well known to many readers is the translation done by Wing-tsit Chan, *The Way of Lao Tzu*, pp. 36–37. For a more recent version, one with detailed annotation, see Ssu-ma Ch'ien [Sima Qian], *The Grand Scribe's Records: Volume 7, The Memoirs of Pre-Han China*, William H. Nienhauser, Jr., ed.; Cheng Tsai-fa, Lu Zongli, William H. Nienhauser, Jr., Robert Reynolds, and Chan Chiu-ming, trans. (Bloomington and Indianapolis: Indiana University Press, 1994), pp. 21–23.

2. This would have been located in the capital city, now Luoyang.

3. Elsewhere in the *Shiji* (in the "Qin benji"), this event is specifically dated to the eleventh year of Duke Xian—374 B.C. But 374 B.C. is not "one hundred and twenty-nine years after the death of Confucius," whose dates—or so we believe—were 551–479 B.C. This inconsistency is rarely noted. Guo Yi mentions it, noting that it would appear that Sima Qian is in error and that the biography ought to say "one hundred and six years after the death of Confucius." (See Guo Yi, "Cong Guodian Chujian *Laozi* kan *Laozi* qiren qishu," p. 54).

4. Qin was enfeoffed as a Zhou state during the reign of King Xiao (孝王, r. 909–985 B.C.). In 325 B.C. the Qin ruler, Huiwen (惠文) started to refer to himself as "king"; he was the first of the feudal lords to assume this title, which was reserved for the ruler in Zhou. Qin eliminated the Zhou in 256 B.C.

5. Duan'gan (段干) was the name of a city in Wei (魏).

6. Quoting the words of Confucius from *Analects* 15:40.

7. These words can be found in chapters 37, 45, and 57 in this edition.

8. There is a good review in English of the various problems that have been noted, in Wing-tsit Chan, *The Way of Lao Tzu*, pp. 35–83.

9. On which see *Zhanguoce* 24.4a, in the *Sibu beiyao* edition (Shanghai: Zhonghua shuju, 1927–35). The passage is translated by J. I. Crump in *Chan-kuo Ts'e* (San Francisco: Chinese Materials Center, 1979), p. 433.

10. "As for *li* (ritual), it's but the thin edge of loyalty and sincerity, and the beginning of disorder" (Henricks, *Lao-tzu Te-tao Ching*, p. 98).

11. The reference here is to four passages in the *Liji* ("The Questions of Zeng Zi," pp. 7.6b–7a, 7.12b–13a, 7.13b, and 7.14a), where Lao Dan appears to be an authority on the minutiae of funeral rites and one of Confucius's teachers. For a translation of these passages, see James Legge, trans., Ch'u Chai and Winberg Chai, ed., *Li Chi: Book of Rites* (New York: New Hyde Park, University Books, 1967), pp. 311–42.

12. Graham translates and comments on this collection in "The Dialogues of Confucius and Old Tan," in his *Chuang Tzu*, pp. 126–34.

13. Lau, *Lao Tzu: Tao Te Ching*, p. 130.

14. A. C. Graham, "The Origins of the Legend of Lao Tan," in *Studies in Chinese*

*Philosophy and Philosophical Literature* (Singapore: Institute of East Asian Philosophies, 1986), pp. 111–24.

15. Graham makes two points worth noting as support for this conclusion. One is
that the Old Dan who knew so much about funeral rites would be more likely to
have served as a "librarian" in the Zhou archives than the Laozi who would write
this kind of book. The other point is that, in chapter 3 of the *Zhuangzi*, "The Essen-
tials of Nourishing Life," the disciples of Old Dan are chided by someone of Daoist
bent for weeping and wailing when Old Dan died. One might infer from this that
Old Dan was known as a specialist on funeral rites, and that if anyone should know
how to mourn correctly, it would be Old Dan's disciples. (For Graham's translation
of this story, see *Chuang Tzu: The Inner Chapters*, p. 65.)

16. See Guo Yi, "Cong Guodian Chujian *Laozi* kan *Laozi* qiren qishu," pp. 53–55.

*Appendix 3. Punctuation Marks and Determination of Chapter Divisions*

1. In the Guodian slips, "chapter 20" (B:3) begins with this line.

2. *Chang* can be read as the first character in the next "chapter," and it is understood that way in the Wenwu transcription (*Guodian Chumu zhujian*, p. 111). For
more on this point, see note 12 in *Laozi* A above.

# Bibliography

Allan, Sarah. *The Shape of the Turtle: Myth, Art, and Cosmos in Early China*. Albany: State University of New York Press, 1991.

Baxter, William H. "Situating the Language of the *Lao-tzu*: The Probable Date of the *Tao-te-ching*." In Livia Kohn and Michael LaFargue, ed., *Lao-tzu and the Tao-te-ching*. Albany: State University of New York Press, 1998, pp. 231–53.

Boltz, William G. "The Study of Early Chinese Manuscripts: Methodological Preliminaries." Paper presented at the international conference on the "Guodian *Laozi*," May 1998.

———. "The *Lao tzu* Text That Wang Pi and Ho-shang Kung Never Saw." *Bulletin of the School of Oriental and African Studies* 48.3 (1985): 493–501.

Chan, Wing-tsit, trans. *The Way of Lao Tzu*. Indianapolis: Bobbs-Merrill, 1963.

———. *A Source Book in Chinese Philosophy*. Princeton: Princeton University Press, 1963.

Chen Guying [朝躬萊]. *Huangdi sijing jinzhu jinyi* [《黃帝四經》今註今譯]. Taibei: Commercial Press, 1995.

———. *Laozi jinzhu jinyi* [《老子》今註今譯]. Taibei: Commercial Press, 1997.

———. "Chu du jianben *Laozi*" [初讀簡本《老子》]. Paper presented at the international conference on the "Guodian *Laozi*," May 1998.

———. *Laozi zhuyi ji pingjie* [《老子》註譯及評介]. Hong Kong: Zhonghua shuju, 1987.

Crump, J. I., trans. *Chan-kuo Ts'e*. San Francisco: Chinese Materials Center, 1979.

Cui Renyi [崔仁義]. "Shilun Jingmen zhujian *Laozi* de niandai" [試論荆門竹簡《老子》的年代]. *Jingmen daxue xuebao* [荆門大學學報], no. 2 (1997): 38–42.

———. "Jingmen Chumu chutude zhujian *Laozi* chutan" [荆門楚墓出土的竹簡《老子》初探]. *Jingmen shehui kexue* [荆門社會科學], no. 5 (1997): 31–35.

Defoort, Carine. *The Pheasant Cap Master (Heguanzi): A Rhetorical Reading*. Albany: State University of New York Press, 1997.

Ding Yuanzhi [丁原植]. *Guodian zhujian Laozi shixi yu yanjiu* [郭店竹簡《老子》釋析與研究]. Taibei: Wanjuanlou, 1998.

Dong Tonghe [董同龢]. *Shanggu yinyun biaogao* [上古音韻表稿]. Taibei: Zhongyang yanjiuyuan lishiyuyan yanjiusuo, 1967.

Fu Juyou [傅舉有] and Chen Songchang [陳松長], ed. *Mawangdui Hanmu wenwu* [馬王堆漢墓文物]. Hunan: Hunan Publishing Co., 1992.

Gao Dalun [高大倫]. "Shi jiandu wenzi zhongde jizhong fuhao" [釋簡牘文字中的幾種符號]. In *Qin Han jiandu lunwenji* [秦漢簡牘論文集]. Gansu: Gansu renmin chubanshe, 1989, pp. 291–301.

Gao Ming [高明]. "Boshu *Laozi* jiayiben yu jinben *Laozi* kanjiao zhaji" [帛書《老子》甲乙本與今本《老子》勘校札記]. In Wenwu bianji weiyuanhui [文物編輯委員會], ed., *Wenwu ziliao congkan* [文物資料叢刊]. Beijing: Wenwu Press, 1978, 2:209–21.

————. *Boshu Laozi jiaozhu* [帛書《老子》校注]. Beijing: Zhonghua shuju, 1996.

Ge Zhaoguang [葛兆光]. "Zhong-miao zhi men—Beiji yu Taiyi, Dao, Taiji" [衆妙之門——北極與太一, 道, 太極]. *Zhongguo wenhua* [中國文化] 3 (1990): 46–65.

Graham, A. C. "A Neglected Pre-Han Philosophical Text: *Ho-kuan-tzu*." *Bulletin of the School of Oriental and African Studies* 52.3 (1989): 497–532.

————. *Disputers of the Tao: Philosophical Argument in Ancient China*. La Salle, IL: Open Court, 1989.

————. *Studies in Chinese Philosophy and Philosophical Literature*. Singapore: Institute of East Asian Philosophies, 1986.

Graham, A. C., trans. *Chuang Tzu: The Inner Chapters*. London: George Allen & Unwin, 1981.

Guojia wenwuju guwenxian yanjiushi [國家文物局古文獻研究室], ed. *Mawangdui Hanmu boshu* [馬王堆漢墓帛書], vol. 1. Beijing: Wenwu Press, 1980.

Guo Yi [郭沂]. "Cong Guodian Chujian *Laozi* kan *Laozi* qiren qishu" [從郭店楚簡《老子》看老子其人其書]. *Zhexue yanjiu* [哲學研究, Philosophical Research] 7 (July 1998): 47–55.

Henricks, Robert G. "On the Chapter Divisions in the *Lao-tzu*." *Bulletin of the School of Oriental and African Studies* 45.3 (1982): 501–24.

————. "The Ma-wang-tui Manuscripts of the *Lao-tzu* and the Problem of Dating the Text." *Chinese Culture* 20.2 (June 1979): 8–12.

————. "The Philosophy of Lao-tzu Based on the Ma-wang-tui Texts: Some Preliminary Observations." *Bulletin of the Society for the Study of Chinese Religions* 9 (October 1981): 60–61.

————. "The Ruler's Agenda: A Proposed Reading of Section One in Document A of the Guodian *Laozi*" [Zhiguo dagang—shidu Guodian *Laozi* jiazu de diyi bufen,

治國大剛——試讀郭店《老子》甲組的第一部分]. *Daojia wenhua yanjiu* [道家文化研究] 17 (1999): 144–88.

———. "The Three-Bodied Shun and the Completion of Creation." *Bulletin of the School of Oriental and African Studies* 59.2 (1996): 268–95.

Henricks, Robert G., trans. *Lao-tzu Te-tao ching: A New Translation Based on the Recently Discovered Ma-wang-tui Texts*. New York: Ballantine Books, 1989.

Hubeisheng Jingmenshi bowuguan [湖北省荊門市博物館], ed. *Guodian Chumu zhujian* [郭店楚墓竹簡]. Beijing: Wenwu Press, 1998.

———. "Jingmen Guodian yihao Chumu" [荊門郭店一號楚墓]. *Wenwu* 7 (1997): 35–48.

Ikeda, Tomohisa [池田知久]. "Jingmenshi bowuguan *Guodian Chumu zhujian* biji" [荊門市博物館《郭店楚墓竹簡》筆記]. Paper presented at the international conference on the "Guodian *Laozi*," May 1998.

———. *Ma-ōtai Hanbo "Goanhen" kenkyū* [馬王堆漢墓帛書《五行篇》研究]. Tokyo: Kyūko shoin, 1993.

Jiang Xichang [蔣錫昌]. *Laozi jiaogu* [老子校詁]. Taibei: Minglun chubanshe, 1971.

Karlgren, Bernhard. *Grammata Serica Recensa*. Stockholm: Museum of Far Eastern Antiquities, 1972.

———. *The Book of Odes*. Stockholm: Museum of Far Eastern Antiquities, 1950.

———. "The Poetical Parts in Lao-Tsï." *Göteborgs Högskolas Årsskrift* 38.3 (1932): 3–45.

La Fargue, Michael. *The Tao of the Tao Te Ching*. Albany: State University of New York Press, 1992.

Lau, D. C., trans. *Chinese Classics: Tao Te Ching*. Hong Kong: Chinese University Press, 1982.

———. *Confucius: The Analects*. Middlesex, UK: Penguin Books, 1979.

———. *Lao Tzu: Tao Te Ching*. Middlesex, UK: Penguin Books, 1963.

Legge, James, trans.; Ch'u Chai and Winberg Chai, ed. *Li Chi: Book of Rites*. New York: New Hyde Park, University Books, 1967.

Li Jiahao [李家浩]. "Du *Guodian Chumu zhujian* yiyi" [讀《郭店楚墓竹簡》遺議]. *Zhongguo zhexue* [中國哲學], no. 20 (October 1998): 339–58.

Li Ling [李零]. "Du Guodian Chujian *Laozi*" [讀郭店楚簡《老子》]. Paper presented at the international conference on the "Guodian *Laozi*," May 1998.

Li Xueqin [李學勤]. "Shenlun *Laozi* de niandai" [申論《老子》的年代]. *Daojia wenhua yanjiu* 6 (1995): 72–79.

———. "Jingmen Guodian Chujian zhongde *Zi Si zi*" [荊門郭店楚簡中的《子思子》]. *Wenwu tiandi* (Cultural Relics World) 2 (1998): 28–30.

———. "Jingmen Guodian Chujian suojian Guanyin yishuo" [荊門郭店楚簡所見關尹遺說]. *Zhongguo wenwubao* [中國文物報], April 8, 1998.

226  Liu An [劉安], comp. *Huainanzi* [淮南子]. *Sibu beiyao* [四部備要] edition. Repr. Shanghai: Zhonghua shuju, 1927–35; Taibei: Zhonghua shuju, 1987.

Liu Xiaogan [劉笑敢]. "*Laozi* zaoqi shuo zhi xin zheng" [《老子》早期說之新證]. *Daojia wenhua yanjiu* 4 (1994): 419–37.

Liu Zuxin [劉祖信]. "Jingmen Guodian yihao mu gailun" [荊門郭店一號墓概論]. Paper presented at the international conference on the "Guodian *Laozi*," May 1998.

Lu Buwei [呂不韋]. *Lushi chunqiu* [呂氏春秋]. *Sibu beiyao* edition. Repr. Shanghai: Zhonghua shuju, 1927–35; Taibei: Zhonghua shuju, 1982.

Luo Genze [羅根澤], ed. *Gushi bian* [古史辨], vol. 4. Repr. Shanghai: Guji, 1982.

Luo Zhufeng [羅竹風], ed. *Hanyu da cidian* [漢語大詞典]. Shanghai: Cishu chubanshe, 1987–94.

Mair, Victor, trans. *Tao Te Ching: The Classic Book of Integrity and the Way*. New York: Bantam Books, 1990.

Pei Xuehai [裴學海]. *Gushu xuzi jishi* [古書虛字集釋]. Shanghai: Commercial Press, 1934. Repr. Taibei: Guangwen shuju, 1962, 1971.

Peng Hao [彭浩]. "Guanyu Guodian Chujian *Laozi* zhengli gongzuo de jidian shuoming" [關于郭店楚簡《老子》整理工作的几點說明]. Paper presented at the international conference on the "Guodian *Laozi*," May 1998.

———. "Guodian Chujian *Laozi* de niandai ji fenzhang" [郭店楚簡《老子》的年代及分章]. Paper presented at the international conference on the "Guodian *Laozi*," May 1998.

———. "Zhanguo shiqi de qiance" [戰國時期的遣策]. In Li Xueqin, ed., *Jianboyanjiu* [簡帛研究]. Beijing: Falu chubanshe, 1996, 2:48–55.

Pulleyblank, Edwin G. *Outline of Classical Chinese Grammar*. Vancouver: University of British Columbia Press, 1995.

Roth, Harold D. "Some Methodological Issues in the Study of the Kuo Tien *Lao Tzu* Parallels." Paper presented at the international conference on the "Guodian *Laozi*," May 1998.

———. "Text and Edition in Early Chinese Philosophical Literature." *Journal of the American Oriental Society* 113.2 (1993): 214–27.

———. "What Is Huang-Lao?" Paper presented at the annual meeting of the Association for Asian Studies, 1991.

Ryden, Edmund. "Guodian Bamboo Slips: An Edition of the Guodian *Laozi*, *Tai Yi Sheng Shui*." Paper presented at the international conference on the "Guodian *Laozi*," May 1998.

Shima Kunio [島邦男]. *Rōshi kōsei* [老子校正]. Tokyo: Kyūko shoin, 1973.

Ssu-ma Ch'ien [Sima Qian]. *The Grand Scribe's Records: Volume 7, The Memoirs of Pre-Han China*. William H. Nienhauser, Jr., ed.; Cheng Tsai-fa, Lu Zongli, William

H. Nienhauser, Jr., Robert Reynolds, and Chan Chiu-ming, trans. Indianapolis and Bloomington: Indiana University Press, 1994.

———. *Shiji* [史記]. Repr. Beijing: Zhonghua shuju, 1959.

Teng Rensheng [滕壬生], ed. *Chuxi jianbo wenzi bian* [楚系簡帛文字編]. Wuhan: Hubei jiaoyu chubanshe, 1995.

Tōdō Akiyasu [藤堂明保]. *Kanwa daijiten* [漢和大字典]. Tokyo: Gakushūkenkyū-sha, 1978.

Wagner, Rudolf G. "The Wang Bi Recension of the *Laozi*." *Early China* 14 (1989): 27–54.

Wang Bi [王弼], comm. *Laozi Daode jing* [老子道德經]. *Sibu beiyao* edition. Repr. Taibei: Zhonghua shuju, 1966.

Wang Bo [王博]. "Guodian *Laozi* weishenma you sanzu?" [郭店《老子》為什麼有三組]. Paper presented at the international conference on the "Guodian *Laozi*," May 1998.

Xia Song [夏竦], ed. *Guwen sisheng yun* [古文四聲韻]. *Siku quanshu* [四庫全書] edition. Vol. 224. Repr. Shanghai: Guji, 1987.

Xie Shouhao [謝守灝]. *Hunyuan shengji* [混元聖記]. In *Zhengtong daozang* [正統道藏]. CT 770 (text no. 770). Repr. Taibei: Yiwen yinshuguan, 1977, vol. 30.

Xing Wen [邢文]. "Lun Guodian *Laozi* yu jinben *Laozi* bu zhu yixi—Chujian 'Taiyi shengshui' ji qi yiyi" [論郭店《老子》與今本《老子》不屬一系——楚簡《太一生水》及其意義]. *Zhongguo zhexue*, no. 20 (October 1998): 165–86.

Xu Kangsheng [許抗生]. "Chudu Guodian zhujian *Laozi*" [初讀郭店竹簡《老子》]. Paper presented at the international conference on the "Guodian *Laozi*," May 1998.

———. *Boshu Laozi zhushi yu yanjiu* [帛書《老子》註譯與研究]. Hangzhou: Zhejiang renmin chubanshe, 1985.

Xu Shen [許慎], comp. *Shuowen jiezi zhu* [說文解字注]. Annotated by Duan Yucai [段玉裁]. Repr. Shanghai: Guji, 1981.

Yan Kejun [嚴可均], ed. *Quan shanggu sandai Qin Han sanguo liuchao wen* [全上古三代秦漢三國六朝文]. Taibei: Zhongwen chubanshe, 1972.

Zhang Shouzhong [張守中]. *Baoshan Chujian wenzibian* [包山楚簡文字編]. Beijing: Wenwu Press, 1996.

Zhang Xuan [張瑄]. *The Etymologies of 3,000 Chinese Characters in Common Usage*. Hong Kong: Hong Kong University Press, 1968.

Zhang Zhengming [張正明]. *Chushi* [楚史]. Wuhan: Hubei jiaoyu chubanshe, 1995.

*Zhanguoce* [駒瓣鄲]. *Sibu beiyao* edition. Repr. Shanghai: Zhonghua shuju, 1927–35; Taibei: Zhonghua shuju, 1966.

Zhou Fagao [周法高], ed. *Hanzi gujin yinhui* [A Pronouncing Dictionary of Chinese

Characters, 漢字古今音彙]. Hong Kong: Chinese University of Hong Kong, 1973.

Zhou Shirong [周世榮]. "Mawangdui Hanmu zhong de renwu tuxiang ji qi minzu tedian chutan" [馬王堆漢墓中的人物圖像及其民族特點初探]. *Wenwu yanjiucongkan* [文物研究叢刊] 2 (December 1986): 71–77.

Zhu Bin [朱彬]. *Liji xunzuan* [禮記訓纂]. *Sibu beiyao* edition. Repr. Shanghai: Zhonghua shuju, 1927–35; Taibei: Zhonghua shuju, 1966.

# Index

# Other Works

*in the Columbia Asian Studies Series*

*Two Plays of Ancient India: The Little Clay Cart and the Minister's Seal*, tr. J. A. B. van Buitenen 1968

*The Complete Works of Chuang Tzu*, tr. Burton Watson 1968

*The Romance of the Western Chamber (Hsi Hsiang chi)*, tr. S. I. Hsiung. Also in paperback ed. 1968

*The Manyōshū*, Nippon Gakujutsu Shinkōkai edition. Paperback ed. only. 1969

*Records of the Historian: Chapters from the Shih chi of Ssu-ma Ch'ien*, tr. Burton Watson. Paperback ed. only. 1969

*Cold Mountain: 100 Poems by the T'ang Poet Han-shan*, tr. Burton Watson. Also in paperback ed. 1970

*Twenty Plays of the Nō Theatre*, ed. Donald Keene. Also in paperback ed. 1970

*Chūshingura: The Treasury of Loyal Retainers*, tr. Donald Keene. Also in paperback ed. 1971; rev. ed. 1997

*The Zen Master Hakuin: Selected Writings*, tr. Philip B. Yampolsky 1971

*Chinese Rhyme-Prose: Poems in the Fu Form from the Han and Six Dynasties Periods*, tr. Burton Watson. Also in paperback ed. 1971

*Kūkai: Major Works*, tr. Yoshito S. Hakeda. Also in paperback ed. 1972

*The Old Man Who Does as He Pleases: Selections from the Poetry and Prose of Lu Yu*, tr. Burton Watson 1973

*The Lion's Roar of Queen Śrīmālā*, tr. Alex and Hideko Wayman 1974

*Courtier and Commoner in Ancient China: Selections from the History of the Former Han by Pan Ku*, tr. Burton Watson. Also in paperback ed. 1974

*Japanese Literature in Chinese, vol. 1: Poetry and Prose in Chinese by Japanese Writers of the Early Period*, tr. Burton Watson 1975

*Japanese Literature in Chinese, vol. 2: Poetry and Prose in Chinese by Japanese Writers of the Later Period*, tr. Burton Watson 1976

*Scripture of the Lotus Blossom of the Fine Dharma*, tr. Leon Hurvitz. Also in paperback ed. 1976

*Love Song of the Dark Lord: Jayadeva's Gītagovinda*, tr. Barbara Stoler Miller. Also in paperback ed. Cloth ed. includes critical text of the Sanskrit. 1977; rev. ed. 1997

*Ryōkan: Zen Monk-Poet of Japan*, tr. Burton Watson 1977

*Calming the Mind and Discerning the Real: From the Lam rim chen mo of Tson-kha-pa*, tr. Alex Wayman 1978

*The Hermit and the Love-Thief: Sanskrit Poems of Bhartrihari and Bilhaṇa*, tr. Barbara Stoler Miller 1978

*The Lute: Kao Ming's P'i-p'a chi*, tr. Jean Mulligan. Also in paperback ed. 1980

*A Chronicle of Gods and Sovereigns: Jinnō Shōtōki of Kitabatake Chikafusa*, tr. H. Paul Varley. 1980

*Among the Flowers: The Hua-chien chi*, tr. Lois Fusek 1982

*Grass Hill: Poems and Prose by the Japanese Monk Gensei*, tr. Burton Watson 1983     

*Doctors, Diviners, and Magicians of Ancient China: Biographies of Fang-shih*, tr. Kenneth J. DeWoskin. Also in paperback ed. 1983

*Theater of Memory: The Plays of Kālidāsa*, ed. Barbara Stoler Miller. Also in paperback ed. 1984

*The Columbia Book of Chinese Poetry: From Early Times to the Thirteenth Century*, ed. and tr. Burton Watson. Also in paperback ed. 1984

*Poems of Love and War: From the Eight Anthologies and the Ten Long Poems of Classical Tamil*, tr. A. K. Ramanujan. Also in paperback ed. 1985

*The Bhagavad Gita: Krishna's Counsel in Time of War*, tr. Barbara Stoler Miller 1986

*The Columbia Book of Later Chinese Poetry*, ed. and tr. Jonathan Chaves. Also in paperback ed. 1986

*The Tso Chuan: Selections from China's Oldest Narrative History*, tr. Burton Watson 1989

*Waiting for the Wind: Thirty-six Poets of Japan's Late Medieval Age*, tr. Steven Carter 1989

*Selected Writings of Nichiren*, ed. Philip B. Yampolsky 1990

*Saigyō, Poems of a Mountain Home*, tr. Burton Watson 1990

*The Book of Lieh Tzu: A Classic of the Tao*, tr. A. C. Graham. Morningside ed. 1990

*The Tale of an Anklet: An Epic of South India—The Cilappatikāram of Iḷaṅkō Aṭikaḷ*, tr. R. Parthasarathy 1993

*Waiting for the Dawn: A Plan for the Prince*, tr. and introduction by Wm. Theodore de Bary 1993

*Yoshitsune and the Thousand Cherry Trees: A Masterpiece of the Eighteenth-Century Japanese Puppet Theater*, tr., annotated, and with introduction by Stanleigh H. Jones, Jr. 1993

*The Lotus Sutra*, tr. Burton Watson. Also in paperback ed. 1993

*The Classic of Changes: A New Translation of the I Ching as Interpreted by Wang Bi*, tr. Richard John Lynn 1994

*Beyond Spring: Tz'u Poems of the Sung Dynasty*, tr. Julie Landau 1994

*The Columbia Anthology of Traditional Chinese Literature*, ed. Victor H. Mair 1994

*Scenes for Mandarins: The Elite Theater of the Ming*, tr. Cyril Birch 1995

*Letters of Nichiren*, ed. Philip B. Yampolsky; tr. Burton Watson et al. 1996

*Unforgotten Dreams: Poems by the Zen Monk Shōtetsu*, tr. Steven D. Carter 1997

*The Vimalakirti Sutra*, tr. Burton Watson 1997

*Japanese and Chinese Poems to Sing: The Wakan rōei shū*, tr. J. Thomas Rimer and Jonathan Chaves 1997

*A Tower for the Summer Heat*, Li Yu, tr. Patrick Hanan 1998

*The Classic of the Way and Virtue: A New Translation of the Tao-te Ching of Laozi as Interpreted by Wang Bi*, tr. Richard John Lynn 1999

238   *The Four Hundred Songs of War and Wisdom: An Anthology of Poems from Classical Tamil,
The Puranāṉūṟu,* eds. and trans. George L. Hart and Hank Heifetz 1999
*Original Tao:* Inward Training (Nei-yeh) *and the Foundations of Taoist Mysticism,* Harold
D. Roth 1999

MODERN ASIAN LITERATURE

*Modern Japanese Drama: An Anthology,* ed. and tr. Ted. Takaya. Also in paperback ed.
1979
*Mask and Sword: Two Plays for the Contemporary Japanese Theater,* by Yamazaki Masakazu,
tr. J. Thomas Rimer 1980
*Yokomitsu Riichi, Modernist,* Dennis Keene 1980
*Nepali Visions, Nepali Dreams: The Poetry of Laxmiprasad Devkota,* tr. David Rubin 1980
*Literature of the Hundred Flowers, vol. 1: Criticism and Polemics,* ed. Hualing Nieh 1981
*Literature of the Hundred Flowers, vol. 2: Poetry and Fiction,* ed. Hualing Nieh 1981
*Modern Chinese Stories and Novellas, 1919–1949,* ed. Joseph S. M. Lau, C. T. Hsia, and
Leo Ou-fan Lee. Also in paperback ed. 1984
*A View by the Sea,* by Yasuoka Shōtarō, tr. Kären Wigen Lewis 1984
*Other Worlds; Arishima Takeo and the Bounds of Modern Japanese Fiction,* by Paul Anderer
1984
*Selected Poems of Sŏ Chŏngju,* tr. with introduction by David R. McCann 1989
*The Sting of Life: Four Contemporary Japanese Novelists,* by Van C. Gessel 1989
*Stories of Osaka Life,* by Oda Sakunosuke, tr. Burton Watson 1990
*The Bodhisattva, or Samantabhadra, by Ishikawa Jun,* tr. with introduction by William
Jefferson Tyler 1990
*The Travels of Lao Ts'an,* by Liu T'ieh-yün, tr. Harold Shadick. Morningside ed. 1990
*Three Plays by Kōbō Abe,* tr. with introduction by Donald Keene 1993
*The Columbia Anthology of Modern Chinese Literature,* ed. Joseph S. M. Lau and Howard
Goldblatt 1995
*Modern Japanese Tanka,* ed. and tr. by Makoto Ueda 1996
*Masaoka Shiki: Selected Poems,* ed. and tr. by Burton Watson 1997
*Writing Women in Modern China: An Anthology of Women's Literature from the Early Twen-
tieth Century,* ed. and tr. by Amy D. Dooling and Kristina M. Torgeson 1998
*American Stories,* by Nagai Kafū, tr. Mitsuko Iriye        2000

STUDIES IN ASIAN CULTURE

*The Ōnin War: History of Its Origins and Background, with a Selective Translation of the
Chronicle of Ōnin,* by H. Paul Varley 1967
*Chinese Government in Ming Times: Seven Studies,* ed. Charles O. Hucker 1969
*The Actors' Analects (Yakusha Rongo),* ed. and tr. by Charles J. Dunn and Bungō Torigoe
1969

*Self and Society in Ming Thought*, by Wm. Theodore de Bary and the Conference on Ming Thought. Also in paperback ed. 1970

*A History of Islamic Philosophy*, by Majid Fakhry, 2d ed. 1983

*Phantasies of a Love Thief: The Caurapañatcāśikā Attributed to Bilhaṇa*, by Barbara Stoler Miller 1971

*Iqbal: Poet-Philosopher of Pakistan*, ed. Hafeez Malik 1971

*The Golden Tradition: An Anthology of Urdu Poetry*, ed. and tr. Ahmed Ali. Also in paperback ed. 1973

*Conquerors and Confucians: Aspects of Political Change in Late Yüan China*, by John W. Dardess 1973

*The Unfolding of Neo-Confucianism*, by Wm. Theodore de Bary and the Conference on Seventeenth-Century Chinese Thought. Also in paperback ed. 1975

*To Acquire Wisdom: The Way of Wang Yang-ming*, by Julia Ching 1976

*Gods, Priests, and Warriors: The Bhṛgus of the Mahābhārata*, by Robert P. Goldman 1977

*Mei Yao-ch'en and the Development of Early Sung Poetry*, by Jonathan Chaves 1976

*The Legend of Semimaru, Blind Musician of Japan*, by Susan Matisoff 1977

*Sir Sayyid Ahmad Khan and Muslim Modernization in India and Pakistan*, by Hafeez Malik 1980

*The Khilafat Movement: Religious Symbolism and Political Mobilization in India*, by Gail Minault 1982

*The World of K'ung Shang-jen: A Man of Letters in Early Ch'ing China*, by Richard Strassberg 1983

*The Lotus Boat: The Origins of Chinese Tz'u Poetry in T'ang Popular Culture*, by Marsha L. Wagner 1984

*Expressions of Self in Chinese Literature*, ed. Robert E. Hegel and Richard C. Hessney 1985

*Songs for the Bride: Women's Voices and Wedding Rites of Rural India*, by W. G. Archer; eds. Barbara Stoler Miller and Mildred Archer 1986

*A Heritage of Kings: One Man's Monarchy in the Confucian World*, by JaHyun Kim Haboush 1988

COMPANIONS TO ASIAN STUDIES

*Approaches to the Oriental Classics*, ed. Wm. Theodore de Bary 1959

*Early Chinese Literature*, by Burton Watson. Also in paperback ed. 1962

*Approaches to Asian Civilizations*, eds. Wm. Theodore de Bary and Ainslie T. Embree 1964

*The Classic Chinese Novel: A Critical Introduction*, by C. T. Hsia. Also in paperback ed. 1968

*Chinese Lyricism: Shih Poetry from the Second to the Twelfth Century*, tr. Burton Watson. Also in paperback ed. 1971

*A Syllabus of Indian Civilization,* by Leonard A. Gordon and Barbara Stoler Miller 1971

*Twentieth-Century Chinese Stories,* ed. C. T. Hsia and Joseph S. M. Lau. Also in paperback ed. 1971

*A Syllabus of Chinese Civilization,* by J. Mason Gentzler, 2d ed. 1972

*A Syllabus of Japanese Civilization,* by H. Paul Varley, 2d ed. 1972

*An Introduction to Chinese Civilization,* ed. John Meskill, with the assistance of J. Mason Gentzler 1973

*An Introduction to Japanese Civilization,* ed. Arthur E. Tiedemann 1974

*Ukifune: Love in the* Tale of Genji, ed. Andrew Pekarik 1982

*The Pleasures of Japanese Literature,* by Donald Keene 1988

*A Guide to Oriental Classics,* eds. Wm. Theodore de Bary and Ainslie T. Embree; 3d edition ed. Amy Vladeck Heinrich, 2 vols. 1989

INTRODUCTION TO ASIAN CIVILIZATIONS

Wm. Theodore de Bary, General Editor

*Sources of Japanese Tradition,* 1958; paperback ed., 2 vols., 1964

*Sources of Indian Tradition,* 1958; paperback ed., 2 vols., 1964; 2d ed., 2 vols., 1988

*Sources of Chinese Tradition,* 1960; paperback ed., 2 vols., 1964; 2d ed., 2 vols., 1999

*Sources of Korean Tradition,* ed. Peter H. Lee and Wm. Theodore de Bary; paperback ed., vol. 1, 1997

NEO-CONFUCIAN STUDIES

*Instructions for Practical Living and Other Neo-Confucian Writings by Wang Yang-ming,* tr. Wing-tsit Chan 1963

*Reflections on Things at Hand: The Neo-Confucian Anthology,* comp. Chu Hsi and Lü Tsu-ch'ien, tr. Wing-tsit Chan 1967

*Self and Society in Ming Thought,* by Wm. Theodore de Bary and the Conference on Ming Thought. Also in paperback ed. 1970

*The Unfolding of Neo-Confucianism,* by Wm. Theodore de Bary and the Conference on Seventeenth-Century Chinese Thought. Also in paperback ed. 1975

*Principle and Practicality: Essays in Neo-Confucianism and Practical Learning,* eds. Wm. Theodore de Bary and Irene Bloom. Also in paperback ed. 1979

*The Syncretic Religion of Lin Chao-en,* by Judith A. Berling 1980

*The Renewal of Buddhism in China: Chu-hung and the Late Ming Synthesis,* by Chün-fang Yü 1981

*Neo-Confucian Orthodoxy and the Learning of the Mind-and-Heart,* by Wm. Theodore de Bary 1981

*Yüan Thought: Chinese Thought and Religion Under the Mongols,* eds. Hok-lam Chan and Wm. Theodore de Bary 1982

*The Liberal Tradition in China*, by Wm. Theodore de Bary 1983

*The Development and Decline of Chinese Cosmology*, by John B. Henderso.

*The Rise of Neo-Confucianism in Korea*, by Wm. Theodore de Bary and Jaн, Haboush 1985

*Chiao Hung and the Restructuring of Neo-Confucianism in Late Ming*, by Edward T. Ch'ien 1985

*Neo-Confucian Terms Explained: Pei-hsi tʒu-i*, by Ch'en Ch'un, ed. and trans. Wing-tsit Chan 1986

*Knowledge Painfully Acquired: K'un-chih chi*, by Lo Ch'in-shun, ed. and trans. Irene Bloom 1987

*To Become a Sage: The Ten Diagrams on Sage Learning*, by Yi T'oegye, ed. and trans. Michael C. Kalton 1988

*The Message of the Mind in Neo-Confucian Thought*, by Wm. Theodore de Bary 1989